OGRE 3D 1.7 Application Development Cookbook

Over 50 recipes to provide world-class 3D graphics
solutions with OGRE 3D

Ilya Grinblat

Alex Peterson

BIRMINGHAM - MUMBAI

OGRE 3D 1.7 Application Development Cookbook

First published: May 2012

Production Reference: 1270412

Published by Packt Publishing Ltd.
Livery Place
35 Livery Street
Birmingham B3 2PB, UK.

ISBN 978-1-84951-456-9

www.packtpub.com

Cover Image by Rakesh Shejwal (shejwal.rakesh@gmail.com)

Credits

Authors
Ilya Grinblat

Alex Peterson

Reviewers
Matthew Casperson

Thomas Trocha

Senior Acquisition Editor
Usha Iyer

Lead Technical Editor
Hyacintha D'souza

Technical Editor
Lubna Shaikh

Project Coordinator
Shubhanjan Chatterjee

Proofreader
Aaron Nash

Mario Cecere

Indexer
Monica Ajmera

Graphics
Manu Joseph

Production Coordinator
Alwin Roy

Shantanu Zagade

Cover Work
Alwin Roy

About the Authors

Ilya Grinblat started to work 35 years ago as developer of control systems, and some years later, he moved to the development of Computer Aided Design software. He was a development manager of the architectural software ARC+, and was working in the development of the 3D city software—a software for 3D editing and management of a 3D printer. Last year, he was working in the development of simulators and the 3D GIS software. He was using Ogre to develop Civil Simulate—a software for 3D modeling of roads and driving simulation.

I would like to thank many people from Packt publishing.

I would also like to thank my wife Irena for giving me the time and support to write this book.

Alex Peterson is a graphics enthusiast with a background in game programming. His work with the Ogre engine is primarily due to programming a universe size game engine, a space skybox creator called **Spacescape**, and most recently, mobile games. Though his current life is filled with his family and running a business, he makes it a point be active musically and spiritually. He aims to promote his faith in God through his work to serve others, whether it is by fueling their creativity, entertaining them, or educating them. You can find Alex online at http://alexcpeterson.com.

I would like to thank my Father, my family, my wife Lydia, the Ogre development team, Steve Streeting, the Ogre forum moderators, Sean O'Neil, Chris, Ava Barneys, and all the kind people who have helped me be a part of this work. Thank you.

About the Reviewers

Matthew Casperson has worked in the IT industry for nearly a decade in a variety of roles, and is the author of *Away3D 3.6 Essentials*. In his spare time, he loves nothing more than to experiment with the latest Web and multimedia technologies. Many of these experiments can be found on Matthew's personal website at `http://goo.gl/2Hgr`.

Thomas Trocha found his passion for the world of computer programming in the mid eighties, using one of the first home computers - TI99/4a. Since then, he has studied computer science, and developed his knowledge in a wide spectrum of computer technologies. Inspired by the great online 48h game coding competition "Ludum Dare", he shifted to 3D game development, which finally ended up in him founding his own game company *ToMaGa*.

www.PacktPub.com

Support files, eBooks, discount offers and more

You might want to visit www.PacktPub.com for support files and downloads related to your book.

Did you know that Packt offers eBook versions of every book published, with PDF and ePub files available? You can upgrade to the eBook version at www.PacktPub.com and as a print book customer, you are entitled to a discount on the eBook copy. Get in touch with us at service@packtpub.com for more details.

At www.PacktPub.com, you can also read a collection of free technical articles, sign up for a range of free newsletters and receive exclusive discounts and offers on Packt books and eBooks.

http://PacktLib.PacktPub.com

Do you need instant solutions to your IT questions? PacktLib is Packt's online digital book library. Here, you can access, read and search across Packt's entire library of books.

Why Subscribe?

- Fully searchable across every book published by Packt
- Copy and paste, print and bookmark content
- On demand and accessible via web browser

Free Access for Packt account holders

If you have an account with Packt at www.PacktPub.com, you can use this to access PacktLib today and view nine entirely free books. Simply use your login credentials for immediate access.

Table of Contents

Preface

Harnessing the power of an elaborate graphics engine, such as Ogre 3D is time-consuming, but a highly rewarding pursuit. Developers, over the world, attest to Ogre's elegance, versatility, and efficiency, not to mention that its code is open source and supported by a thriving online community. This book explores many useful and fun ways to leverage Ogre 3D, to make your graphics application fully-featured and entertaining.

What this book covers

Chapter 1, Delving Deep into Application Design, covers how to create various types of basic Ogre 3D Windows applications and plugins.

Chapter 2, Let us be Multimodal, shows how to use the keyboard, the mouse, and the voice input to control a 3D application.

Chapter 3, Managing Objects and Scenes, contains recipes to build a rudimentary Ogre 3D scene editor in which you can create various types of meshes, terrain, and save the scene information to an XML file.

Chapter 4, Let There Be Light, explores lighting, shadows, and particle effects.

Chapter 5, Playing with Materials, covers advanced techniques to manipulate materials and textures, using Ogre 3D.

Chapter 6, Learning to Move, provides methods for moving meshes in a scene and basic collision detection.

Chapter 7, Implementing Animations, covers skeletal, morph, and pose animations. It also covers various methods of animating programmatically, using controllers.

Chapter 8, Flashy Multimedia, shows how to render to texture, and use audio and video in Ogre 3D.

Chapter 9, Queries and Views, covers selecting objects in a scene with the mouse and zooming with the camera.

What you need for this book

To follow the recipes in this book, and compile the various applications, you will need Microsoft Visual C++ 2010 on a machine running MS Windows with a DirectX 9 or higher graphics card.

Who this book is for

If you have ever wanted to develop 3D applications with OGRE 3D, then this example-driven book will enable you to do so. An understanding of C++ is needed to follow the examples in the book.

Conventions

In this book, you will find a number of styles of text that distinguish between different kinds of information. Here are some examples of these styles, and an explanation of their meaning.

Code words in text are shown as follows: "Executables for every sample project will be output in the `bin/debug` or `bin/release` folders depending on the project's build configuration".

A block of code is set as follows:

```
case WM_PAINT:
   hdc = BeginPaint(hWnd, &ps);
   m_Engine->m_Root->renderOneFrame();
   EndPaint(hWnd, &ps);
break;
```

When we wish to draw your attention to a particular part of a code block, the relevant lines or items are set in bold:

```
facet normal ni nj nk
  outer loop
    vertex v1x v1y v1z
    vertex v2x v2y v2z
    vertex v3x v3y v3z'
  endloop
endfacet
```

New terms and important words are shown in bold. Words that you see on the screen, in menus or dialog boxes for example, appear in the text like this: "In the **New Project** dialog-box, expand **Visual C++**, and click on **Win32 Project**.".

 Warnings or important notes appear in a box like this.

Tips and tricks appear like this.

Reader feedback

Feedback from our readers is always welcome. Let us know what you think about this book—what you liked or may have disliked. Reader feedback is important for us to develop titles that you really get the most out of.

To send us general feedback, simply send an e-mail to feedback@packtpub.com, and mention the book title through the subject of your message.

If there is a topic that you have expertise in and you are interested in either writing or contributing to a book, see our author guide on www.packtpub.com/authors.

Customer support

Now that you are the proud owner of a Packt book, we have a number of things to help you to get the most from your purchase.

Downloading the example code

You can download the example code files for all Packt books you have purchased from your account at http://www.packtpub.com. If you purchased this book elsewhere, you can visit http://www.packtpub.com/support and register to have the files e-mailed directly to you.

Errata

Although we have taken every care to ensure the accuracy of our content, mistakes do happen. If you find a mistake in one of our books—maybe a mistake in the text or the code—we would be grateful if you would report this to us. By doing so, you can save other readers from frustration and help us improve subsequent versions of this book. If you find any errata, please report them by visiting http://www.packtpub.com/support, selecting your book, clicking on the **errata submission form** link, and entering the details of your errata. Once your errata are verified, your submission will be accepted and the errata will be uploaded to our website, or added to any list of existing errata, under the Errata section of that title.

Piracy

Piracy of copyright material on the Internet is an ongoing problem across all media. At Packt, we take the protection of our copyright and licenses very seriously. If you come across any illegal copies of our works, in any form, on the Internet, please provide us with the location address or website name immediately so that we can pursue a remedy.

Please contact us at `copyright@packtpub.com` with a link to the suspected pirated material.

We appreciate your help in protecting our authors, and our ability to bring you valuable content.

Questions

You can contact us at `questions@packtpub.com` if you are having a problem with any aspect of the book, and we will do our best to address it.

1
Delving Deep into Application Design

In this chapter, we will cover the following recipes:

- ▸ Creating a Win32 Ogre application
- ▸ Creating an MFC Ogre application
- ▸ Creating an MFC Ogre application with a ribbon
- ▸ Creating a Windows Forms Ogre application
- ▸ Creating an Ogre plugin
- ▸ Creating a custom resource manager

Introduction

In this chapter, we'll show you how to create an Ogre 3D Windows application in Visual Studio 2010 using the Win32 API, the **Microsoft Foundation Classes** (**MFC**), and the .NET framework. We'll show you how to configure your project settings to support Ogre, and how to integrate Ogre into each type of application. We'll also create a custom Ogre plugin and a custom resource manager.

Before we get started, please note the folder structure that we'll be using. This will help you quickly find the files referred to in each recipe.

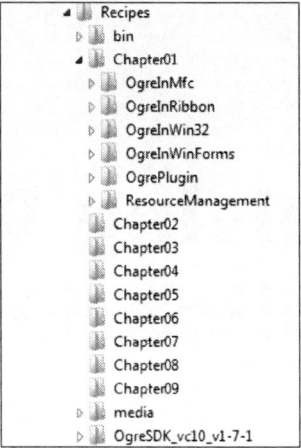

Executables for every sample project will be output in the `bin/debug` or `bin/release` folders depending on the project's build configuration. These folders also contain the following required DLLs and configuration files:

File name	Description
OgreMain.dll	Main Ogre DLL.
RenderSystem_Direct3D9.dll	DirectX 9 Ogre render system DLL. This is necessary only if you want Ogre to use the DirectX 9 graphics library.
RenderSystem_GL.dll	OpenGL Ogre render system DLL. This is necessary only if you want Ogre to use the OpenGL graphics library.
Plugin_OctreeSceneManager.dll	Octree scene manager Ogre plugin DLL.
Plugin_ParticleFX.dll	Particle effects Ogre plugin DLL.
ogre.cfg	Ogre main configuration file that includes render system settings.
resources.cfg	Ogre resource configuration file that contains paths to all resource locations. Resources include graphics files, shaders, material files, mesh files, and so on.
plugins.cfg	Ogre plugin configuration file that contains a list of all the plugins we want Ogre to use. Typical plugins include the `Plugin_OctreeSceneManager`, `RenderSystem_Direct3D9`, `RenderSystem_GL`, and so on.

In the `bin/debug` folder, you'll notice that the debug versions of the Ogre plugin DLLs all have a `_d` appended to the filename. For example, the debug version of `OgreMain.dll` is `OgreMain_d.dll`. This is the standard method for naming debug versions of Ogre DLLs.

The `media` folder contains all the Ogre resource files, and the `OgreSDK_vc10_v1-7-1` folder contains the Ogre header and library files.

Creating a Win32 Ogre application

The Win32 application is the leanest and meanest of windowed applications, which makes it a good candidate for graphics. In this recipe, we will create a simple Win32 application that displays a 3D robot model that comes with Ogre, in a window. Because these steps are identical for all Win32 Ogre applications, you can use the completed project as a starting point for new Win32 applications.

Getting ready

To follow along with this recipe, open the solution located in the `Recipes/Chapter01/OgreInWin32` folder in the code bundle available on the Packt website.

How to do it...

We'll start off by creating a new Win32 application using the Visual C++ Win32 application wizard.

1. Create a new project by clicking on **File | New | Project**. In the **New Project** dialog-box, expand **Visual C++**, and click on **Win32 Project**. Name the project `OgreInWin32`. For **Location**, browse to the `Recipes` folder and append `\Chapter_01_Examples`, then click on **OK**.

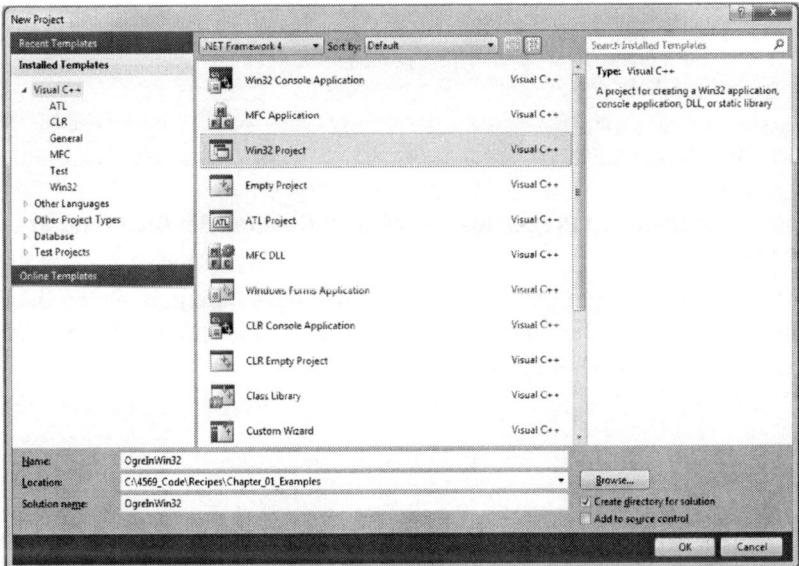

2. In the **Win32 Application Wizard** that appears, click on **Next**. For **Application type**, select Windows application, and then click on **Finish** to create the project. At this point, we have everything we need for a bare-bones Win32 application without Ogre.

3. Next, we need to adjust our project properties, so that the compiler and linker know where to put our executable and find the Ogre header and library files.

4. Open the **Property Pages** dialog-box, by selecting the **Project** menu and clicking on **Properties**.

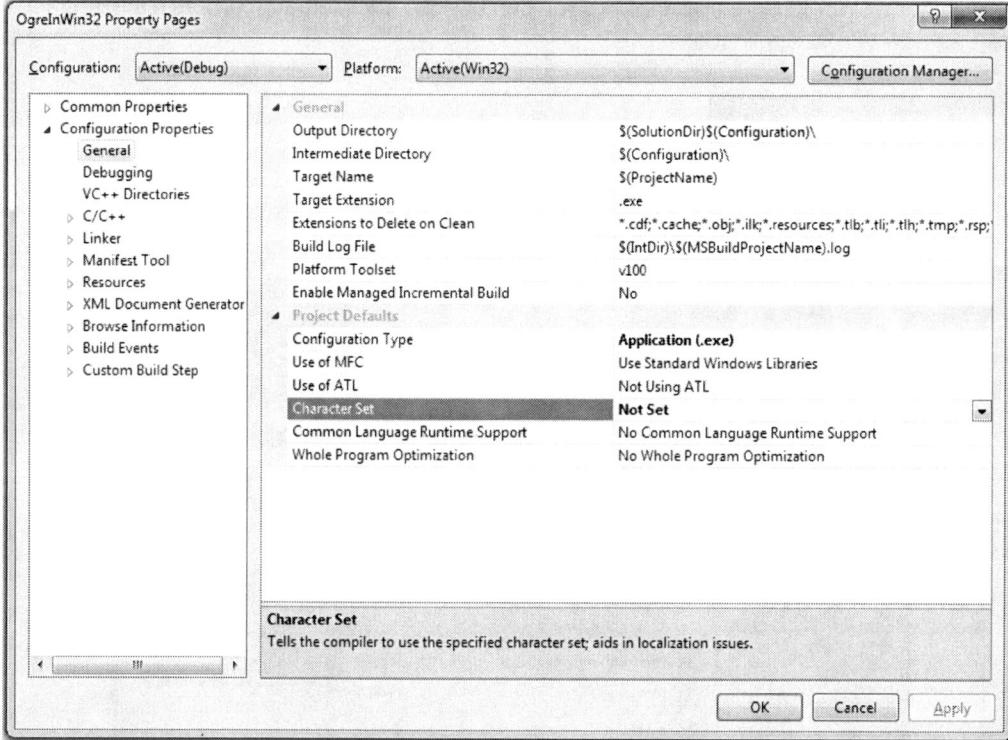

5. Expand **Configuration Properties** and click on **General**. Set **Character Set** to **Not Set**.

6. Next, click on **Debugging**. Select the **Local Windows Debugger** as the **Debugger to launch**, then specify the **Command** for starting the application as `..\..\..\bin\debug\$(TargetName)$(TargetExt)`.

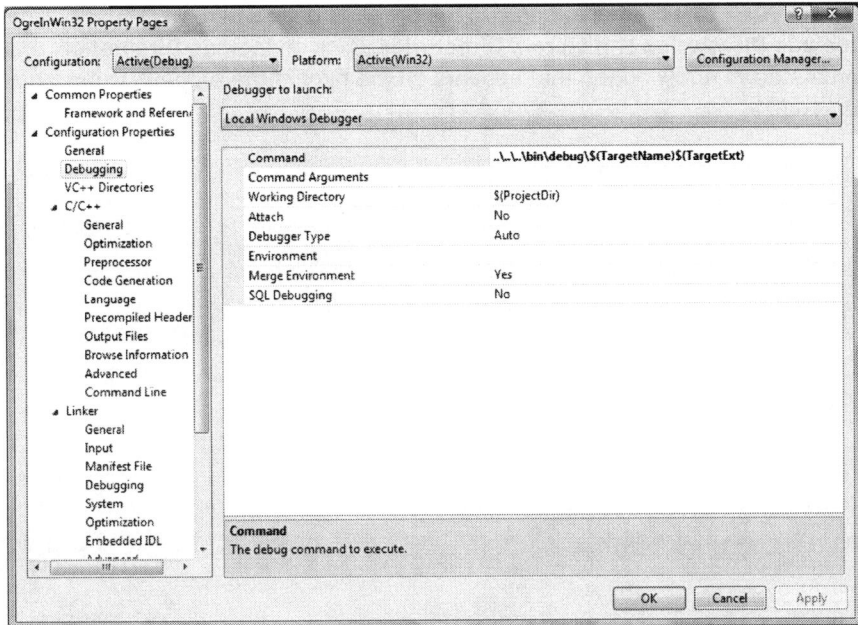

 Each project property setting is automatically written to a **per-user** file with the extension `.vcxproj.user`, whenever you save the solution.

7. Next we'll specify our **VC++ Directories**, so they match our Cookbook folder structure.

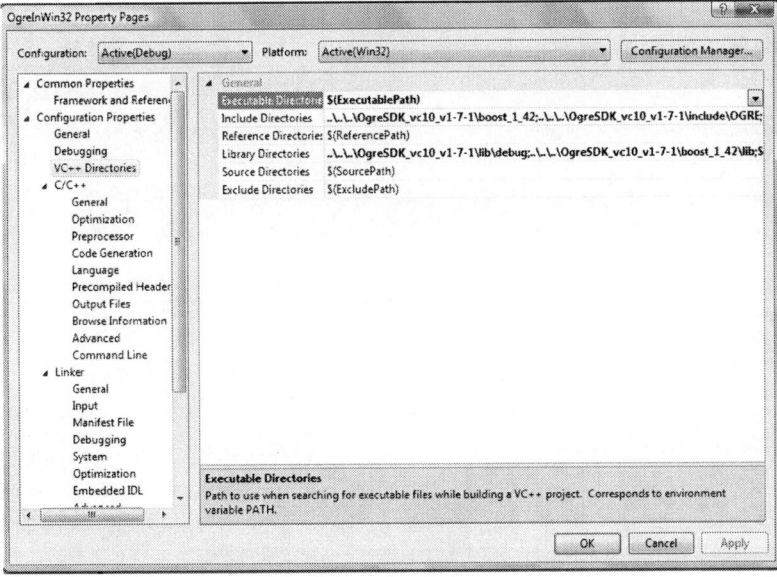

8. Select **VC++ Directories** to bring up the property page where we'll specify general **Include Directories** and **Library Directories**. Click on **Include Directories**, then click on the down arrow button that appears on the right of the property value, and click on **<edit>.**

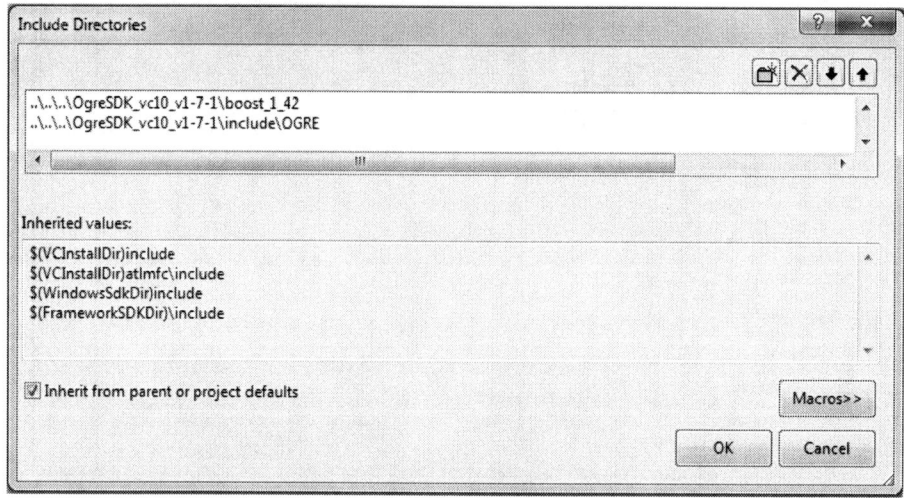

9. In the **Include Directories** dialog-box that appears, click on the first line of the text area, and enter the relative path to the Boost header files: `..\..\..\OgreSDK_vc10_v1-7-1\boost_1_42`.

10. Click on the second line, and enter the relative path to the Ogre header files `..\..\..\OgreSDK_vc10_v1-7-1\include\OGRE`, and click **OK**.

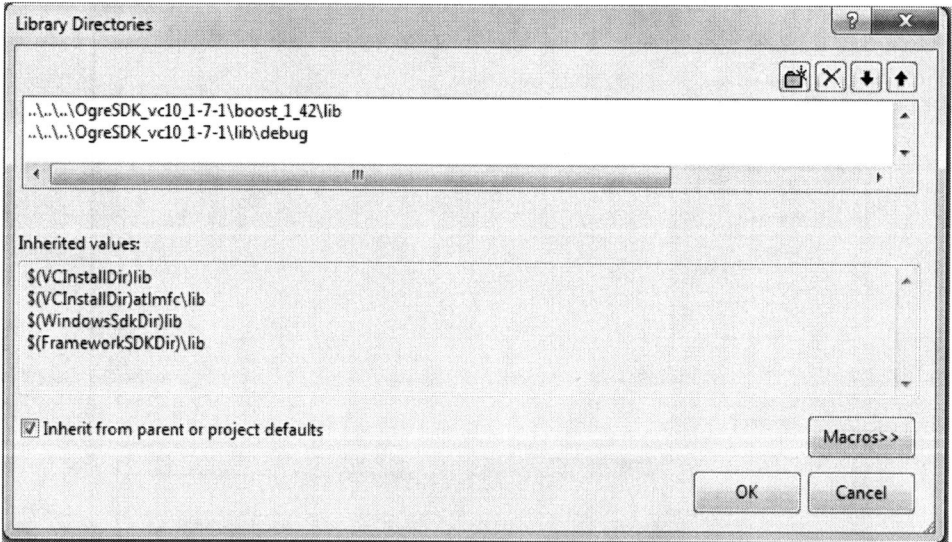

11. Edit the **Library Directories** property in the same way. Add the library directory `..\..\..\OgreSDK_vc10_v1-7-1\boost_1_42\lib` for Boost, and `..\..\..\OgreSDK_vc10_v1-7-1\lib\debug` for Ogre, then click **OK**.

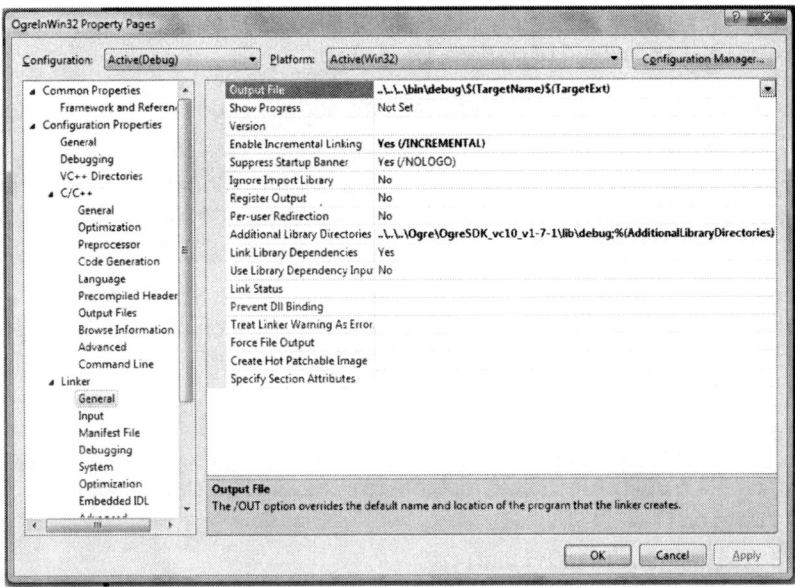

12. Next, expand the **Linker** section, and select **General**. Change the **Output File** property to `..\..\..\bin\debug\$(TargetName)$(TargetExt)`.

13. Then, change the **Additional Library Directories** property to `..\..\..\Ogre\OgreSDK_vc10_v1-7-1\lib\debug`.

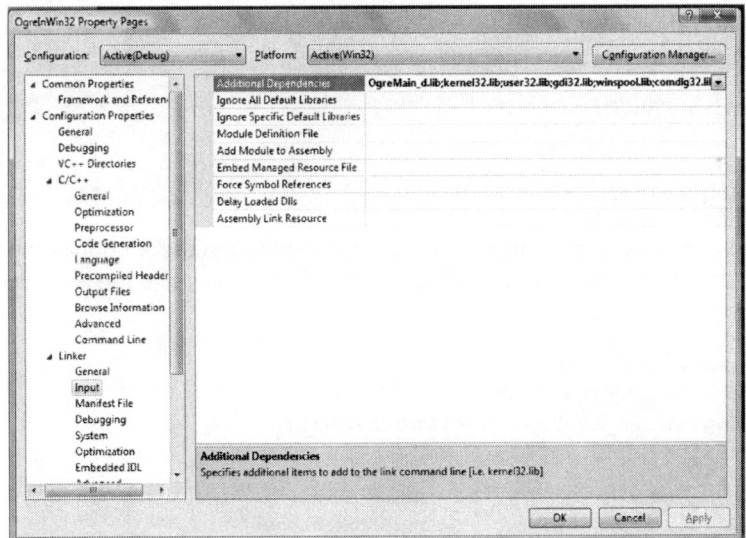

14. Finally, provide the linker with the location of the main Ogre code library. Select the **Input properties** section, and prepend `OgreMain_d.lib;` at the beginning of the line.

    Note that if we were setting properties for the release configuration, we would use `OgreMain.lib` instead of `OgreMain_d.lib`.

15. Now that the project properties are set, let's add the code necessary to integrate Ogre in our Win32 application.

    Copy the `Engine.cpp` and `Engine.h` files from the Cookbook sample files to your new project folder, and add them to the project. These files contain the `CEngine` wrapper class that we'll be using to interface with Ogre.

16. Open the `OgreInWin32.cpp` file, and include `Engine.h`, then declare a global instance of the `CEngine` class, and a forward declaration of our `InitEngine()` function with the other globals at the top of the file.

```
CEngine *m_Engine = NULL;
void InitEngine(HWND hWnd);
```

17. Next, create a utility function to instantiate our `CEngine` class, called `InitEngine()`.

```
void InitEngine(HWND hWnd){
  m_Engine = new CEngine(hWnd);
}
```

18. Then, call `InitEngine()` from inside the `InitInstance()` function, just after the window handle has been created successfully, as follows:

```
hWnd = CreateWindow(szWindowClass, szTitle, WS_OVERLAPPEDWINDOW,
  CW_USEDEFAULT, 0, CW_USEDEFAULT, 0, NULL, NULL, hInstance,
  NULL);

if (!hWnd){
  return FALSE;
}

InitEngine(hWnd);
```

19. Our last task is to render the 3D scene and display it in the window when we receive a `WM_PAINT` message. Add a call to `renderOneFrame()` to the `WndProc()` function, as follows:

```
case WM_PAINT:
  hdc = BeginPaint(hWnd, &ps);
  m_Engine->m_Root->renderOneFrame();
  EndPaint(hWnd, &ps);
break;
```

And that's it!

How it works...

Let's look at the CEngine class to see how we create and initialize an instance of the Ogre engine, and add a camera and robot model to the scene.

Open Engine.cpp, and look at the constructor for CEngine. In the constructor, we create an instance of the Ogre engine, and store it in the m_Root class member variable.

```
m_Root = new Ogre::Root("", "", Ogre::String(ApplicationPath +
    Ogre::String("OgreInWin32.log")));
```

An instance of Ogre::Root must exist before any other Ogre functions are called. The first parameter to the constructor is the **plugins configuration filename**, which defaults to plugins.cfg, but we pass it an empty string because we are going to load that file manually later. The second parameter is the **main configuration filename**, which defaults to ogre. cfg, but we pass it an empty string, also because we'll be loading that file manually as well. The third parameter is the **name of the log file** where Ogre will write the debugging and the hardware information.

> Once the Ogre::Root instance has been created, it can be globally accessed by Root::getSingleton(), which returns a reference or Root::getSingletonPtr(), which returns a pointer.

Next, we manually load the configuration file ogre.cfg, which resides in the same directory as our application executable.

```
OgreConfigFile.load(Ogre::String(ApplicationPath +
    Ogre::String("ogre.cfg")), "\t:=", false);
```

The ogre.cfg configuration file contains Ogre 3D engine graphics settings and typically looks as follows:

```
# Render System indicates which of the render systems
# in this configuration file we'll be using.
Render System=Direct3D9 Rendering Subsystem

[Direct3D9 Rendering Subsystem]
Allow NVPerfHUD=No
Anti aliasing=None
Floating-point mode=Fastest
Full Screen=Yes
Rendering Device=NVIDIA GeForce 7600 GS (Microsoft Corporation - WDDM)
VSync=No
Video Mode=800 x 600 @ 32-bit colour
```

```
[OpenGL Rendering Subsystem]
Colour Depth=32
Display Frequency=60
FSAA=0
Full Screen=Yes
RTT Preferred Mode=FBO
VSync=No
Video Mode=1024 x 768
```

Once the main configuration file is loaded, we manually load the correct render system plugin and tell Ogre which render system to use.

```
Ogre::String RenderSystemName;
RenderSystemName = OgreConfigFile.getSetting("Render System");


m_Root->loadPlugin("RenderSystem_Direct3D9_d);


Ogre::RenderSystemList RendersList = m_Root->getAvailableRenderers();
m_Root->setRenderSystem(RendersList[0]);
```

There's actually a little more code in `Engine.cpp` for selecting the correct render system plugin to load, but for our render system settings the `RenderSystem_Direct3D9_d` plugin is all we need.

Next, we load the `resources.cfg` configuration file.

```
Ogre::ConfigFile cf;
Ogre::String ResourcePath = ApplicationPath + Ogre::String("resources.
cfg");
cf.load(ResourcePath);
```

The `resources.cfg` file contains a list of all the paths where Ogre should search for graphic resources.

Then, we go through all the sections and settings in the resource configuration file, and add every location to the Ogre resource manager.

```
Ogre::ConfigFile::SectionIterator seci = cf.getSectionIterator();
Ogre::String secName, typeName, archName;


while (seci.hasMoreElements()){
  secName = seci.peekNextKey();
  Ogre::ConfigFile::SettingsMultiMap *settings = seci.getNext();
  Ogre::ConfigFile::SettingsMultiMap::iterator i;

  for(i = settings->begin(); i != settings->end(); ++i){
    typeName = i->first;
```

```
        archName = i->second;
        archName = ApplicationPath + archName;
        Ogre::ResourceGroupManager::getSingleton().
          addResourceLocation(archName, typeName, secName);
    }
}
```

Now, we are ready to initialize the engine.

```
m_Root->initialise(false);
```

We pass in `false` to the `initialize()` function, to indicate that we don't want Ogre to create a render window for us. We'll be manually creating a render window later, using the `hWnd` window handle from our Win32 Application.

Every graphics object in the scene including all meshes, lights, and cameras are managed by the **Ogre scene manager**. There are several scene managers to choose from, and each specializes in managing certain types of scenes of varying sizes. Some scene managers support rendering vast landscapes, while others are best for enclosed spaces. We'll use the generic scene manager for this recipe, because we don't need any extra features.

```
m_SceneManager = m_Root->createSceneManager(Ogre::ST_GENERIC,
  "Win32Ogre");
```

Remember when we initialized `Ogre::Root`, and specifically told it not to auto-create a render window? We did that because we create a render window manually using the `externalWindowHandle` parameter.

```
Ogre::NameValuePairList params;
params["externalWindowHandle"] =
  Ogre::StringConverter::toString((long)hWnd);
params["vsync"] = "true";

RECT   rect;
GetClientRect(hWnd, &rect);

Ogre::RenderTarget *RenderWindow = NULL;

try{
  m_RenderWindow = m_Root->createRenderWindow("Ogre in Win32", rect.
right
    - rect.left, rect.bottom - rect.top, false, &params);
}
catch(...){
  MessageBox(hWnd, "Failed to create the Ogre::RenderWindow\nCheck that
    your graphics card driver is up-to-date", "Initialize Render
System",
    MB_OK | MB_ICONSTOP);
exit(EXIT_SUCCESS);
}
```

As you have probably guessed, the `createRenderWindow()` method creates a new `RenderWindow` instance. The first parameter is the **name** of the window. The second and third parameters are the **width** and **height** of the window, respectively. The fourth parameter is set to `false` to indicate that we don't want to run in full-screen mode. The last parameter is our `NameValuePair` list, in which we provide the external window handle for embedding the Ogre renderer in our application window.

If we want to see anything, we need to create a camera, and add it to our scene. The next bit of code does just that.

```
m_Camera = m_SceneManager->createCamera("Camera");
m_Camera->setNearClipDistance(0.5);
m_Camera->setFarClipDistance(5000);
m_Camera->setCastShadows(false);
m_Camera->setUseRenderingDistance(true);
m_Camera->setPosition(Ogre::Vector3(200.0, 50.0, 100.0));
Ogre::SceneNode *CameraNode = NULL;
CameraNode = m_SceneManager->getRootSceneNode()-
>createChildSceneNode("CameraNode");
```

First, we tell the scene manager to create a camera, and give it the highly controversial name `Camera`. Next, we set some basic camera properties, such as the near and far clip distances, whether to cast shadows or not, and where to put the camera in the scene. Now that the camera is created and configured, we still have to attach it to a scene node for Ogre to consider it a part of the scene graph, so we create a new child scene node named `CameraNode`, and attach our camera to that node.

The last bit of the camera-related code involves us telling Ogre that we want the content for our camera to end up in our render window. We do this by defining a viewport that gets its content from the camera, and displays it in the render window.

```
Ogre::Viewport* Viewport = NULL;

if (0 == m_RenderWindow->getNumViewports()){
  Viewport = m_RenderWindow->addViewport(m_Camera);
  Viewport->setBackgroundColour(Ogre::ColourValue(0.8f, 1.0f, 0.8f));
}

m_Camera->setAspectRatio(Ogre::Real(rect.right - rect.left) /
  Ogre::Real(rect.bottom - rect.top));
```

The first line of code checks whether we have already created a viewport for our render window or not; if not, it creates one with a greenish background color.

We also set the aspect ratio of the camera to match the aspect ratio of our viewport. Without setting the aspect ratio, we could end up with some really squashed or stretched-looking scenes.

 You may wonder why you might want to have multiple viewports for a single render window. Consider a car racing game where you want to display the rear view mirror in the top portion of your render window. One way to accomplish, this would be to define a viewport that draws to the entire render window, and gets its content from a camera facing out the front windshield of the car, and another viewport that draws to a small subsection of the render window and gets its content from a camera facing out the back windshield.

The last lines of code in the `CEngine` constructor are for loading and creating the 3D robot model that comes with the Ogre SDK.

```
Ogre::Entity *RobotEntity = m_SceneManager->createEntity("Robot",
  "robot.mesh");
Ogre::SceneNode *RobotNode = m_SceneManager->getRootSceneNode()-
  >createChildSceneNode();
RobotNode->attachObject(RobotEntity);

Ogre::AxisAlignedBox RobotBox = RobotEntity->getBoundingBox();
Ogre::Vector3 RobotCenter = RobotBox.getCenter();
m_Camera->lookAt(RobotCenter);
```

We tell the scene manager to create a new entity named `Robot`, and to load the `robot.mesh` resource file for this new entity. The `robot.mesh` file is a model file in the Ogre `.mesh` format that describes the triangles, textures, and texture mappings for the robot model. We then create a new scene node just like we did for the camera, and attach our robot entity to this new scene node, making our killer robot visible in our scene graph. Finally, we tell the camera to look at the center of our robot's bounding box.

Finally, we tell Ogre to render the scene.

```
m_Root->renderOneFrame();
```

We also tell Ogre to render the scene in `OgreInWin32.cpp` whenever our application receives a `WM_PAINT` message. The `WM_PAINT` message is sent when the operating system, or another application, makes a request that our application paints a portion of its window. Let's take a look at the `WM_PAINT` specific code in the `WndProc()` function again.

```
case WM_PAINT:
  hdc = BeginPaint(hWnd, &ps);
  m_Engine->m_Root->renderOneFrame();
  EndPaint(hWnd, &ps);
break;
```

The `BeginPaint()` function prepares the window for painting, and the corresponding `EndPaint()` function denotes the end of painting. In between those two calls is the Ogre function call to `renderOneFrame()`, which will draw the contents of our viewport in our application window.

During the `renderOneFrame()` function call, Ogre gathers all the objects, lights, and materials that are to be drawn from the scene manager based on the camera's frustum or visible bounds. It then passes that information to the render system, which executes the 3D library function calls that run on your system's graphics hardware, to do the actual drawing on a render surface. In our case, the 3D library is **Direct X** and the render surface is the `hdc`, or **Handle to the device context**, of our application window.

The result of all our hard work can be seen in the following screenshot:

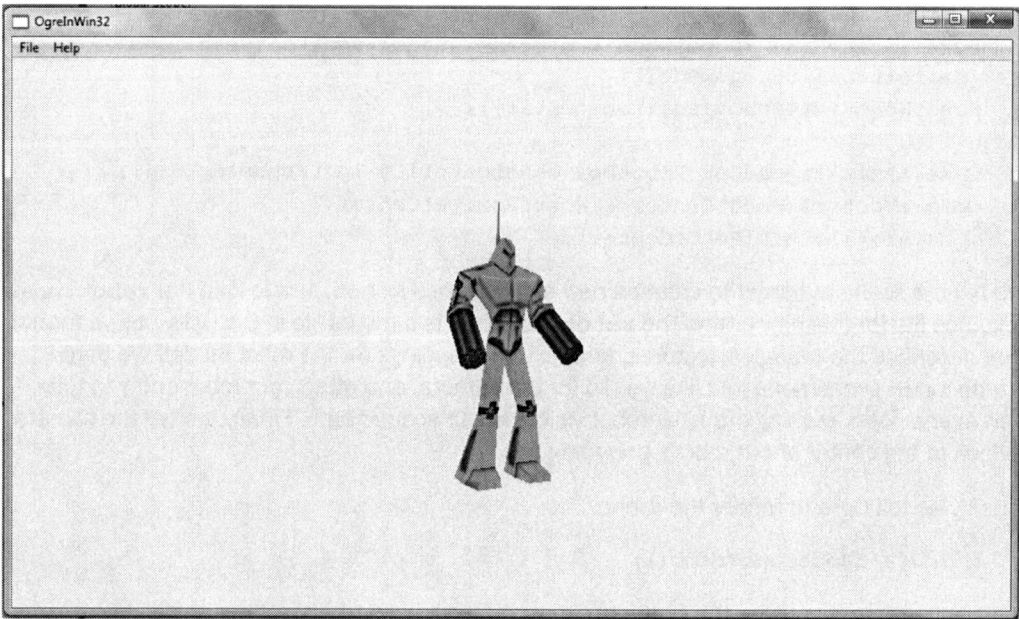

Flee in terror earthling!

There's more...

If you want to use the release configuration instead of debug, change the **Configuration type** to **Release** in the project properties, substitute the word `release` where you see the word `debug` in this recipe, and link the `OgreMain.lib` instead of `OgreMain_d.lib` in the linker settings.

It is likely that at some point you will want to use a newer version of the Ogre SDK. If you download a newer version and extract it to the `Recipes` folder, you will need to change the paths in the project settings so that they match the paths for the version of the SDK you downloaded.

Creating an MFC Ogre application

In the previous recipe, we showed you how to create a simple Win32 application. By incorporating the **Microsoft Foundation Classes** (**MFC**) library into our application, we gain access to a lot of extra functionality and user interface tools. In this recipe, we will show you how to create an Ogre MFC application that displays a 3D robot in a window.

Getting ready

To follow along with this recipe, open the solution located in the `Recipes/Chapter01/OgreInMFC folder` in the code bundle available on the Packt website.

How to do it...

We'll start by creating a new MFC application using the **MFC Application Wizard**.

1. Create a new project by clicking **File | New | Project**. In the **New Project** dialog-box, expand **Visual C++**, and click on **MFC Application**. Name the project `OgreInMFC`. For **Location**, browse to your `Recipes` folder, append `\Chapter_01_Examples`, and click on **OK**.

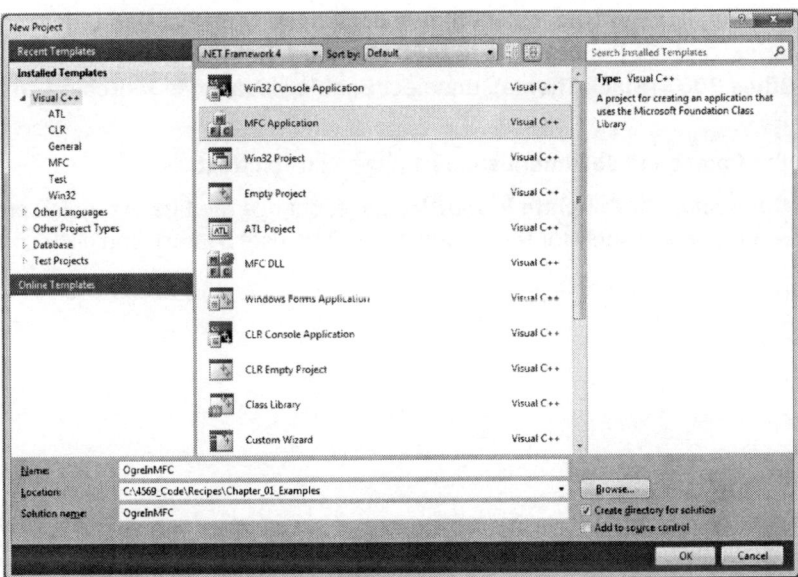

2. In the **MFC Application Wizard**, click on **Next**.

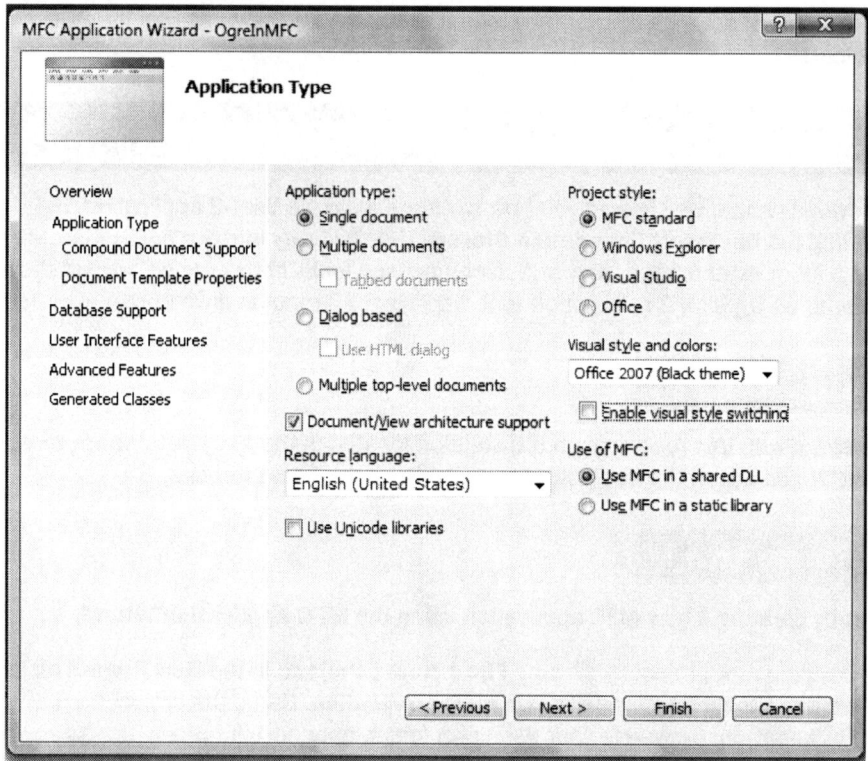

For the **Application type**, select **Single document**. Unselect **Use Unicode libraries**, and set **Project style** to **MFC standard**. Set the **Visual style and colors** to **Office 2007 (Black Theme)**, unselect **Enable visual style switching**, and click on **Next**.

3. On the **Compound document support** page, click on **Next**.

4. On the **Document Template Properties** page, change the **File extension** property to scene (not necessarily for this recipe, but will be useful later), and click on **Next**.

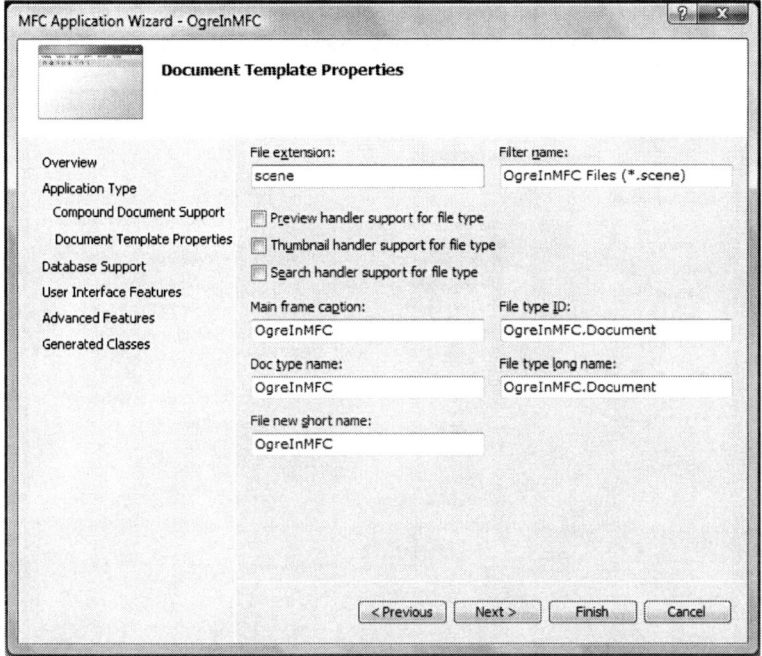

5. On the **Database Support** page, click on **Next**.

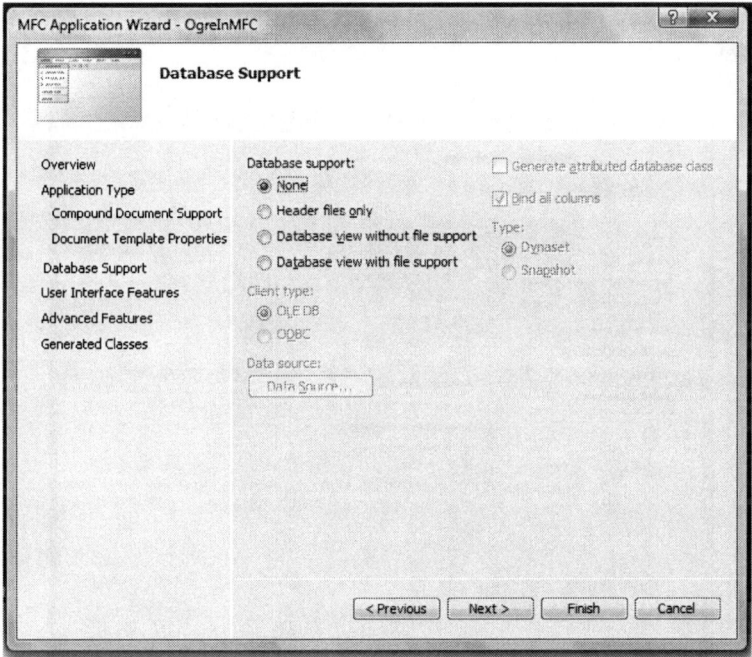

6. On the **User Interface Features** page, select **Maximized** so the application will start with its window maximized. Select **Use a classic menu**, and click on **Next**.

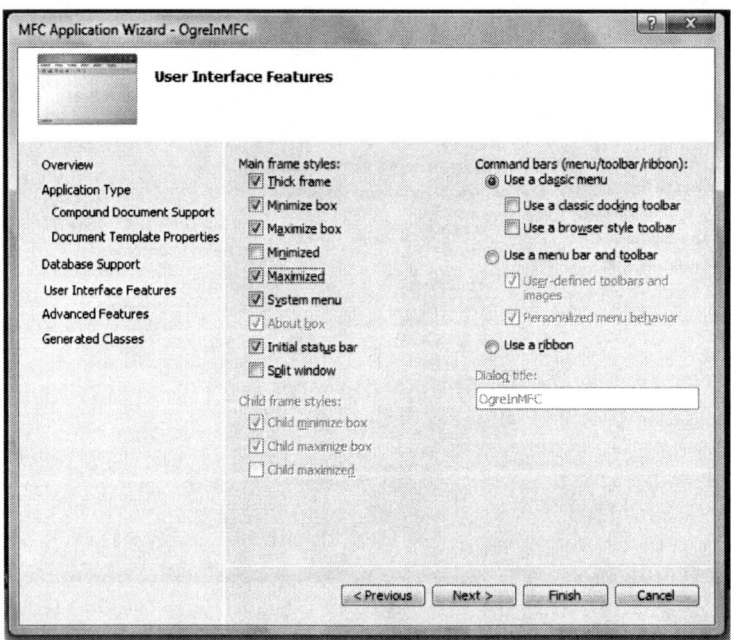

7. On the **Advanced Features** page, un-select **Printing and print preview**, and click on **Next**.

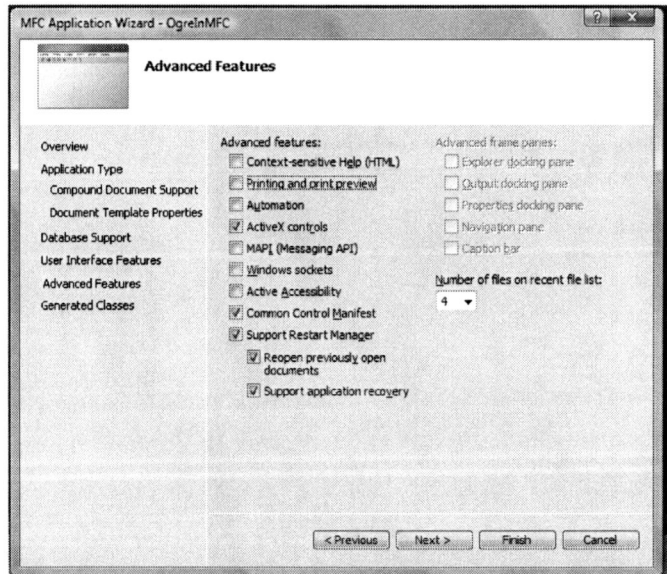

8. On the **Generated Classes** page, click on **Finish** to create the project.

9. The next step is to configure the project properties just like we did for our Win32 application, so that the compiler and linker know where to find the Ogre header and library files. Examine the project properties for the sample MFC application, and you will see that the properties are the same as in our Win32 application.

10. Next, copy the `Engine.cpp` and `Engine.h` files from the Cookbook sample MFC application to our new project folder, and add them to the project.

11. Open `OgreInMfc.h`, and add a new member variable for our `CEngine` instance, and a declaration of the `InitEngine()` function that we'll be adding.

```
public:
  CEngine* m_Engine;
  void InitEngine(void);
```

12. Now, in `OgreInMfc.cpp`, modify the `COgreInMfcApp` constructor to give our new member variable a default value.

```
COgreInMfcApp::COgreInMfcApp()
  : m_Engine(NULL)
```

13. Then, add our familiar `InitEngine()` function.

```
void COgreInMfcApp::InitEngine(void){
  m_Engine = new CEngine();
}
```

14. Finally, call `InitEngine()` at the end of `COgreInMfcApp::InitInstance()`.

```
InitEngine();
```

In our Win32 application, all of our Ogre setup code was done in the `CEngine` constructor. This time, we do not have a window handle in `InitInstance()`, so we can't set up the render window here. The `CEngine` constructor only creates the Ogre engine instance and initializes it.

15. Now, add a function to the `OgreInMfcView` class in `OgreInMfcView.h` called `EngineSetup()` that will contain the rest of our Ogre setup code.

```
void EngineSetup(void);
```

While we're here, let's add a few more member variables that we'll need.

```
bool m_First;

Ogre::Camera*m_Camera;
Ogre::RenderWindow*m_RenderWindow;
```

Now open `OgreInMfcView.cpp`, and create the `EngineSetup()` function.

```
void COgreInMfcView::EngineSetup(void)
{}
```

16. First, we need to get the `Ogre::Root` instance from CEngine, and use it to create a scene manager named `MFCOgre`.

```
Ogre::Root *Root = ((COgreInMfcApp*)AfxGetApp())->m_Engine-
  >GetRoot();

Ogre::SceneManager *SceneManager = NULL;
SceneManager = Root->createSceneManager(Ogre::ST_GENERIC,
  "MFCOgre");
```

We also create a generic scene manager, and name it `MFCOgre`.

17. Next, we create a render window with our window handle, just as we did in the Ogre Win32 application.

```
Ogre::NameValuePairList parms;
parms["externalWindowHandle"] =
  Ogre::StringConverter::toString((long)m_hWnd);
parms["vsync"] = "true";

CRect    rect;
GetClientRect(&rect);

Ogre::RenderTarget *RenderWindow = Root->getRenderTarget("Ogre in
  MFC");

if (RenderWindow == NULL){
  try{
    m_RenderWindow = Root->createRenderWindow("Ogre in MFC",
      rect.Width(), rect.Height(), false, &parms);
  }
  catch(...){
    MessageBox("Cannot initialize\nCheck that graphic-card driver
      is up-to-date", "Initialize Render System", MB_OK |
      MB_ICONSTOP);
    exit(EXIT_SUCCESS);
  }
}
```

18. Then, we instruct the `Ogre::ResourceGroupManager` to initialize all resource groups.

```
// Load resources
Ogre::ResourceGroupManager::getSingleton().
initialiseAllResourceGroups();
```

19. Next, we create and initialize our camera. We also add it to a new scene node.

```
// Create the camera
m_Camera = SceneManager->createCamera("Camera");
m_Camera->setNearClipDistance(0.5);
m_Camera->setFarClipDistance(5000);
m_Camera->setCastShadows(false);
m_Camera->setUseRenderingDistance(true);
m_Camera->setPosition(Ogre::Vector3(200.0, 50.0, 100.0));
Ogre::SceneNode *CameraNode = NULL;
CameraNode = SceneManager->getRootSceneNode()-
   >createChildSceneNode("CameraNode");
```

20. After the camera is set up, we need to create a viewport that will take the contents of the camera's view, and draw it in our render window. We also need to set the camera's aspect ratio to match the aspect ratio of the render window.

```
Ogre::Viewport* Viewport = NULL;

if (0 == m_RenderWindow->getNumViewports()){
  Viewport = m_RenderWindow->addViewport(m_Camera);
  Viewport->setBackgroundColour(Ogre::ColourValue(0.8f, 1.0f,
    0.8f));
}

m_Camera->setAspectRatio(Ogre::Real(rect.Width()) /
  Ogre::Real(rect.Height()));
```

The last lines of code in `EngineSetup()` create a robot entity that uses the `robot.mesh` resource, and attach it to a new scene node. They also point the camera at the center of the robot's bounding box.

```
Ogre::Entity *RobotEntity = SceneManager->createEntity("Robot",
  "robot.mesh");
Ogre::SceneNode *RobotNode = SceneManager->getRootSceneNode()-
  >createChildSceneNode();
RobotNode->attachObject(RobotEntity);

Ogre::AxisAlignedBox Box = RobotEntity->getBoundingBox();
Ogre::Vector3 Center = Box.getCenter();
m_Camera->lookAt(Center);
```

21. Next, we need to add a message handler for the `WM_PAINT` message, and call `EngineSetup()` the first time the Ogre engine instance is available.

22. To add the `WM_PAINT` message handler, open the **Class View** and expand **OgreInMfc**. Then right-click on **COgreInMfcView**, and select `Properties`. In the **Properties** window, click on the **Messages** icon, then scroll down till you find `WM_PAINT`. Click in the box next to **WM_PAINT**, and click on `<add>OnPaint`. Inside the resulting `OnPaint()` function, we add the following code:

```
CEngine *Engine = ((COgreInMfcApp*)AfxGetApp())->m_Engine;
if (Engine == NULL)
   return;

Ogre::Root *Root = Engine->GetRoot();

if (m_First && Root != NULL){
   m_First = false;
   EngineSetup();
}
```

23. Once the Ogre engine instance is available, we need to instruct Ogre to render by calling `renderOneFrame()`, so add the following code to the end of the `OnPaint()`.

```
if (Root != NULL){
   Root->renderOneFrame();
}
```

24. Open `OgreInMfcDoc.cpp`, and add a call to `UpdateAllViews()` in `COgreInMfcDoc::OnNewDocument()`, so that our view's `OnPaint` method is called every time the user clicks on the **New document** button.

```
BOOL COgreInMfcDoc::OnNewDocument(){
   if (!CDocument::OnNewDocument())
      return FALSE;

   UpdateAllViews(NULL);
   return TRUE;
}
```

How it works...

In this recipe, we divide the process of setting up Ogre into two steps. First, we create an instance of the Ogre engine and initialize it in the `CEngine` constructor, just as we do in the *Creating a Win32 Ogre application* recipe. The rest of the setup happens in the `COgreInMfcView::EngineSetup()` function.

When the user runs the program and clicks on the **New** button, the resulting `COgreInMfcDoc::OnNewDocument()` function call contains `UpdateAllViews(NULL);`, which will call our `COgreInMfcView::OnPaint()` method, and display our 3D scene. The following is a screenshot from our new MFC application:

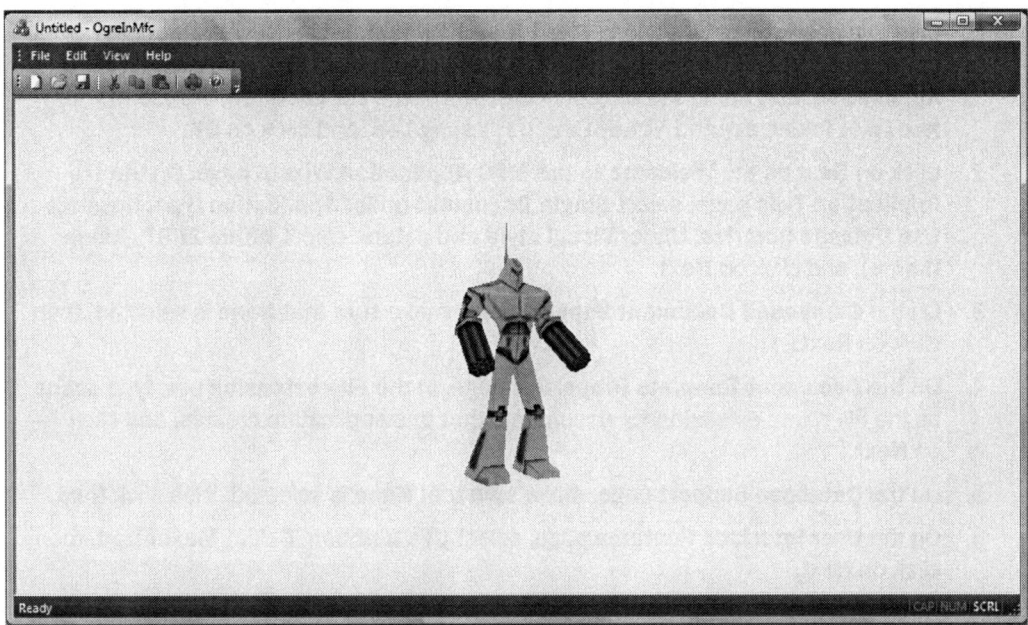

Creating an MFC Ogre application with a ribbon

Adding the **ribbon** to your MFC application is a great way to organize the user interface when your application has a lot of menus and options. In this recipe, we show how to use the **MFC Application Wizard** to create an application with a ribbon. We also show you how to add ribbon categories, category panels, and add controls to category panels.

Getting ready

To follow along with this recipe, open the solution located in the `Recipes/Chapter01/OgreInRibbon` folder in the code bundle available on the Packt website.

How to do it...

Let's start by creating a new MFC application using the MFC Application Wizard. During the wizard process, we'll customize our application to include a ribbon.

1. Create a new project by clicking **File | New | Project**. In the **New Project** dialog-box, expand **Visual C++** under Installed Templates, select MFC and click on **MFC Application**, and name the project `OgreInRibbon`. For **Location**, browse to your `Recipes` folder, append `\Chapter_01_Examples`, and click on **OK**.

2. Click on **Next** on the **Welcome to the MFC Application Wizard** page. On the **Application Type** page, select **Single Document** under **Application type**. Unselect **Use Unicode libraries**. Under **Visual style and colors**, select **Office 2007 (Black theme)**, and click on **Next**.

3. On the **Compound Document Support** page, make sure that **None** is selected, then click on **Next**.

4. On the **Document Template Properties** page, in the **File extension** box, type **scene** as the file name extension for documents that this application creates, and click on **Next**.

5. On the **Database Support** page, make sure that **None** is selected, then click **Next**.

6. On the **User Interface Features** page, select **Use a ribbon**. Select **Maximized**, then click on **Next**.

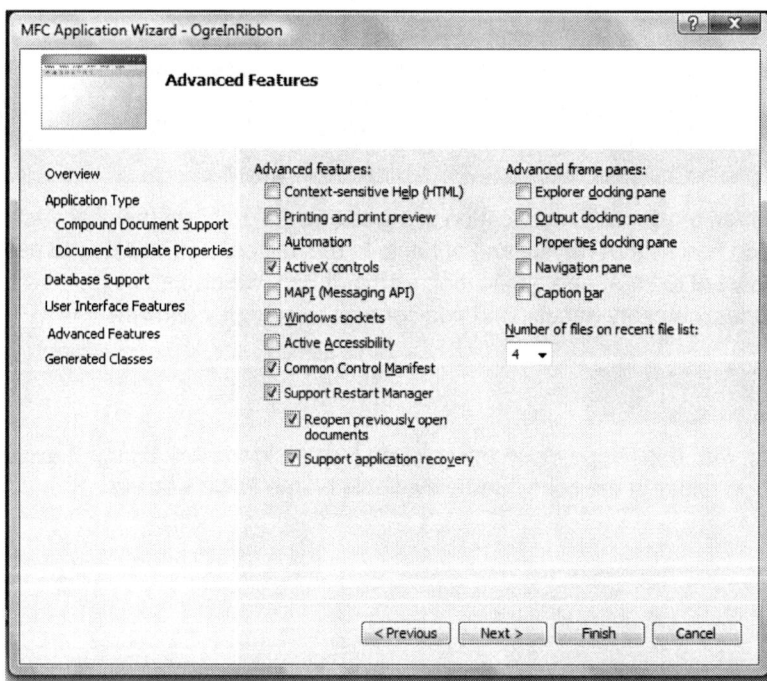

7. Remove **Printing and print preview**, and uncheck all **Advanced frame panes** checkboxes, then click on **Next**.

8. On the **Generated Classes** page, click on **Finish** to create the MFC application.

9. At this point, configure the project properties, just as we did for the *Creating a Win32 Ogre application* recipe.

10. Next, create a message handler for the WM_PAINT message and insert our InitEngine() and EngineSetup() functions, exactly as we did in the *Creating an MFC Ogre application* recipe.

How it works...

The MFC Application Wizard automatically adds a ribbon to the application window with one ribbon category named Home.

We created the Ogre engine instance, and initialize it just as we did in the *Creating a MFC Ogre application* recipe.

There's more...

To add categories and panels to the ribbon, open the ribbon resource in the **Resource View**, by selecting the **View** menu, then click on **Resource View**. Expand **OgreInRibbon**, and then expand **Ribbon**. Double-click on **IDR_RIBBON** to bring up the **Ribbon Editor**.

Next, add a new category by double-clicking **Category** in the **Toolbox**. Right-click the new category, and click on **Properties**. In the **Properties** panel, change the **Caption** to Scene Management. Then, add two panels to this category by double-clicking **Panel** in the **Toolbox**. Change the **Caption** of one panel to Weather Management and the other to Terrain Management.

Now, we can add controls to each panel to manage weather and terrain resources.

The following is a screenshot of our Ogre MFC Application with a customized ribbon:

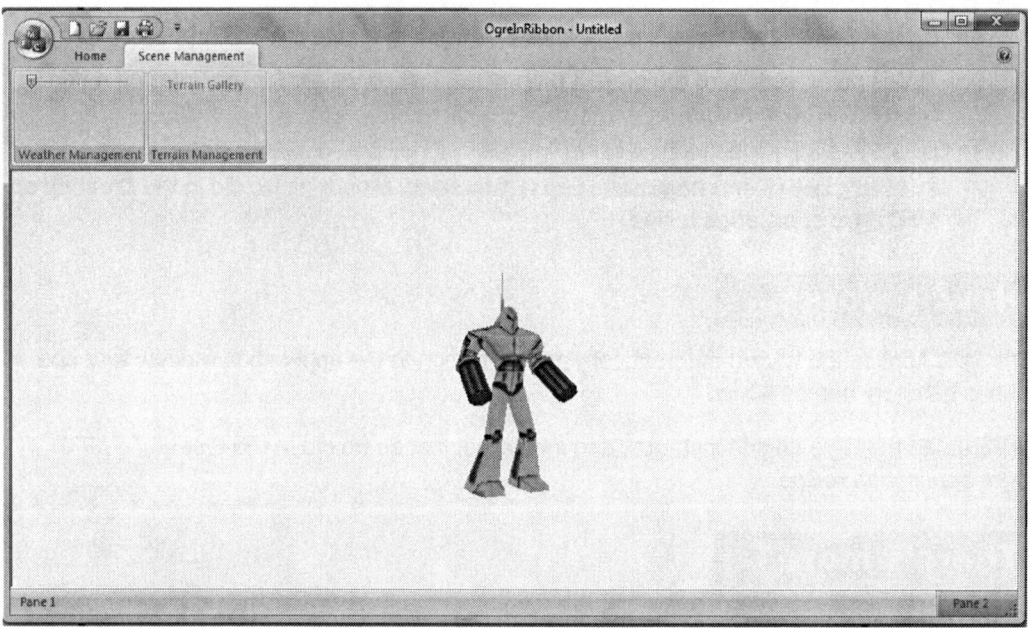

Creating a Windows Forms Ogre application

Windows Forms are a lightweight alternative to MFC, and in this recipe, we'll show you how to create a Windows Forms application that uses Ogre to render a 3D robot model.

Getting ready

To follow along with this recipe, open the solution located in the `Recipes/Chapter01/ OgreInWinForms` folder in the code bundle available on the Packt website.

How to do it...

First, we'll create a new Windows Forms application using the **New Project** wizard.

1. Create a new project by clicking **File | New | Project**. In the **Project Types** pane, expand **Visual C++**, select **CLR**, then select **Windows Forms Application** in the **Templates** pane. Name the project `OgreInWinForms`. For **Location**, browse to your `Recipes` folder, append `\Chapter_01_Examples`, and click on **OK**.

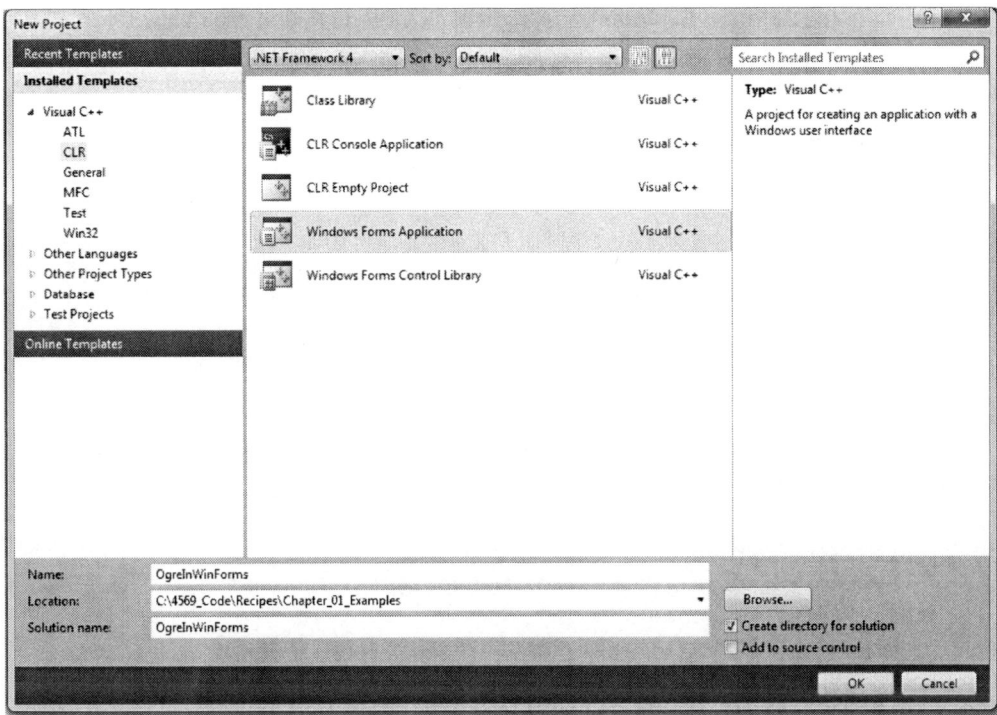

The **Windows Forms Designer** will appear showing **Form1** of the Windows Forms application that we just created.

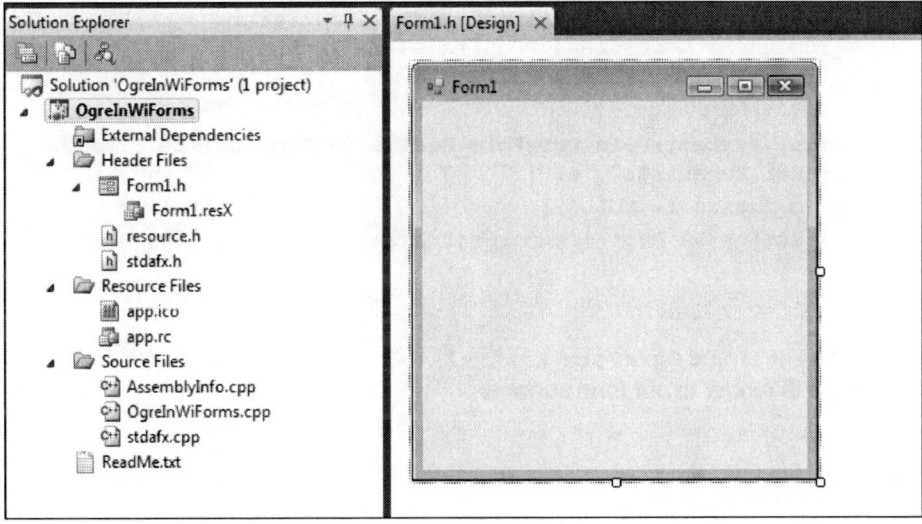

2. Next, in the **Solution Explorer** pane, right-click `Form1.h`, and click **View Code**.

   In `Form1.h`, add a new `CEngine` member instance variable.

   ```
   public:
       CEngine *m_Engine;
   ```

3. In the constructor, create an instance of our `CEngine` class, and pass it our window handle.

   ```
   OgreForm(void)
       : m_Engine(NULL){
       InitializeComponent();
       m_Engine = new CEngine((HWND)this->Handle.ToPointer());
   }
   ```

4. Next, we add a `PaintEventHandler` function and `Resize EventHandler` function to the `InitializeComponent()` method, and set the default window state to `maximized`.

   ```
   this->WindowState =
       System::Windows::Forms::FormWindowState::Maximized;
   this->Paint += gcnew
       System::Windows::Forms::PaintEventHandler(this,
       &OgreForm::Ogre_Paint);
   this->Resize += gcnew System::EventHandler(this,
       &OgreForm::OgreForm_Resize);
   ```

5. Create the functions for the event handlers we just added.

   ```
   private: System::Void Ogre_Paint(System::Object^  sender,
       System::Windows::Forms::PaintEventArgs^  e) {
       m_Engine->m_Root->renderOneFrame();
   }

   private: System::Void OgreForm_Resize(System::Object^  sender,
       System::EventArgs^  e) {
       if (m_Engine != NULL) {
         m_Engine->m_Root->renderOneFrame();
       }
   }
   ```

In the `Ogre_Paint()` and `OgreForm_Resize()` methods, we call `renderOneFrame()`, instructing Ogre to render to our form surface.

How it works...

Windows Forms is a smart client technology for the .NET framework, a set of managed libraries that simplify common application tasks. In Windows Forms, a **form** is a visual surface on which you display information to the user. You ordinarily build Windows Forms applications by adding controls to forms and those controls respond to user actions, such as mouse clicks or key presses. A **control** is a discrete **User Interface** (**UI**) element that displays data or accepts data input. In this basic Windows Forms application, we have Ogre draw the contents of our 3D scene on a form surface.

The following is a screenshot of our Ogre Windows Forms application in action:

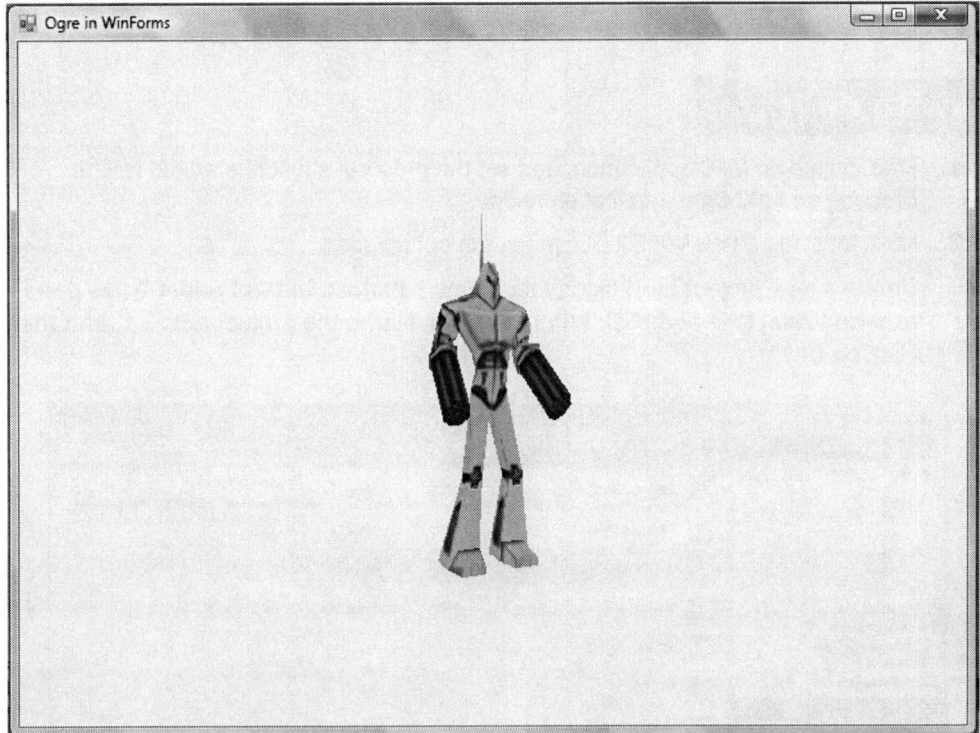

There's more...

It's easy to add controls to our form. In the **Toolbox**, click on the control you want to add. Then, on the form, click where you want the upper-left corner of the control to be located, and drag to where you want the lower-right corner of the control to be. When you let go, the control will be added to the form.

You can also add a control to the form, programmatically, at runtime.

Creating an Ogre plugin

Ogre supports a plugin system for loading and unloading DLLs that provide additional functionality or override existing functionality. You may have already noticed that Ogre relies on the render system and scene manager plugins to render scenes and manage scene objects. In this recipe, we'll show how to create an Ogre plugin that loads a 3D robot and adds it to the scene when the plugin's `initialise()` function is called.

Getting ready

To follow along with this recipe, open the solution located in the `Recipes/Chapter01/OgrePlugin` folder in the code bundle available on the Packt website.

How to do it...

1. First, create an MFC application, and set the properties just like we did for the *Creating an MFC Ogre application* recipe.

2. Next, let's add a new Win32 DLL project to our solution.

   Create a new project by clicking **File | New | Project**. In the **Project Types** pane, expand **Visual C++** and click **Win32 Project**. Name the project `Robot3`, and then click on **OK**.

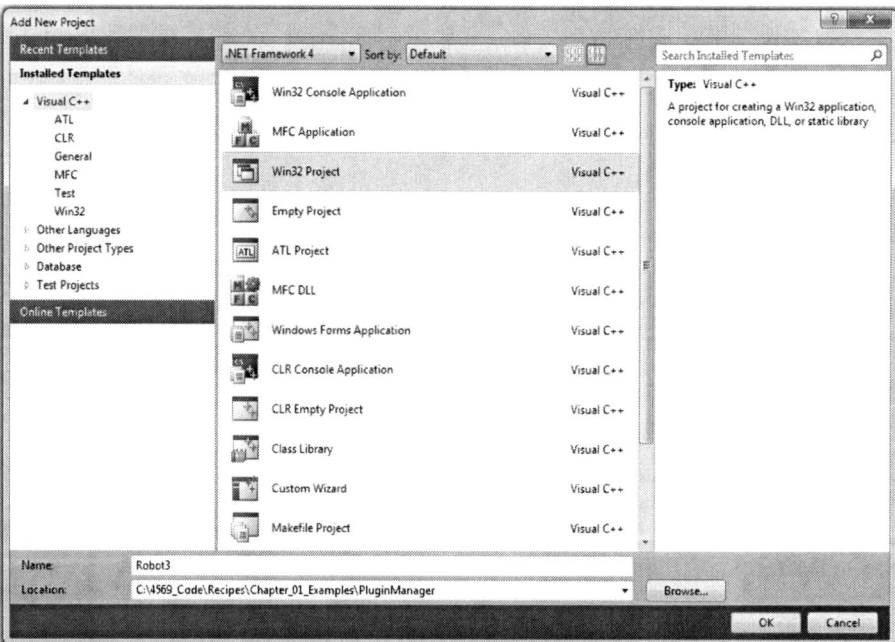

3. Click on **OK** on the **Win32 Application Wizard** welcome page.

4. On the **Application Settings** page, set the **Application type** to **DLL**, check **Empty project** in **Additional options**, and click on **Finish**.

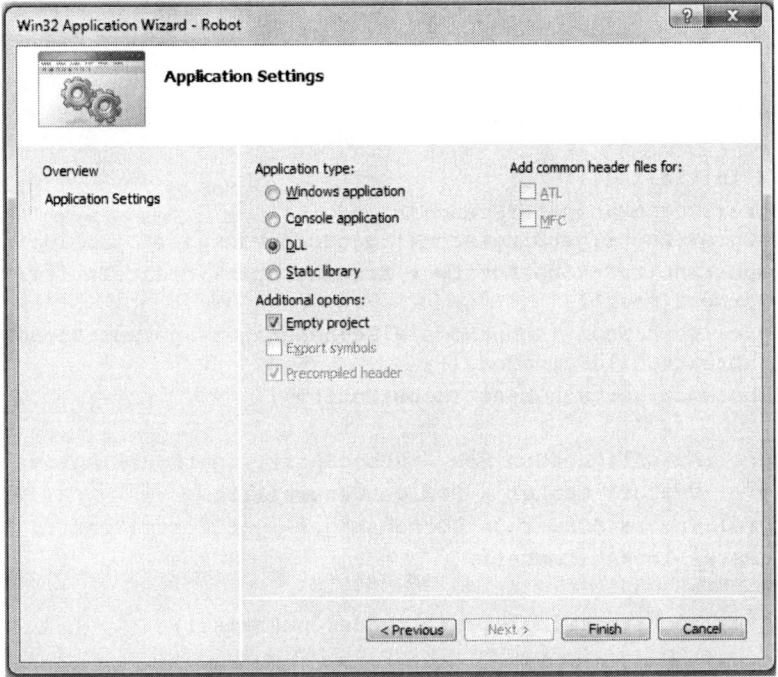

5. Next, modify the project properties, just like for the Win32 application project, and be sure to set the **Linker Output File** property, so our DLL ends up in the same folder as our MFC application executable.

6. Next, create an empty header file named Robot.h, and add it to the **Robot** project. In the new header file, create a new class called Robot3Plugin that derives from Ogre::Plugin.

```cpp
#include "Ogre.h"
#include "OgrePlugin.h"

class Robot3Plugin : public Ogre::Plugin{
  public:
    Ogre::String m_Name;

  Robot3Plugin(){
    m_Name = "Robot";
  }
};
```

7. Every subclass of `Ogre::Plugin` must implement the `getName()`, `install()`, `initialise()`, `shutdown()`, and `uninstall()` methods, so add the following code to our new `Robot3Plugin` class:

```
const Ogre::String& getName() const {
  return m_Name;
}

void install(){}

void initialise(){
  Ogre::SceneManager *SceneManager =
    Ogre::Root::getSingleton().getSceneManager("OgrePlugin");
  Ogre::Entity *RobotEntity = SceneManager->createEntity("Robot",
    "robot.mesh");
  Ogre::SceneNode *RobotNode = SceneManager->getRootSceneNode()-
    >createChildSceneNode();
  RobotNode->attachObject(RobotEntity);

  Ogre::AxisAlignedBox Box = RobotEntity->getBoundingBox();
  Ogre::Vector3 Center = Box.getCenter();
  Ogre::Camera *Camera = SceneManager->getCamera("Camera");
  Camera->lookAt(Center);

  Ogre::Root::getSingleton().renderOneFrame();
}

void shutdown(){}

void uninstall(){}
```

The `getName()` function simply returns the unique name of our plugin. Every other method, except for `initialise()`, we leave empty.

In the `initialise()` method, we load our robot mesh, create the robot entity, and attach it to a `scene` node. We also point the camera at the center of the robot's bounding box, and then call `renderOneFrame()`, which will result in Ogre drawing the scene to our application window.

8. Create an empty file called `Robot3.cpp`, and add it to the project.

At the top of the `Robot3.cpp` file, import the necessary headers and declare a global instance variable of our `Robot3Plugin` class.

```
#include "Robot3.h"
#include "Ogre.h"
#include "OgrePlugin.h"

Robot3Plugin *Robot;
```

9. Next, define two functions, `dllStartPlugin()` and `dllStopPlugin()`.

    ```
    extern "C" __declspec(dllexport) void dllStartPlugin(){
      Robot = OGRE_NEW Robot3Plugin();
      Ogre::Root::getSingleton().installPlugin(Robot);
    }

    extern "C" __declspec(dllexport) void dllStopPlugin(){
      Ogre::Root::getSingleton().uninstallPlugin(Robot);
      OGRE_DELETE Robot;
    }
    ```

    The `dllStartPlugin()` will be called by Ogre when it loads our plugin, and `dllStopPlugin()` will be called when the plugin is unloaded.

10. Now we need to add a menu item, so that we can test loading the `Robot` plugin.

    In the **Resource View**, expand **Plugin Manager**, **PluginManager.rc**, and then **Menu**. Double-click on the **IDR_MAINFRAME** resource item to open the menu editor.

    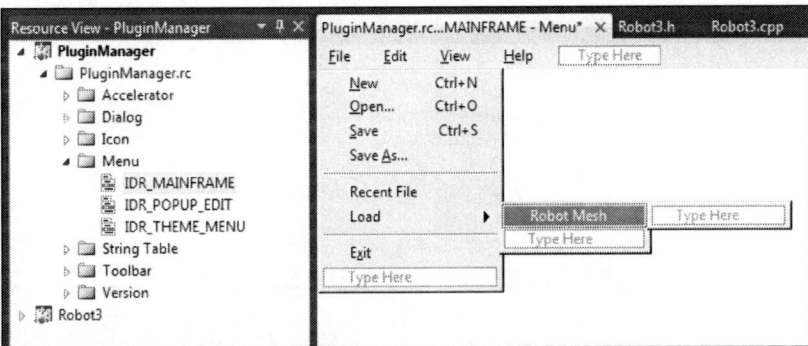

11. Add the submenu `Load` to the main menu, expand it, and add a new item named `Robot Mesh`.

12. Next, we need to add an event handler for when the user selects the new menu item. Right-click on the **RobotMesh** menu item, and choose **Add Event Handler**.

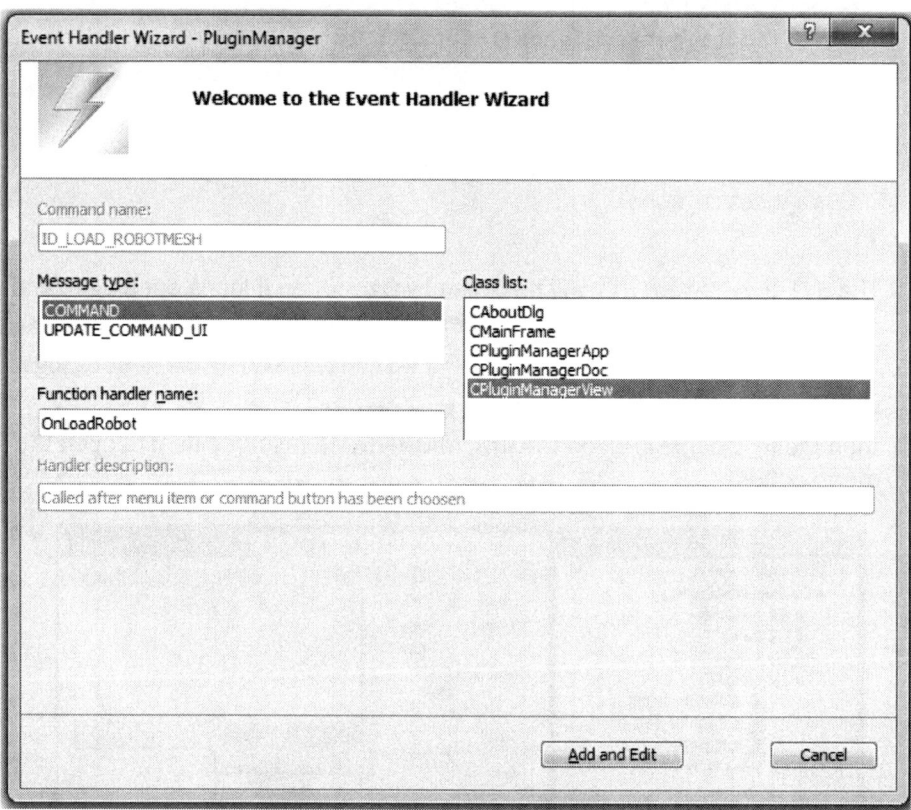

13. In the **Event Handler Wizard** that appears, set the **Function handler** name to OnLoadRobot, select **CPluginManagerView** from the **Class List**, and then press **Add and Edit**.

Our event handler function looks like this:

```
void CPluginManagerView::OnLoadRobot(){
    Ogre::Root::getSingleton().loadPlugin("Robot3");
}
```

When we call loadPlugin(), Ogre will load our Robot plugin and call dll-StartPlugin(), after which, Ogre will call initialize(), and our robot will appear in our application window.

How it works...

The process of creating an instance of the Ogre engine and initializing it is the same as in previous recipes. The main difference in this recipe is that we moved the loading of our robot mesh and creation of the robot entity into a plugin. Our plugin gets loaded when the user clicks our **Load | Robot Mesh** menu item.

The following is a screenshot from our sample project, featuring a killer robot after the user clicks the **Load | Robot Mesh** menu item:

There's more...

In this recipe, we've chosen to load the robot 3d mesh in our plugin, but a more practical use would be to register an object factory or a scene manager. The Ogre **Octree scene manager** plugin and **RenderSystem_GL** plugin are good examples of full-featured Ogre plugins.

See also

In this chapter:

- ▶ *Creating an MFC Ogre application*

If you're interested in how to create a specific type of plugin, such as a scene manager, go to `http://ogre3d.org,` and download the Ogre source code. Within, you will find the source code for the Octree scene manager.

Creating a custom resource manager

A common task for many graphics applications is loading and saving custom resources. In this recipe, we show you how to create a custom resource manager that loads Ogre 3D models from STL files.

The STL file format is used by the stereo lithography CAD software created by 3D Systems. This file format is supported by many other software packages, and is widely used for rapid prototyping and computer-aided manufacturing. STL files describe only the surface geometry of a three-dimensional object, without any representation of color, texture, or other common CAD model attributes. It contains the raw unstructured triangulated surface information as a series of unit normals and vertices, ordered by the right-hand rule.

Getting ready

To follow along with this recipe, open the solution located in the `Recipes/Chapter01/ResourceManagement` folder in the code bundle available on the Packt website.

How to do it...

1. First, create a new Ogre MFC application named `ResourceManager`, by following the *Creating an MFC Ogre application* recipe.

2. Next, we need the following three new classes.

    ❑   `StlFile`: It's derived from `Ogre::Resource`, and will represent our custom resource.

    ❑   `StlFileManager`: It's derived from `Ogre::ResourceManager` and `Ogre::Singleton<StlFileManger>`. This is our custom resource manager for `STLFile` resources.

    ❑   `StlFileSerializer`: It's derived from `Ogre::Serializer`, and is responsible for loading STL files, parsing them and creating meshes from the data.

3. Copy the `StlFile`, `StlFileManager`, `StlFileSerialzer` headers, and `.cpp` files into your projects folder, and add them to the project.

Any resource type we create that we want to add to an `Ogre::ResourceManager` must derive from the `Ogre::Resource` class. It must implement the `loadImpl()` and `unloadImpl()` functions, which will be called when a resource manager attempts to load or unload the resource. The `StlFileSerializer` does all the heavy lifting in terms of parsing the file data and creating Ogre 3D models. Our `StlFileManager` simply keeps track of existing `StlFile` resources, and provides an interface for creating entities from `StlFile` resources.

4. Let's create an instance of our new resource manager, and register it with Ogre.

    Add a new `StlFileManager` member variable in `Engine.h` called `m_StlFile-Manager`, and include `StlFileManager.h`, then open `Engine.cpp` and add the following code just after we create `m_Root`:

    ```
    m_StlFileManager = OGRE_NEW StlFileManager();
    ```

5. Next add the following code just before we call `m_Root->initialize()`:

    ```
    Ogre::ResourceGroupManager::getSingleton().
      createResourceGroup("StlFile", true);
    Ogre::ResourceGroupManager::getSingleton().
      initialiseResourceGroup("StlFile");

    Ogre::ResourceGroupManager::getSingleton().
      addResourceLocation(Ogre::String(ApplicationPath) +
      Ogre::String("..\\..\\media\\stl\\Tubes\\hoses\\curvature"),
      "FileSystem","StlFile");
    ```

    Here, we add a new resource group for our `StlFile` resources, and add a `FileSystem` resource location where Ogre can find `StlFiles`.

6. Next, we modify our MFC view's `EngineSetup()` function, and add code at the end, to create a new entity using the `StlFileManager`.

    ```
    Ogre::Entity *MobiusEntity = Engine->m_StlFileManager-
      >createEntity("Mobius", "1_4.stl");
    Ogre::SceneNode *MobiusNode = SceneManager->getRootSceneNode()-
      >createChildSceneNode();
    MobiusNode->attachObject(MobiusEntity);

    Ogre::AxisAlignedBox MobiusBox = MobiusEntity->getBoundingBox();
    Ogre::Vector3 MobiusCenter = MobiusBox.getCenter();

    m_Camera->lookAt(MobiusCenter);
    m_Camera->setPosition(300, 100, 200);
    ```

We create the entity and attach it to the scene, just as we did for the robot model in previous recipes. In this recipe, we call `m_Camera->setPosition()`, to move the camera further away, because the Mobius model is larger than the robot model.

How it works...

Let's look at the `StlFile` resource class first.

```
class StlFile : public Ogre::Resource{
protected:
  void loadImpl();
  void unloadImpl();
  size_t calculateSize() const;
  Ogre::MeshPtr mMesh;

public:
  StlFile(Ogre::ResourceManager *creator,
    const Ogre::String &name,
    Ogre::ResourceHandle handle,
    const Ogre::String &group,
    bool isManual = false,
    Ogre::ManualResourceLoader *loader = 0
  );

  virtual ~StlFile();

  void setMesh(Ogre::MeshPtr mesh);
  Ogre::MeshPtr getMesh() const;
};
```

Any resource type we create that we want to add to an `Ogre::ResourceManager` must derive from the `Ogre::Resource` class. We must also implement the `loadImpl()` and `unloadImpl()` functions, which will be called when our resource manager attempts to load or unload our custom resource. Our resource is bare-bones, it only has a shared pointer to a mesh.

The `loadImpl()` for our `StlFile` resource looks like the following:

```
void StlFile::loadImpl() {
  if(Ogre::MeshManager::getSingleton().resourceExists(this->mName)) {
    setMesh(Ogre::MeshManager::getSingleton().getByName(this->mName));
  }
  else {
    StlFileSerializer serializer;
    Ogre::DataStreamPtr stream =
      Ogre::ResourceGroupManager::getSingleton().openResource(mName,
      mGroup, true, this);
    serializer.importStlFile(stream, this);
  }
}
```

In our `loadImpl()` function, we check to see if our mesh has already been loaded, and if not, we load one using our `StlFileSerializer`. The `StlFileSerializer` class has one key function called `importStlFile()`, which is where we parse the STL file and create a mesh object.

The STL file format is an ASCII file format that begins with the line:

```
solid name
```

The file then contains series of triangles, each represented as follows:

```
facet normal ni nj nk
  outer loop
    vertex v1x v1y v1z
    vertex v2x v2y v2z
    vertex v3x v3y v3z'
  endloop
endfacet
```

The file concludes with:

```
endsolid name
```

Here's how we parse the file:

```
void StlFileSerializer::importStlFile(Ogre::DataStreamPtr &stream,
  StlFile *pDest) {
  Ogre::SceneManager *sceneManager =
    Ogre::Root::getSingleton().getSceneManagerIterator().begin()-
>second;

  Ogre::ManualObject* ManualObject = sceneManager-
    >createManualObject(pDest->getName());
  ManualObject->setDynamic(false);
  ManualObject->begin("BaseWhiteNoLighting",
    Ogre::RenderOperation::OT_TRIANGLE_LIST);

  float x,y,z,nx,ny,nz;

  // first line is solid name (skip)
  stream->getLine();

  int TriangleIndex = 0;
  while(!stream->eof()) {
    // facet normal nx ny nz
    int ret = sscanf(stream->getLine().c_str(), "%*s %*s %f %f %f\n",
      &nx, &ny, &nz);
    if (ret!=3) continue;
    // skip outer loop declaration
    stream->getLine();
```

```
        for(int i = 0; i < 3; ++i) {
          //vertex x y z
          ret = sscanf(stream->getLine().c_str(), "%*s %f %f %f\n",
            &x, &y, &z);
          if (ret != 3) return;

          ManualObject->position(x, y, z);
          ManualObject->normal(nx, ny, nz);
          ManualObject->colour(Ogre::ColourValue(0.0f, 0.0f, 0.0f, 1.0f));
        }

        ManualObject->triangle(TriangleIndex * 3 + 0, TriangleIndex *
          3 + 1, TriangleIndex * 3 + 2);
        TriangleIndex++;

        // skip outer loop end
        stream->getLine();

        // skip facet end
        stream->getLine();
      }

    ManualObject->end();

    pDest->setMesh( ManualObject->convertToMesh(pDest->getName()) );
  }
```

In this function, we parse the STL file line-by-line, and feed the data into a `ManualObject` instance. `ManualObject` exists to make it easier to create meshes using thr code. Once we are finished parsing the file, we convert the `ManualObject` to a mesh, and pass it back to our `StlFile` instance.

Now let's look at the `StlFileManager` class.

```
StlFileManager::StlFileManager() {
  mResourceType = "StlFile";

  mLoadOrder = 30.0f;
  Ogre::ResourceGroupManager::getSingleton()._
    registerResourceManager(mResourceType, this);
}
```

We must register our resource manager with Ogre's resource group manager, so we do that in the constructor. The first parameter we pass to `_registerResourceManager()`, is the type of resource our manager supports, `StlFile` resources.

Finally, we have the `StlFileManager::createEntity()` method.

```
Ogre::Entity* StlFileManager::createEntity(const Ogre::String
  &entityName, const Ogre::String &meshName){
  // load the resource first
  StlFilePtr stlFile = load(meshName, "StlFile");
  if(stlFile.isNull()) {
    return NULL;
  }

  // get the first available scene manager
  Ogre::SceneManager* sceneManager =
    Ogre::Root::getSingleton().getSceneManagerIterator().begin()-
>second;
  return sceneManager->createEntity(meshName);
}
```

All that we're doing here is loading the requested `StlFile` resource, and then creating an entity using the mesh of the `StlFile`.

The following is a screenshot from the sample application, which has the `camera` mode set to `wireframe`, to better display the unusual shape of the Mobius.

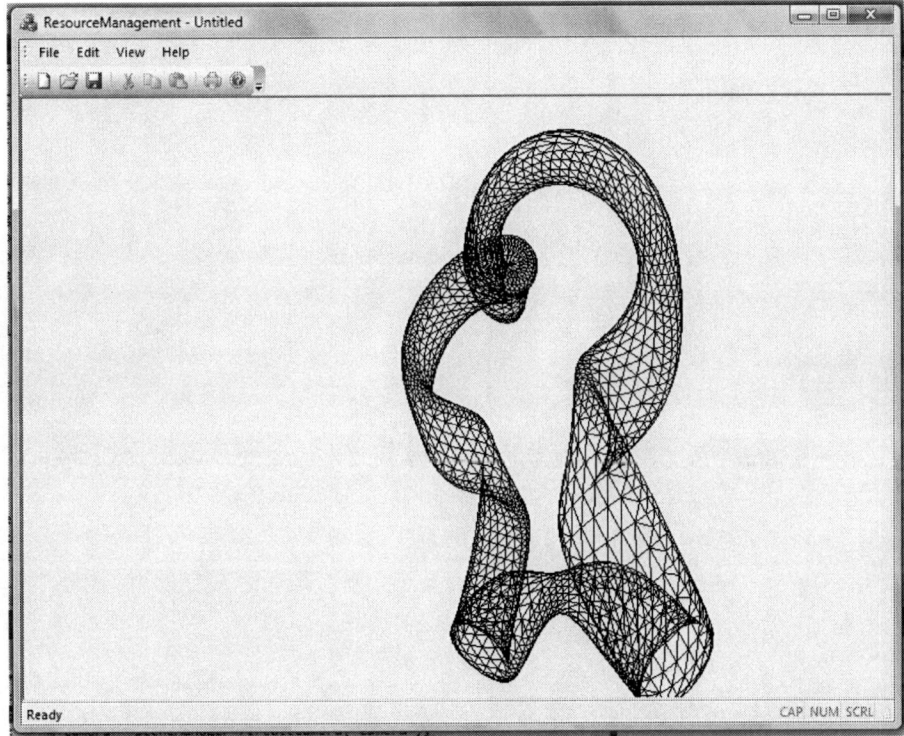

There's more...

Normally, we would not create a specific resource type to load a custom mesh format. The preferred method is to run the STL file through a converter first that saves it as a native Ogre `.mesh` format, and have our program import that.

2
Let Us Be Multimodal

In this chapter, we will cover the following recipes:

- ▶ Using the keyboard input to navigate an Ogre scene
- ▶ Using the mouse input to navigate an Ogre scene
- ▶ Using voice input with static grammar
- ▶ Using voice input with dynamic grammar
- ▶ Using text-to-speech to make the application speak

Introduction

Multimodal interactions with a scene are a necessity for a majority of 3D applications. At the very least, an Ogre 3D application should support the keyboard and the mouse input to move and rotate the camera. This chapter focuses on how to use a keyboard, a mouse, and speech to control various aspects of a 3D scene, such as movement and animation. We also show you how to make a model talk, using the speech API.

Using the keyboard input to navigate an Ogre scene

In this recipe, we will learn how to navigate an Ogre scene using the keyboard input in an MFC environment. MFC uses **message maps** to map messages to distinct class member functions instead of the traditional windows messaging approach, where all messages are handled in a `WndProc` callback function.

Getting ready

To follow along with this recipe, open the solution located in the `Recipes\Chapter02\`
`KeyboardInput` folder in the code bundle available on the Packt website.

How to do it...

We'll create an MFC Ogre application named `KeyboardInput`, by following the *Creating an*
MFC Ogre application recipe from *Chapter 1, Delving Deep into Application Design*, and we'll
add the keyboard input to move the camera in the 3D scene.

1. First, let's add keyboard message handlers to the `CKeyboardInputView` class in our
   project. To open the **MFC Class Wizard**, on the **Project** menu, click on **Class Wizard**.
   Alternatively, to open the wizard with a keyboard shortcut, type *Ctrl + Shift + X*.

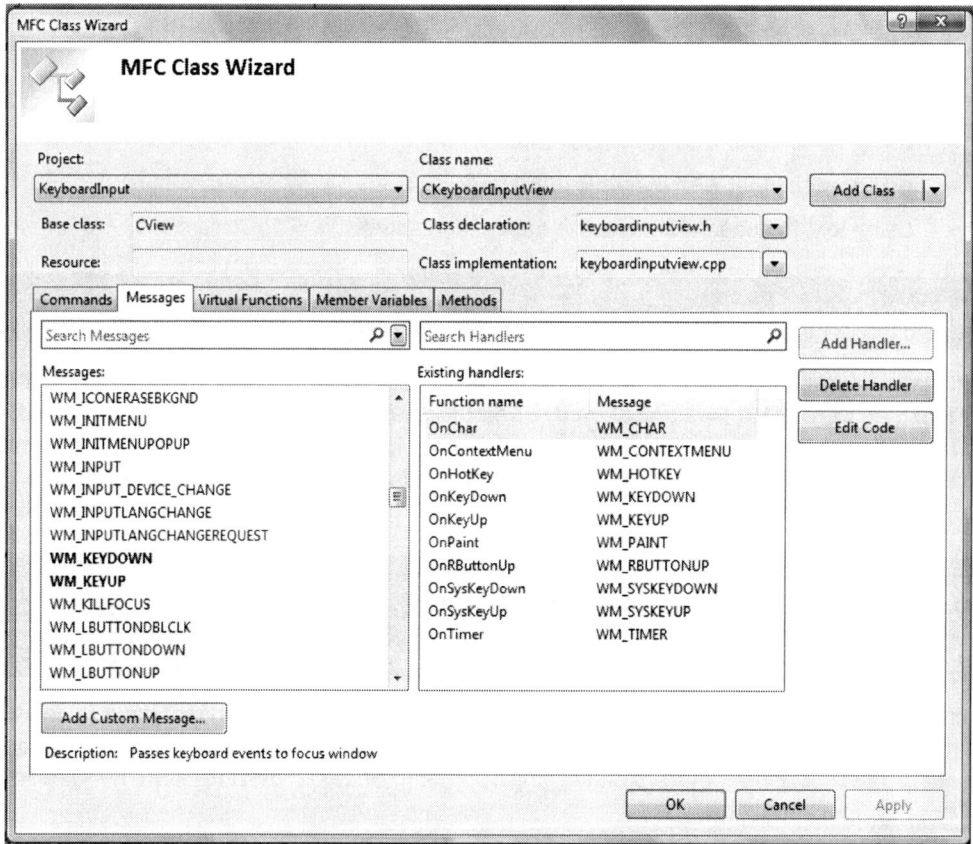

2. Select `KeyboardInput` in the **Project** drop-down listbox, and then select
   `CKeyboardInputView` in the **Class** name listbox.

3. Next, select each message that we will be mapping in the **Messages** list, and then add a handler by clicking on **Add Handler…**, or by double-clicking on the selected message in the **Messages** list. Create message map handlers for all the messages in the following list:

   - ON_WM_CONTEXTMENU()
   - ON_WM_RBUTTONUP()
   - ON_WM_PAINT()
   - ON_WM_CHAR()
   - ON_WM_HOTKEY()
   - ON_WM_KEYDOWN()
   - ON_WM_KEYUP()
   - ON_WM_SYSKEYDOWN()
   - ON_WM_SYSKEYUP()
   - ON_WM_TIMER()

4. The first message handler we implement is the WM_KEYDOWN message handler, which is called when a non-system key is pressed. For our application, the virtual key codes that we will use are: VK_LEFT, VK_UP, VK_RIGHT, VK_DOWN, and WSAD to move the camera.

```
switch (nChar){
  case VK_LEFT: //left
  case 65: //A
  case 97: //a

    m_WorkingTimer = 1;

  break;

  case VK_UP:  //up
  case 87:  //W
  case 119: //w

    m_WorkingTimer = 2;

  break;

  case VK_RIGHT: //right
  case 68: //D
  case 100: //d

    m_WorkingTimer = 3;
```

```
    break;

    case VK_DOWN: //down
    case 83: //S
    case 115://s

      m_WorkingTimer = 4;

    break;
}
```

Notice that we do not directly move the camera each time we receive a WM_KEY-DOWN message. Instead, we start a timer, so that we move the camera regularly at timed intervals, until we receive a WM_KEYUP message.

```
if (m_WorkingTimer != 0)
  SetTimer(m_WorkingTimer, 10, NULL);
```

5. The OnTimer function handles the WM_TIMER event, and contains the code for actually moving the camera.

```
Ogre::Vector3 CameraMove;

switch (nIDEvent){
  case 1:
    CameraMove[0] = -10;
    CameraMove[1] = 0;
    CameraMove[2] = 0;
  break;

  case 2:
    CameraMove[0] = 0;
    CameraMove[1] = 10;
    CameraMove[2] = 0;
  break;

  case 3:
    CameraMove[0] = 10;
    CameraMove[1] = 0;
    CameraMove[2] = 0;
  break;

  case 4:
    CameraMove[0] = 0;
    CameraMove[1] = -10;
    CameraMove[2] = 0;
```

```
    break;
  }

  Ogre::Root *Root = ((CKeyboardInputApp*)AfxGetApp())->
    m_Engine->GetRoot();
  m_Camera->moveRelative(CameraMove);
  Root->renderOneFrame();
```

6. The `OnKeyUp` function handles the `WM_KEYUP` message and stops the timer, which stops camera movement.

7. The `OnSysKeyDown` function handles the `WM_SYSKEYDOWN` message, which is called when the user holds down the *ALT* key and then presses another key. We use this input to change the `polygon` mode used in rendering. The valid `polygon` modes are `PM_SOLID` (the default), `PM_WIREFRAME`, and `PM_POINTS`.

```
  switch (nChar){
    case 'W':
      m_Camera->setPolygonMode(Ogre::PM_WIREFRAME);
    break;

    case 'S':
      m_Camera->setPolygonMode(Ogre::PM_SOLID);
    break;

    case 'P':
      m_Camera->setPolygonMode(Ogre::PM_POINTS);
    break;
  }

  Ogre::Root *Root = ((CKeyboardInputApp*)AfxGetApp())->
    m_Engine->GetRoot();
  Root->renderOneFrame();
```

8. The `OnHotKey` function handles the `WM_HOTKEY` message, and is called when the user presses a system-wide hot key. We use the `RegisterHotKey` function to register system-wide hot keys that trigger the `WM_HOTKEY` message when the user presses *CTRL + I* and *CTRL + O*.

```
  RegisterHotKey(this->m_hWnd, 1, MOD_CONTROL, 'I');
  RegisterHotKey(this->m_hWnd, 2, MOD_CONTROL, 'O');
```

9. In the `OnHotKey` function, we move the camera forward and backwards.

```
Ogre::Vector3 CameraMove;

switch (nHotKeyId){
  case 1:
    CameraMove[0] = 0;
    CameraMove[1] = 0;
    CameraMove[2] = -10;
  break;

  case 2:
    CameraMove[0] = 0;
    CameraMove[1] = 0;
    CameraMove[2] = 10;
  break;
}

Ogre::Root *Root = ((CKeyboardInputApp*)AfxGetApp())->
  m_Engine->GetRoot();
m_Camera->moveRelative(CameraMove);
Root->renderOneFrame();
```

How it works...

When the user presses a key, a `WM_KEYDOWN` or `WM_SYSKEYDOWN` message is placed in the message queue. In the same way, releasing the key results in a `WM_KEYUP` or `WM_SYSKEYUP` message being placed in the message queue. If the user holds down a key for an extended period of time, multiple `WM_KEYDOWN` or `WM_SYSKEYDOWN` messages are generated. However, generating multiple key down messages does not affect how the `OnKeyDown` function works, because our application uses a timer to convert the keyboard input to camera movement at specific intervals.

The hot key combinations that we register for the forward and backward movement take precedence over normal messages, such as `WM_KEYDOWN`. We ensure that they take priority by placing them at the top of the message queue, to be handled before any other pending messages.

While running the application, you may notice that the camera rotates around the head, and moving forward and backward zooms in and out on the head object. This is because when we initialize the camera in `CKeyboardInputView::EngineSetup()`, we set the camera to always look at the head model.

```
Ogre::AxisAlignedBox Box = m_HeadEntity->getBoundingBox();
Ogre::Vector3 HeadCenter = Box.getCenter();
```

```
m_Camera->lookAt(HeadCenter);
m_Camera->setAutoTracking(true, HeadNode);
m_Camera->setFixedYawAxis(true);
```

Using the mouse input to navigate an Ogre scene

In this recipe, we will learn how to navigate an Ogre scene using a mouse input in an MFC environment.

How to do it...

We'll start by following the *Creating an MFC Ogre application* recipe from *Chapter 1, Delving Deep into Application Design*, to create an Ogre MFC application named `MouseInput`, and we'll add a mouse input to move the camera in the 3D scene.

1. The first thing to do is open the **MFC Class Wizard**, by clicking on **Class Wizard** on the **Project** menu. Select **MouseInput** in the **Project** listbox, and then **CMouseInputView** in the **Class name** list-box.

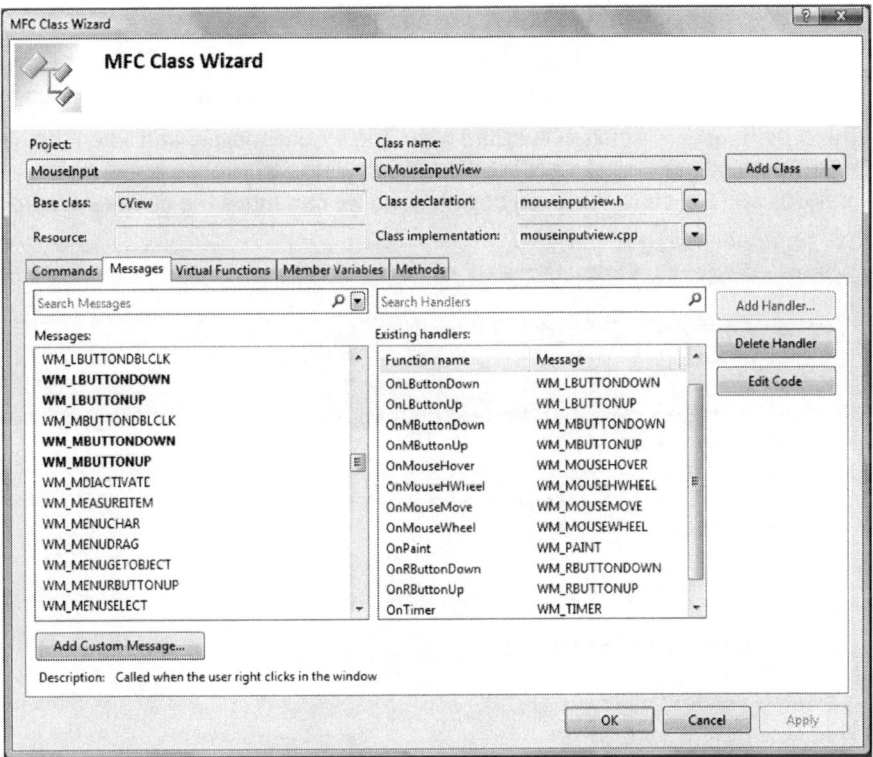

2. Next, we add message handlers for several mouse messages and end up with a message map that looks similar to the following:

```
BEGIN_MESSAGE_MAP(CMouseInputView, CView)
    ON_WM_CONTEXTMENU()
    ON_WM_RBUTTONUP()
    ON_WM_PAINT()
    ON_WM_TIMER()
    ON_WM_LBUTTONDOWN()
    ON_WM_LBUTTONUP()
    ON_WM_MBUTTONDOWN()
    ON_WM_MBUTTONUP()
    ON_WM_MOUSEHOVER()
    ON_WM_MOUSEHWHEEL()
    ON_WM_MOUSEMOVE()
    ON_WM_MOUSEWHEEL()
    ON_WM_RBUTTONDOWN()
END_MESSAGE_MAP()
```

3. Before going over the code for the message handlers, let's turn on the Sonar accessibility feature for the mouse to make tracking the mouse easier. In `CMouseInputView::EngineSetup()`, we add the following code to set up `Sonar`:

```
bool Sonar = TRUE;
SystemParametersInfo(SPI_SETMOUSESONAR, 0, &Sonar, 0);
```

4. Next, we implement the `OnLButtonDown` and `OnLButtonUp` functions to toggle the `m_MouseNavigation` flag, when the user presses or releases the left mouse button.

5. The `OnMouseMove` function is called when the mouse moves, and when the `m_MouseNavigationFlag` is enabled, it calculates difference between the previous and the current mouse positions, so we can move the camera accordingly.

```
if (m_MouseNavigation){
  Ogre::Vector3 CameraMove(0.0, 0.0, 0.0);

  CameraMove[0] = -(m_MousePosition.x - point.x);
  CameraMove[1] = m_MousePosition.y - point.y;

  CEngine * Engine = ((CMouseInputApp*)AfxGetApp())->m_Engine;
  if (Engine == NULL)
    return;
  Ogre::Root *Root = Engine->GetRoot();
  if (m_Camera == NULL)
    return;
  m_Camera->moveRelative(CameraMove);

  m_MousePosition = point;

  Root->renderOneFrame();
}
```

6. The `OnMouseWheel` function handles the `WM_MOUSEWHEEL` message, and is used for moving the camera forwards and backwards.

```
Ogre::Vector3 CameraMove(0.0, 0.0, 0.0);

CameraMove[2] = 0.1 * zDelta;

CEngine * Engine = ((CMouseInputApp*)AfxGetApp())->m_Engine;
if (Engine == NULL)
   return false;
Ogre::Root *Root = Engine->GetRoot();
if (m_Camera == NULL)
   return false;
m_Camera->moveRelative(CameraMove);

Root->renderOneFrame();
```

Use the MFC global function `AfxGetApp()` to get a pointer to our application for easy access to our engine object.

Getting ready

To follow along with this recipe, open the solution located in the `Recipes\Chapter02\MouseInput` folder in the code bundle available on the Packt website.

How it works...

The framework calls the `OnLButtonDown` function when the user presses the left mouse button and `OnLButtonUp` when the user releases the left mouse button. While the left mouse button is down, we sample the mouse position in `OnMouseMove`, by examining the point parameter, which specifies the x and y-coordinate of the cursor, relative to the upper-left corner of our application window.

We use the `OnMouseWheel` function to zoom the camera, based on the `zDelta` parameter that indicates the distance the mouse wheel was rotated. A negative `zDelta` indicates rotation back toward the user, and a positive value indicates forward rotation away from the user.

The optional Sonar accessibility feature is useful for highlighting the mouse position on a cluttered screen or when the screen resolution is high. To activate the Sonar visual circles around the mouse, the user simply presses and then releases the *Ctrl* key.

Using voice input with static grammar

In this recipe, we'll use the Microsoft Speech SDK to enable voice input in an Ogre 3D application, and use voice commands to set the pose animation of our model. The facial mesh that we'll be using in our application resides in the `media/models` folder, and contains the following poses: `neutral`, `happy`, `sad`, and `mad`.

Getting ready

To follow along with this recipe, open the solution located in the `Recipes\Chapter02\ StaticGrammar` folder in the code bundle available on the Packt website.

How to do it...

We start by following the *Creating an MFC Ogre application* recipe from *Chapter 1, Delving Deep into Application Design*, to create an Ogre MFC application named `StaticGrammar`, then we add the speech SDK, create a grammar, and use it to set the poses for a 3D model.

1. When creating the MFC Ogre application, be sure to check the **Automation** checkbox on the **Advanced features** page of the **MFC Application Wizard**.

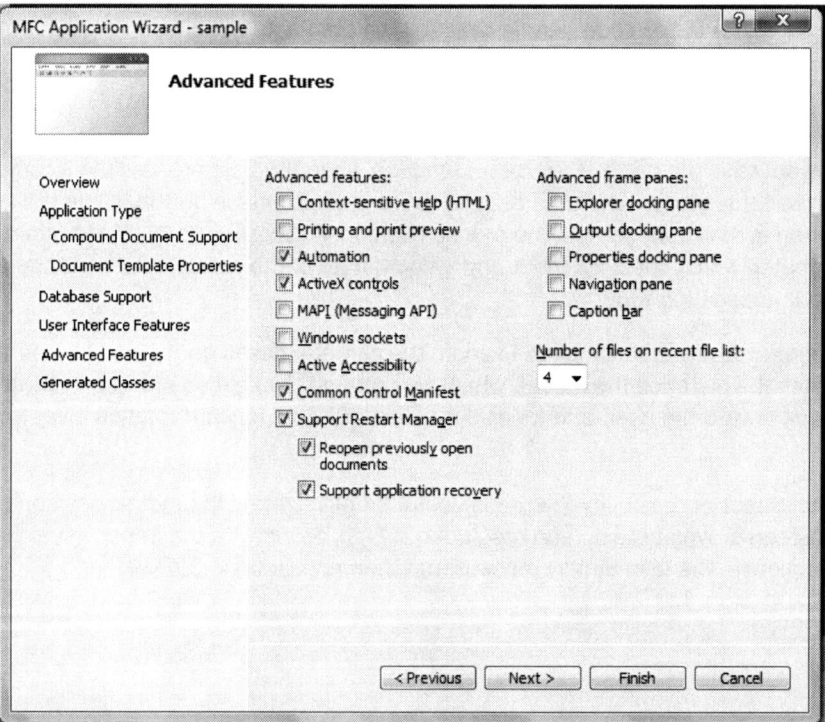

2. After clicking on **Finish** on the **MFC Application Wizard** dialog-box, open the **Project** property pages, and add the path to the `Speech SDK`.

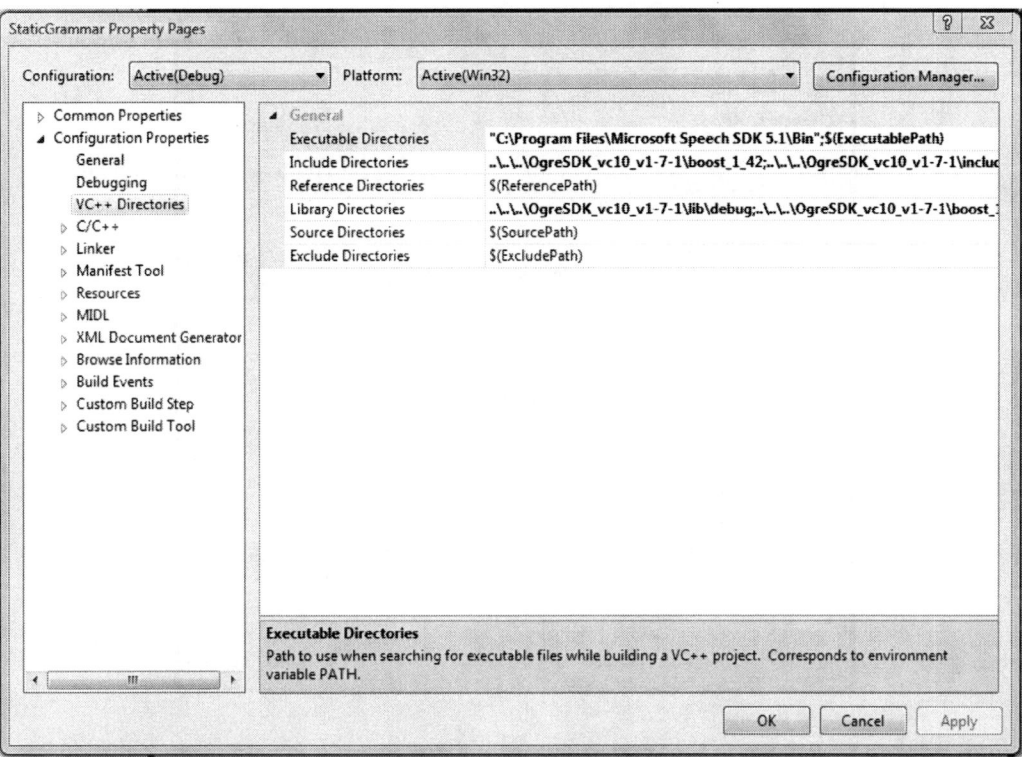

3. Next, select **External Tools** from the **Tools** menu, and add a `Speech Help` menu item that points to `sapi.chm`.

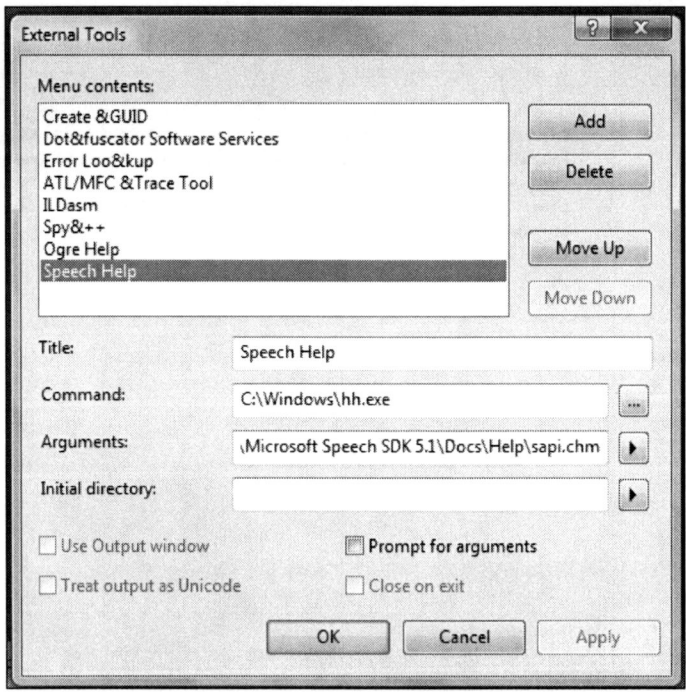

4. Before we add any of the code to interact with the `Speech` API, we need to include the `Speech` API main header in `StaticGrammer.h` and `StaticGrammarView.cpp`.

    ```
    #include <sphelper.h>
    ```

    We also include `Expression.h` in `StaticGrammarView.cpp`. `Expression.h` is automatically generated by the grammar compiler `gc.exe`, and is used to handle various speech events.

    ```
    #include "Expression.h"
    ```

5. Next, we add the following variables to the `CStaticGrammerApp` class:

    ```
    CComPtr<ISpRecognizer> m_cpEngine;
    CComPtr<ISpRecoContext> m_cpRecoCtxt;
    CComPtr<ISpRecoGrammar> m_cpCmdGrammar;
    ```

    These are the engine, recognition context, and grammar `Speech` API variables, respectively.

6. When the `Speech` API processes the speech input, it will send a `WM_RECOEVENT` message to our application. We define the `WM_RECOEVENT` message as `WM_USER+1`:

```
#define WM_RECOEVENT WM_USER+1
```

7. Next, we declare our event handler in `StaticGrammarView.cpp`.

```
ON_MESSAGE(WM_RECOEVENT, &CStaticGrammarView::OnRecoEvent)
```

Now, it's time to create the grammar rules to describe the speech input we want to support in our application. The grammar rules used by the **Speech API (SAPI)** are defined using XML. The entire grammar is surrounding by a GRAMMAR XML tag. The first section is the DEFINE section, in which we declare various ID elements that can be associated with phrases.

```
<GRAMMAR LANGID="409">
  <DEFINE>
    <ID NAME="VID_Sad" VAL="1"/>
    <ID NAME="VID_Mad" VAL="2"/>
    <ID NAME="VID_Neutral" VAL="3"/>
    <ID NAME="VID_Happy" VAL="4"/>
    <ID NAME="VID_ShowExpression" VAL="21"/>
    <ID NAME="VID_ExpressionType" VAL="22"/>
  </DEFINE>
  <RULE ID="VID_ShowExpression" TOPLEVEL="ACTIVE">
    <O>Please</O>
    <O>show</O>
    <P>
      <RULEREF REFID="VID_ExpressionType"/>
    </P>
    <O>expression</O>
  </RULE>
  <RULE ID="VID_ExpressionType">
    <L PROPID="VID_ExpressionType">
      <P VAL="VID_Sad">sad</P>
      <P VAL="VID_Mad">mad</P>
      <P VAL="VID_Neutral">neutral</P>
      <P VAL="VID_Happy">happy</P>
    </L>
  </RULE>
</GRAMMAR>
```

The RULE section describes the different phrases and their associated ID. The first RULE is the VID_ShowExpression, which has an ACTIVE tag, meaning this is something the speech recognition engine should expect to hear. The VID_ShowExpression rule describes a phrase in the format:

```
(Please)->(show)->sad | mad | neutral | happy->(expression)
```

Any words in parenthesis are optional, and any set of words separated by a '|' are words that can be said in that position.

The `<O>` tag denotes an optional word, and the `<P>` denotes a phrase.

In order to make use of our grammar XML file, we must compile it into a `.cfg` file. To compile the grammar, we add a custom build tool command.

1. First, add the XML file to the project. Then, select the file, right-click and select `Properties`, and fill in the **Command Line** and **Outputs** properties on the **Custom Build Tool** property page. Set **Command Line** to `gc /h Expression.h %(Filename)`, and **Outputs** to `$(ProjectDir)Expression. cfg;$(ProjectDir)Expression.h;%(Outputs)`.

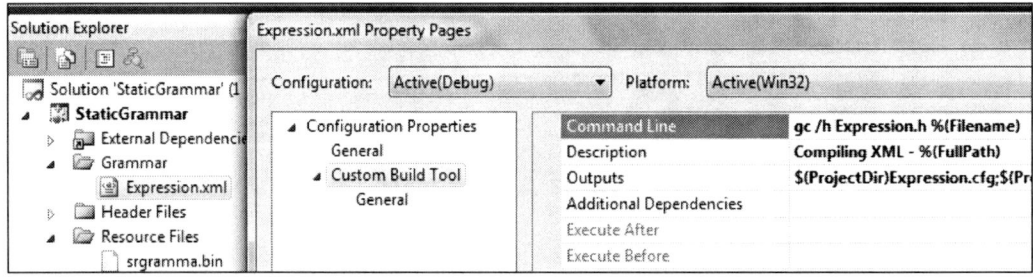

2. Now we must add the compiled grammar file to the project. Go to **Resource View** and select **Add Resource**, then **Import**. Open `Expression.cfg`, and when it prompts for a custom type, enter "SRGRAMMAR".

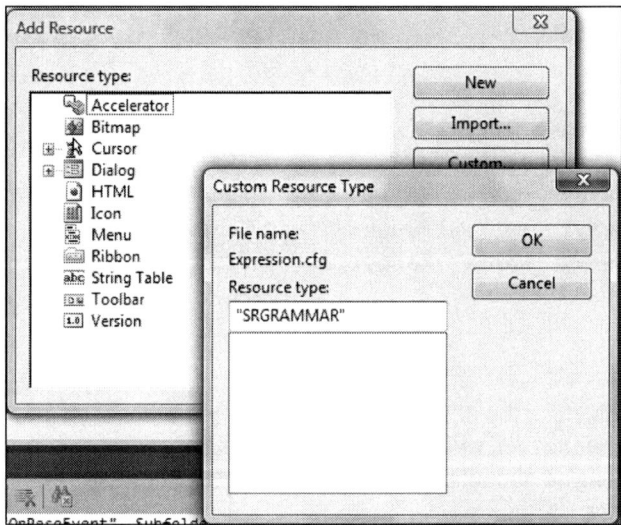

3. Next, rename the new resource to "IDR_EXPRESSION".

4. In StaticGrammar.cpp, we initialize the Speech API COM in a function called InitializeSpeechRecognition().

```
if (FAILED(CoInitialize(NULL))){
  AfxMessageBox("Error starting COM");
  return false;
}
```

5. First, we create the **engine** using a **shared recognizer**. This means that the other applications will be able to use the recognizer simultaneously.

```
HRESULT hRes = m_cpEngine.
  CoCreateInstance(CLSID_SpSharedRecognizer);
```

6. Then we create a **Speech Recognition context**.

```
hRes = m_cpEngine->CreateRecoContext(&m_cpRecoCtxt);
```

7. We then specify which window will receive notifications from the Speech Recognition Engine. In this case, it is our only window.

```
hRes = m_cpRecoCtxt->SetNotifyWindowMessage(m_pMainWnd->m_
hWnd, WM_RECOEVENT, 0, 0);
```

8. Next, we indicate that we are only interested in speech recognition events.

```
hRes = m_cpRecoCtxt->SetInterest(SPFEI(SPEI_RECOGNITION),
SPFEI(SPEI_RECOGNITION));
```

9. We then load our grammar resource with LoadCmdFromResource().

```
hRes = m_cpCmdGrammar->LoadCmdFromResource(
  NULL,
MAKEINTRESOURCEW(IDR_EXPRESSION),
  L"SRGRAMMAR",
  MAKELANGID(LANG_NEUTRAL, SUBLANG_NEUTRAL),
  SPLO_DYNAMIC);
hRes = m_cpCmdGrammar->SetRuleState(NULL, NULL, SPRS_ACTIVE );
```

The first parameter is a **handle** to the module, but we pass in NULL because we want to use the default path, which is the path to the file containing the current process. The second parameter is the **name** of the resource, and the third parameter is the **type** of the resource. The fourth parameter is the **language ID**, and the last parameter is a **flag**, indicating that the resource file should be loaded dynamically.

10. Finally, we add our grammar and set our grammar rule state to active.

```
hRes = m_cpRecoCtxt->CreateGrammar(0, &m_cpCmdGrammar);
```

11. To handle the speech recognition, we add code to the `OnRecoEvent()` function in `StaticGrammarView.cpp`.

```
while (event.GetFrom(((CStaticGrammarApp*)AfxGetApp())-
  >m_cpRecoCtxt) == S_OK) {
// Look at recognition event only
switch (event.eEventId) {
  case SPEI_RECOGNITION:
    ExecuteCommand(event.RecoResult());
  break;
  }
}
```

12. When we get a `SPEI_RECOGNITION` event, we run a utility function called `ExecuteCommand()` that changes the model pose, based on the input speech phrase.

```
SPPHRASE *pElements;
Ogre::Root *Root = ((CStaticGrammarApp*)AfxGetApp())->
  m_Engine->GetRoot();

if (SUCCEEDED(Phrase->GetPhrase(&pElements))) {
  switch (pElements->Rule.ulId) {
    case VID_ExpressionType:
    {
      const SPPHRASEPROPERTY *pProp = pElements->pProperties;

      while (pProp) {
        switch(pProp->vValue.ulVal){
          case VID_Sad:
            m_ManualKeyFrame->updatePoseReference(0, 0.0);
            m_ManualKeyFrame->updatePoseReference(1, 0.0);
            m_ManualKeyFrame->updatePoseReference(2, 1.0);
            m_ManualKeyFrame->updatePoseReference(3, 0.0);
            m_ManualAnimState->getParent()->_notifyDirty();
            Root->renderOneFrame();
          break;

          case VID_Mad:
            m_ManualKeyFrame->updatePoseReference(0, 0.0);
            m_ManualKeyFrame->updatePoseReference(1, 0.0);
            m_ManualKeyFrame->updatePoseReference(2, 0.0);
            m_ManualKeyFrame->updatePoseReference(3, 1.0);
            m_ManualAnimState->getParent()->_notifyDirty();
            Root->renderOneFrame();
          break;
```

```
        case VID_Neutral:
          m_ManualKeyFrame->updatePoseReference(0, 1.0);
          m_ManualKeyFrame->updatePoseReference(1, 0.0);
          m_ManualKeyFrame->updatePoseReference(2, 0.0);
          m_ManualKeyFrame->updatePoseReference(3, 0.0);
          m_ManualAnimState->getParent()->_notifyDirty();
          Root->renderOneFrame();
        break;

        case VID_Happy:
          m_ManualKeyFrame->updatePoseReference(0, 0.0);
          m_ManualKeyFrame->updatePoseReference(1, 1.0);
          m_ManualKeyFrame->updatePoseReference(2, 0.0);
          m_ManualKeyFrame->updatePoseReference(3, 0.0);
          m_ManualAnimState->getParent()->_notifyDirty();
          Root->renderOneFrame();
        break;
      }

      pProp = pProp->pNextSibling;
    }
  }
  break;
}
```

Ogre 3D supports blending of poses, and the `updatePoseReference()` function updates the influence of a pose. An influence value of `1` means that the pose should be fully visible, and a value of `0` means the pose should have no effect. The first parameter is the pose index, and the second parameter is the amount of influence. We set the influence value to `1` for the pose we want to use, and the influence value to `0` for poses we don't want.

How it works...

We inspect the elements from the input phrase to determine which rule was recognized. Then we cycle through the words, update the pose influence appropriately, and render the frame.

The following screenshot shows the facial mesh in a **neutral** pose:

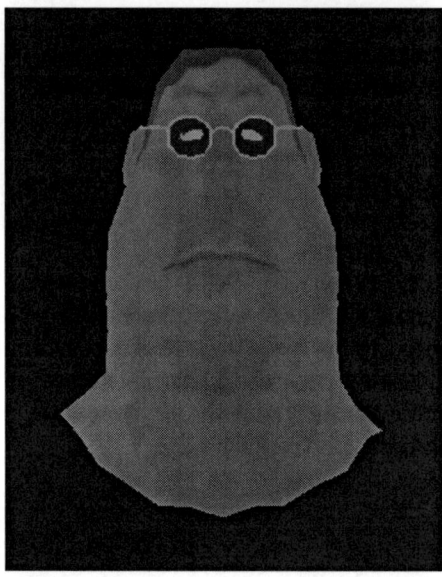

The following screenshot shows the facial mesh in a **happy** pose:

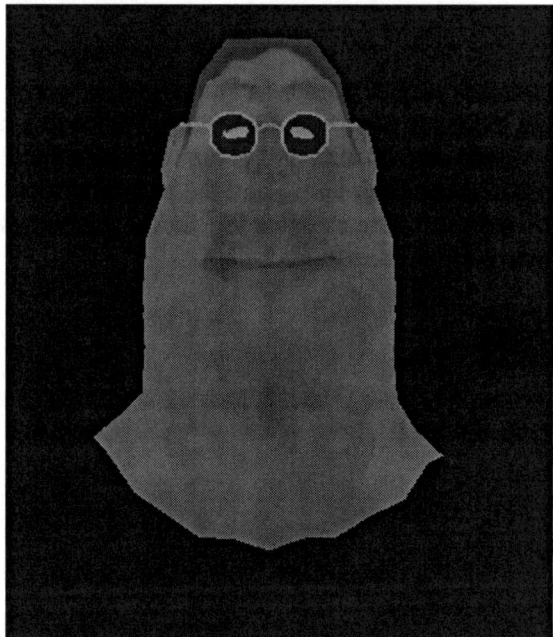

The following screenshot shows the facial mesh in a **sad** pose:

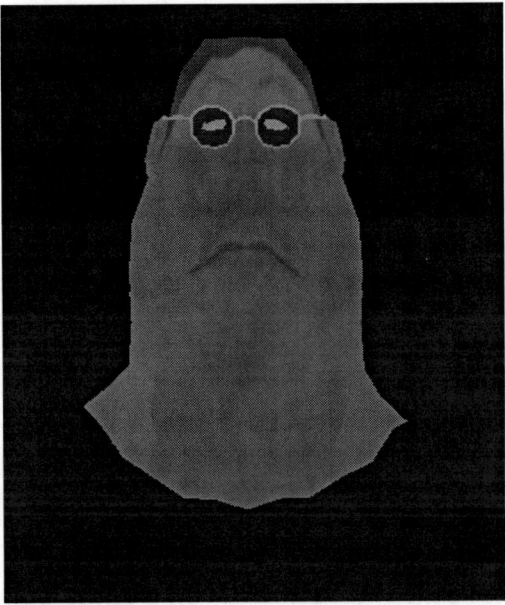

The following screenshot shows the facial mesh in a **mad** pose:

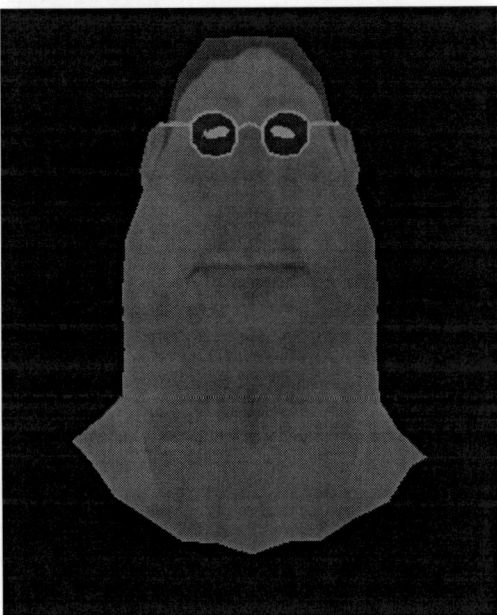

There's more...

We can also change the grammar to combine multiple phrases, such as *happy and mad* and then blend the *happy and mad* poses together, by setting the amount of influence to 0.5 for the *happy and mad* poses.

Using voice input with dynamic grammar

This recipe is very similar to the previous recipe. However, in this recipe, we show you how to dynamically set valid phrases, based on the names of the poses in a 3D mesh.

Getting ready

To follow along with this recipe, open the solution located in the Recipes\Chapter02\ DynamicGrammar folder in the code bundle available on the Packt website.

How to do it...

Instead of using a static expression list, as we did in the previous recipe, we can iterate over the list of poses in the facial mesh, and dynamically create expressions based on the names of the poses. First, we create our project following the previous recipe and name the project DynamicGrammer, then we add the code to dynamically create our expressions.

1. We start by cleaning up the grammar, so that we can insert our expression rules. In CDynamicGrammarView::EngineSetup(), we clear the VID_ExpressionType rule, then we add new word transitions for every pose in our mesh. In each new word transition, we store the index of the pose, adding the expressions we commit the grammar modifications, and mark them as active.

    ```
    SPSTATEHANDLE hDynamicRuleHandle;

    ((CDynamicGrammarApp*)AfxGetApp())->
      m_cpCmdGrammar->GetRule(L"VID_ExpressionType", NULL,
      SPRAF_Dynamic, FALSE, &hDynamicRuleHandle);

    ((CDynamicGrammarApp*)AfxGetApp())->
      m_cpCmdGrammar->ClearRule(hDynamicRuleHandle);

    ((CDynamicGrammarApp*)AfxGetApp())->m_cpCmdGrammar->Commit(0);

    for (unsigned int i = 0;
      i < m_ManualKeyFrame->getPoseReferences().size(); i++){
      Ogre::String poseName = m_HeadMesh->getPose(i)->getName();
      CSpDynamicString ds(poseName.c_str());
    ```

```
SPPROPERTYINFO prop;
prop.pszName = L"Id";
prop.pszValue = L"Property";
prop.vValue.vt = VT_I4;
prop.vValue.ulVal = i;

((CDynamicGrammarApp*)AfxGetApp())->
  m_cpCmdGrammar->AddWordTransition(hDynamicRuleHandle, NULL,
    ds , L" -.",SPWT_LEXICAL, 1.0, &prop);
}


((CDynamicGrammarApp*)AfxGetApp())->m_cpCmdGrammar->Commit(0);
((CDynamicGrammarApp*)AfxGetApp())->
  m_cpCmdGrammar->SetRuleIdState(VID_ExpressionType, SPRS_ACTIVE);
```

2. Finally, we modify the `CDynamicGrammarView::ExecuteCommand()` function, so that it reads the pose index from the input phrase, and set the influence value to 1 for that pose.

```
SPPHRASE *pElements;
Ogre::Root *Root = ((CDynamicGrammarApp*)AfxGetApp())->
  m_Engine->GetRoot();

if (SUCCEEDED(Phrase->GetPhrase(&pElements))) {
  switch (pElements->Rule.ulId) {
    case VID_ExpressionType:
    {
      const SPPHRASEPROPERTY *pProp = pElements->pProperties;

      while (pProp) {
        m_ManualKeyFrame->updatePoseReference(pProp->
          vValue.ulVal, 1.0);
        m_ManualAnimState->getParent()->_notifyDirty();
        Root->renderOneFrame();

        pProp = pProp->pNextSibling;
      }
    }

    break;
  }

  // Free the pElements memory which was allocated for us
  ::CoTaskMemFree(pElements);
}
```

Using text-to-speech to make the application speak

Text-to-speech is a useful tool for making models communicate and interact with the user. Unlike voice acting, the speech API voices will rarely fool anyone, but for robotic and other synthetic voices, it can be highly appropriate. In this recipe, we will use the speech features of the Microsoft Speech SDK to make our application speak to the user. We also animate the mouth of our mesh so it opens and closes.

Getting ready

To follow along with this recipe, open the solution located in the `Recipes\Chapter02\` `Speech` folder in the code bundle available on the Packt website.

How to do it...

We start by following the previous recipe to create an Ogre MFC application named `Speech`, and then we configure the speech API to select a voice, speak phrases, and animate the model.

1. First we have to create the voice as a `COM` object. In `Speech.h`, we add an `include` for the `Speech` API.

   ```
   #include <sapi.h>
   ```

2. We also declare an instance of a com pointer for the `Speech` API.

   ```
   CComPtr<ISpVoice>    m_cpVoice;
   ```

3. Next, we initialize the object in `CSpeechApp::InitInstance()`.

   ```
   m_cpVoice.CoCreateInstance(CLSID_SpVoice);
   ```

4. In `CSpeechView::EngineSetup()`, we enumerate all the available voices and select one.

   ```
   CComPtr<ISpObjectToken> cpVoiceToken;
   CComPtr<IEnumSpObjectTokens> cpEnum;
   ULONG ulCount = 0;

   SpEnumTokens(SPCAT_VOICES, NULL, NULL, &cpEnum);

   cpEnum->GetCount(&ulCount);

   while (ulCount -- ){
     cpVoiceToken.Release();
   ```

```
cpEnum->Next( 1, &cpVoiceToken, NULL );
Voice->SetVoice(cpVoiceToken);
Voice->Speak( L"How are you?<silence msec='1000'/>",
SPF_ASYNC | SPF_IS_XML, NULL);
}
```

5. Now we are ready to make our application speak. To do this, we simply call the `Speak()` method along with the text to speak, as follows:

```
((CSpeechApp*)AfxGetApp())->m_cpVoice->Speak(L"This is the demo of
    the text to speech in the Ogre application", SPF_ASYNC, NULL);
```

6. The last step is to animate the face mesh. We set the animation state and then start a timer to update the animation time every 10 milliseconds.

```
m_AnimationState = m_HeadEntity->getAnimationState("Speak");
m_AnimationState->setLoop(false);
m_AnimationState->setEnabled(true);
SetTimer(1, 10, 0);
```

The timer we set, calls the `CSpeechView::OnTimer()` function in which we increment the time position and render the scene. Each time we do this, the animation will progress by a certain amount, and then we render the updated model.

```
m_AnimationState->addTime(Ogre::Real(0.01));
Ogre::Root *Root = Engine->GetRoot();
Root->renderOneFrame();
```

There's more...

In addition to simple speech, we can control the volume, rate, pitch, and emphasis of the voice that speaks. The simplest way to modify the voice is with XML tags within the text passed to the `Speak()` method.

In `SpeechView.cpp`, we demonstrate how to manipulate the voice with several examples.

▶ **Voice State Control**

```
Voice->Speak(L"This is the demo of the voice state control<silence
    msec='1000'/>", SPF_ASYNC | SPF_IS_XML, NULL);
```

▶ **Voice Volume Control**

```
Voice->Speak(L"<volume level = '50'>This text should be spoken at
    volume level fifty</volume><silence msec='1000'/>", SPF_ASYNC |
    SPF_IS_XML, NULL);
```

▶ **Voice Emphasis Control**

```
Voice->Speak(L"The following word should be
    emphasized<emph>boo</emph>!<silence msec='1000'/>", SPF_ASYNC |
SPF_IS_XML, NULL);
```

See also

Chapter 7, Implementing Animations: This chapter provides more detailed information about various animation techniques in Ogre

3
Managing Objects and Scenes

In this chapter, we will cover the following recipes:

- ▶ Creating terrain from a LandXML file
- ▶ Creating Delaunay triangulation
- ▶ Creating manual objects
- ▶ Creating parametric superellipsoids
- ▶ Adding meshes on the terrain
- ▶ Adding trees as billboards
- ▶ Creating and editing a scene
- ▶ Saving a scene to an XML file
- ▶ Loading a scene from an XML file

Introduction

In this chapter, we'll show you how to create various meshes including terrain, billboards, and superellipsoids. We will also show you how to create an interface to manage a scene and the objects in it, and how to save and load a scene from a XML file. By the end of this chapter, you will have a basic Ogre 3D scene editor.

Creating terrain from a LandXML file

In this recipe, we will load terrain data from a `LandXML` file, and then convert it into an Ogre 3D mesh using a `ManualObject`. The `LandXML` file format is a non-proprietary format used in civil engineering and surveying communities, to exchange data regarding terrain, roads, and other surfaces. `LandXML` is supported by many popular CAD programs, including those made by Autodesk.

Getting ready

You'll need the `LandXML` SDK from `http://www.landxml.org` for this recipe. Download it and place the SDK folder in the `Recipes` folder.

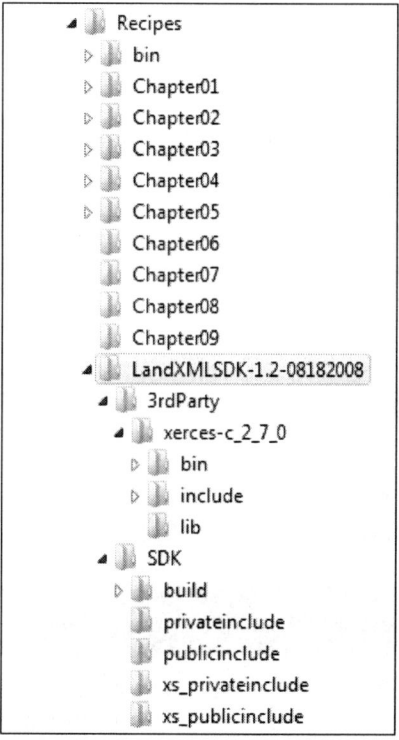

Put `LandXMLSDK1.2.dll` and `xerces-c_2_7_LX.dll` into `bin\debug` and `bin\release` folders.

To follow along with this recipe, open the solution located in the `Recipes/Chapter03/LandXml` folder in the code bundle available on the Packt website.

How to do it...

We begin with a base MFC Ogre application, and add a utility function named `CLandXmlView::GetManualObject()` that will load a `LandXML` file and return a `ManualObject`.

1. First, we create a `ManualObject` named `Topography`.

    ```
    Ogre::ManualObject *Topography =
      SceneManager->createManualObject("Topography");
    Topography->setDynamic(false);
    Topography->begin("BaseWhiteNoLighting",
      Ogre::RenderOperation::OT_TRIANGLE_LIST);
    ```

    We set the dynamic property of our `ManualObject` to `false`, because we will not be changing the mesh dynamically after we create it. We also use the default `BaseWhiteNoLighting` material, and indicate that the render operation should be `OT_TRIANGLE_LIST`, because our mesh data will use a simple triangle list format instead of something like a triangle strip format.

2. Next, we use the `LandXML` API to create a `LandXML` document object, and load our `LandXML` file for us.

    ```
    LX::Document* LxDocument = NULL;
    LX::ILxNode* LxRootNode = NULL;
    LX::LandXML* LandXml = NULL;
    LX::Surfaces* Surfaces = NULL;
    LX::Surface* Surface = NULL;
    LX::Faces* Faces = NULL;
    LX::String Name(T2W(SurfaceName));
    LxDocument = LX::createDocumentObject();
    LPWSTR Path = T2W(LandXmlPath);
    LxDocument->loadXml(Path);
    LxDocument->releaseDOMDocument();
    ```

    You may also notice that we create an `LX::String` object called `Name`, which will hold the surface name for the surface we want to read from the `LandXML` file. The `SurfaceName` variable is one of the variables we pass to our `GetManualObject()` utility function.

3. Next, we find the surface structure using the `LxDocument` object that represents the `LandXML` file we just loaded, and we add all the vertex positions from that surface to the `ManualObject`.

    ```
    Surface = LxDocument->getGlobalObjects().getSurfaceCollection().
      findFirstMatch(Name);
    LX::FacesCollection& FacesCollection =
      Surface->getDefinition()->Faces();
    LX::Pnts* Points = Surface->getDefinition()->getPnts();
    ```

```
LX::PCollection& PointsCollection = Points->P();
LX::PCollectionIterator* PointsCollectionIterator =
  PointsCollection.iterator();

LX::P* P = NULL;

double x;
double y;
double z;

/////////////////////////////Points/////////////////////////////////
while (!PointsCollectionIterator->atEnd()){
  P = PointsCollectionIterator->current();
  unsignedint id = P->getId();

  LX::IndexedListValueCollection<double>& Coordinates =
    P->value();

x = Coordinates[0];
y = Coordinates[1];
z = Coordinates[2];

Topography->position(x, y, z);
PointsCollectionIterator->next();
}

PointsCollectionIterator->release();
```

4. Now that we have all the vertex positions defined, we need to define the triangles that use those vertices.

```
LX::FacesCollectionIterator* FacesCollectionIterator =
  FacesCollection.iterator();

LX::FCollectionIterator* FCollectionIterator = NULL;
LX::F* F = NULL;

longint V[3];
```

```
while (!FacesCollectionIterator->atEnd()){
  Faces = FacesCollectionIterator->current();
  LX::FCollection& FCollection = Faces->F();
  FCollectionIterator = FCollection.iterator();

  while(!FCollectionIterator->atEnd()){
    F = FCollectionIterator->current();

    LX::IndexedListValueCollection<int>& Verteces = F->value();

    V[0] = Vertices[0];
    V[1] = Vertices[1];
    V[2] = Vertices[2];

    Topography->triangle(V[0], V[1], V[2]);
    FCollectionIterator->next();
  }

  FCollectionIterator->release();
  FacesCollectionIterator->next();
}

Topography->end();
```

The `ManualObject` is now complete, and all that remains to do is attach it to the scene graph:

```
Ogre::ManualObject *Topography = GetManualObject(
  "\\zigzag creek.xml", "Topography");

Ogre::SceneNode *Node =
  SceneManager->getRootSceneNode()->createChildSceneNode();

Node->attachObject(Topography);
```

How it works...

The following screenshot shows the structure and content of the LandXML file format:

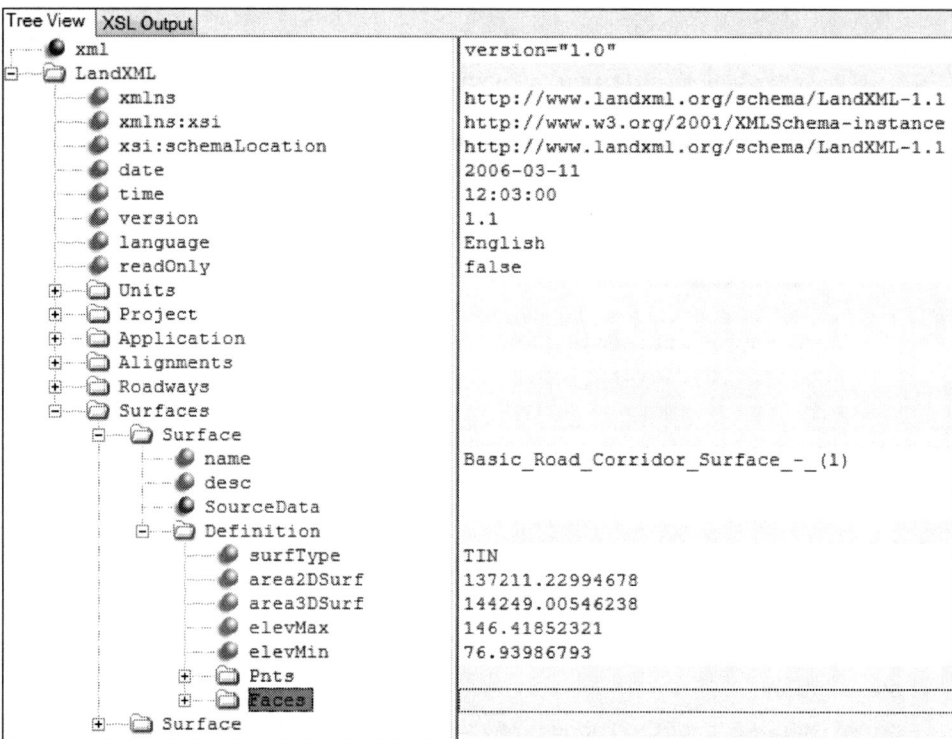

The **Surfaces** XML node has been expanded in the following screenshot to show an example **Surface** and the type of data within:

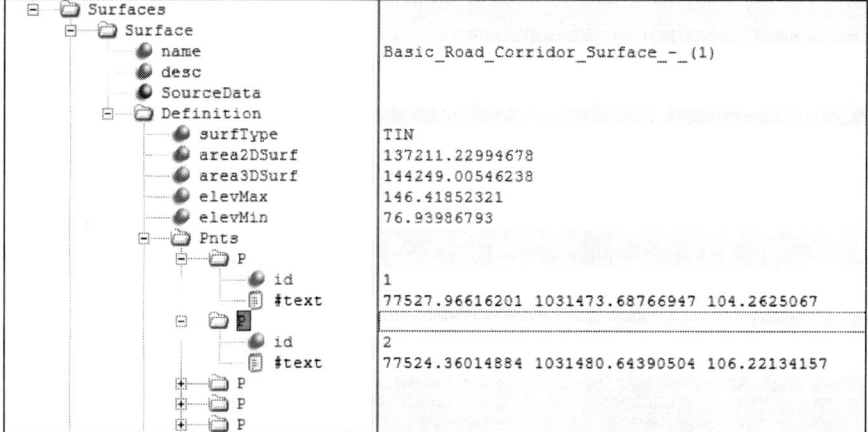

All the points data for each surface is contained within the **Points** XML node for each surface.

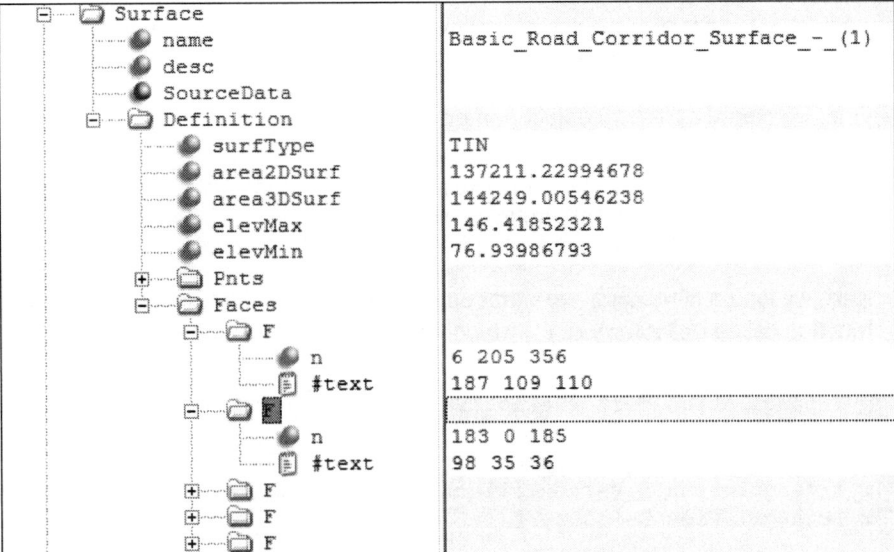

Similarly, the faces data is contained in a **Faces** XML node for each surface. We use the faces data to create triangles in our `MeshObject`.

There's more...

The `LandXML` file format is capable of holding other kinds of data, such as roads and bridges. Visit the `LandXML` website at `http://www.landxml.org` for further details, examples, and documentation.

Creating Delaunay triangulation

In this recipe, we show you how to create a Delaunay triangulation from a triangle vertex data. The usefulness of a mesh that satisfies the Delaunay triangulation is that such an arrangement tends to avoid skinny triangles. We will also be using Delaunay triangulation on mesh vertices, later, to find the height of a point on the surface of the terrain.

Getting ready

To follow along with this recipe, open the solution located in the `Recipes/Chapter03/ Delaunay` folder in the code bundle available on the Packt website.

How to do it...

We start with a basic MFC Ogre application, then add the functionality to load the vertices, and create a mesh with Delaunay triangulation.

1. First, we create a manual object named `Topography` with a generic white material.

```
m_Topography = SceneManager->createManualObject("Topography");
m_Topography->setDynamic(false);
m_Topography->begin("BaseWhiteNoLighting",
  Ogre::RenderOperation::OT_TRIANGLE_LIST);
```

2. Next, we load a file `test2.xyz` that contains our vertex data, and run a utility function called `DelaunayIt()`, which will convert the structure of the triangulation data into a Delaunay triangulation.

```
m_Triangulation.VertexSerialize(CString("test2.xyz"),
  CArchive::load);
m_Triangulation.m_VertexNumber = 0;
m_Triangulation.m_VertexCollection.m_VertexNumber = 0;
m_Triangulation.DelaunayIt();
```

3. Finally, we iterate over the triangulation data, and add all the vertex position data and triangle data to the `ManualObject`.

```
for (longintEdgeIndex = 0;
  EdgeIndex<m_Triangulation.m_EdgeCollection.
  m_Collection.GetCount(); EdgeIndex++) {

Edge1 = (CEdge *) m_Triangulation.m_EdgeCollection.
  m_Collection[EdgeIndex];
Vertex1 = Edge1->m_Origin;
Edge2 = Edge1->m_Left;
Vertex2 = Edge2->m_Origin;
Edge3 = Edge2->m_Left;

// Code omitted here that skips "virtual" edges and
// edges that have already been printed

Edge1->m_Printed = true;
Edge2->m_Printed = true;
Edge3->m_Printed = true;

m_Topography->position(Vertex1->m_Coordinate[0] - this->
  m_Triangulation.m_VertexCollection.m_Min.m_Coordinate[0],
  Vertex1->m_Coordinate[1] - this->m_Triangulation.
  m_VertexCollection.m_Min.m_Coordinate[1],
  (Vertex1->m_Coordinate[2] - this->m_Triangulation.
  m_VertexCollection.m_Min.m_Coordinate[2])/100);

m_Topography->position(Vertex2->m_Coordinate[0] - this->
  m_Triangulation.m_VertexCollection.m_Min.m_Coordinate[0],
```

```
        Vertex2->m_Coordinate[1] - this->m_Triangulation.
        m_VertexCollection.m_Min.m_Coordinate[1],
        (Vertex2->m_Coordinate[2] - this->m_Triangulation.
        m_VertexCollection.m_Min.m_Coordinate[2])/100);

    m_Topography->position(Vertex3->m_Coordinate[0] - this->
        m_Triangulation.m_VertexCollection.m_Min.m_Coordinate[0],
        Vertex3->m_Coordinate[1] - this->m_Triangulation.
        m_VertexCollection.m_Min.m_Coordinate[1],
        (Vertex3->m_Coordinate[2] - this->m_Triangulation.
        m_VertexCollection.m_Min.m_Coordinate[2])/100);

    m_Topography->triangle(TriangleIndex * 3 + 0,
        TriangleIndex * 3 + 1, TriangleIndex * 3 + 2);
    TriangleIndex++;
}

m_Topography->end();
```

4. Once all the triangle data for `ManualObject` has been defined, we add the object to the scene graph.

```
Ogre::SceneNode *Node = SceneManager->
    getRootSceneNode()->createChildSceneNode(
    Ogre::Vector3(626145.0,4539495.0,1459.992));
DelaunayIt();

Node->attachObject(m_Topography);
```

How it works...

For each edge of triangulation, there are two oriented edges. For each oriented edge, we define its vertex of origin, its destination, its left neighbor in the triangle, and the same edge with the opposite direction. In this case, we have a triangle of edge, `edge.left`, `edge.left.left`, and a neighboring triangle with `edge.sym`.

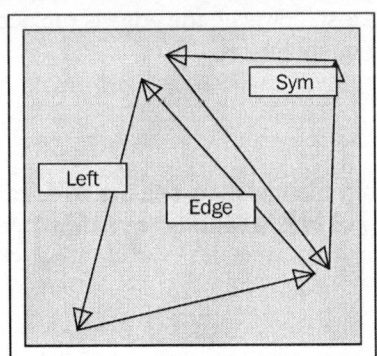

We use an **incremental algorithm** to create the Delaunay triangulation. Initially, we create a bounding frame from our set of 3D points, and then insert points one at a time. When we insert a point, we first determine what triangle edge the point belongs to, using the `CTriangu lation::LocateTriangle()` method. This method looks in the edge collections for a valid neighbor edge, and determines if the point is actually on the edge.

Once a valid neighbor is found, new `CEdge` objects are created, using the new vertex, and then are added to the edge collection. Finally, a test is performed to determine if the new arrangement satisfies the `DelaunayInCircle` condition. The condition states that *every edge must have a point-free circle passing through its endpoints*.

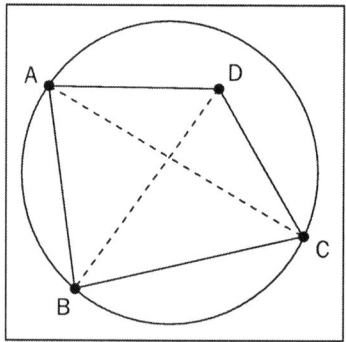

For those interested in the math behind this, the `InCircle` condition is as follows:

$$\mathscr{D}(A, B, C, D) = \begin{vmatrix} x_A & y_A & x_A^2 + y_A^2 & 1 \\ x_B & y_B & x_B^2 + y_B^2 & 1 \\ x_C & y_C & x_C^2 + y_C^2 & 1 \\ x_D & y_D & x_D^2 + y_D^2 & 1 \end{vmatrix} > 0$$

If the edge passes the test, it is guaranteed to be a Delaunay edge, and need not be considered further. If it fails the test, however, the edge is replaced by another edge that is the other diagonal of the quadrilateral.

See also

For more information on Delaunay triangulation, see the Wikipedia page at `http://en.wikipedia.org/wiki/Delaunay_triangulation`.

Creating manual objects

In this recipe, we'll show you how to create a **Mebius** mesh with multiple sections, using a `ManualObject`. We'll also add menu items to our application's user interface, so that the user can change the material used by each section at runtime.

Getting ready

To follow along with this recipe, open the solution located in the `Recipes/Chapter03/ManualObject` folder in the code bundle available on the Packt website.

How to do it...

1. First, we create an MFC Ogre application named `ManualObject`.

2. Next, we create a Mebius mesh with multiple sections using code similar to what we used in the *Creating a custom resource manager* recipe, from *Chapter 1, Delving Deep into Application Design*. The `Materials` array contains the names of all the materials we will be using.

```
Ogre::String Materials[] =
{
  "Examples/SphereMappedRustySteel",
  "Examples/OgreLogo",
  "Examples/BeachStones",
  "Examples/TrippySkyBox",
  "Examples/SpaceSkyBox",
  "Examples/DynamicCubeMap",
  "Examples/RustySteel",
  "Examples/Chrome",
  "Examples/WaterStream",
  "Examples/Flare"
};
```

The code for creating the `ManualObject` is very similar to what we have used in previous recipes, except that we set the dynamic property to `true`, because we intend to change the mesh at runtime.

```
m_MaterialIndex = 0;
m_ManualObject = m_SceneManager->createManualObject("stl");
m_ManualObject->setDynamic(true);
m_ManualObject->begin(Materials[m_MaterialIndex++],
  Ogre::RenderOperation::OT_TRIANGLE_LIST);
```

3. When parsing the Mebius file, we start a new section after every `1000` triangles, and assign a different material.

```
while (!feof(fp)) {
  int ret = fscanf(fp, "%*s %*s %f %f %f\n", &nx,
    &ny, &nz); //facet normal nx ny nz

  ret = fscanf(fp, "%*s %*s"); //outer loop
  ret = fscanf(fp, "%*s %f %f %f\n", &x,  &y,  &z); //vertex x y z

  m_ManualObject->position(x, y, z);
  m_ManualObject->normal(nx, ny, nz);
  m_ManualObject->colour(Ogre::ColourValue(0.0f, 0.0f,
    0.0f, 1.0f));
  ret=fscanf(fp, "%*s %f %f %f\n", &x,  &y,  &z); //vertex x y z

  m_ManualObject->position(x, y, z);
  m_ManualObject->normal(nx, ny, nz);
  m_ManualObject->colour(Ogre::ColourValue(0.0f, 0.0f,
    0.0f, 1.0f));
ret=fscanf(fp, "%*s %f %f %f\n", &x,  &y,  &z); //vertex x y z

  m_ManualObject->position(x, y, z);
  m_ManualObject->normal(nx, ny, nz);
  m_ManualObject->colour(Ogre::ColourValue(0.0f, 0.0f,
    0.0f, 1.0f));

  m_ManualObject->triangle(TriangleIndex * 3 + 0, TriangleIndex *
    3 + 1, TriangleIndex * 3 + 2);
  TriangleIndex++;

  ret=fscanf(fp, "%*s"); //endloop
  ret=fscanf(fp, "%*s"); //endfacet

  if (feof(fp))
    break;

  if (TriangleIndex % 1000 == 0) {
    m_ManualObject->end();
    m_ManualObject->begin(Materials[m_MaterialIndex++],
      Ogre::RenderOperation::OT_TRIANGLE_LIST);
    TriangleIndex = 0;
  }
}

fclose(fp);

m_ManualObject->end();
```

4. Finally, we add a submenu called `Actions` with two items: `Change materials` and `Reset`. The `CManualObjectView::OnActionsMaterials()` method changes the material name used by each section in the `ManualObject`, and the `CManual ObjectView::OnActionsReset()` method resets the material names to their original state.

```
for (int Index = 0; Index < m_ManualObject->getNumSections();
  Index++) {
  m_ManualObject->setMaterialName(Index,
    Materials[m_ManualObject->getNumSections() - Index]);
}
```

The `ManualObject` has a function named `setMaterialName()`, which is used to change the material for a section.

How it works...

`ManualObject` is a utility class designed to simplify the process of creating custom geometry. All of the functionality in `ManualObject` can be accomplished with lower-level Ogre API calls, memory buffer manipulation, and more code, but `ManualObject` makes all that unnecessary.

In this recipe, we used the basic `ManualObject` functionality to define vertex positions, normals, and `colors`. We also used `ManualObject::begin()` and `ManualObject::end()` to create multiple `ManualObjectSections`. Each `ManualObjectSection` represents a separate renderable, and in our recipe, we gave each of these a different `Material`, and then showed you how to change the `Material` for each section during runtime, by calling `ManualObject::setMaterialName()`.

See also

In this chapter:

▶ *Creating parametric superellipsoids*

Creating parametric superellipsoids

Superellipsoids are graphical primitives that take a variety of ellipsoid shapes, depending on the parameters in the equation used to generate the shape. In this recipe, we will show you how to create a superellipsoid with a `ManualObject`, and modify the shape at runtime.

Getting ready

To follow along with this recipe, open the solution located in the `Recipes/Chapter03/` `SuperEllipsoid` folder in the code bundle available on the Packt website.

How to do it...

1. First, we create an MFC with Ribbon Ogre application named `SuperEllipsoid`.
2. Next, we add the controls that we'll be using to adjust the superellipsoid shape.

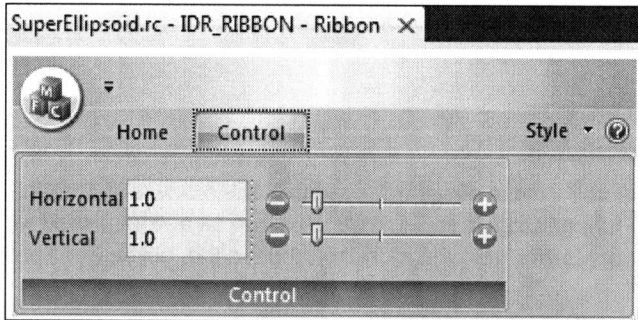

3. Use the Ribbon editor to create a new panel named `Control`. Then, create a linked pair of edit boxes and sliders for both superellipsoid parameters.

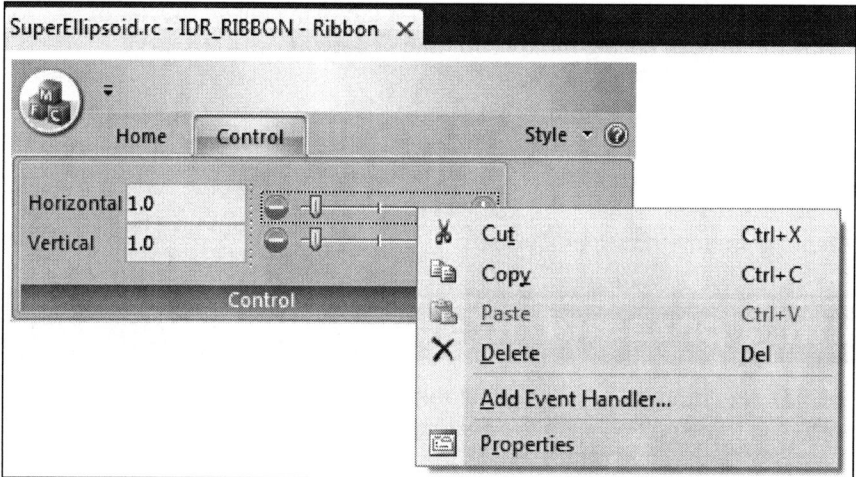

4. Next, add event handlers by right-clicking on each control and selecting **Add event handler**.

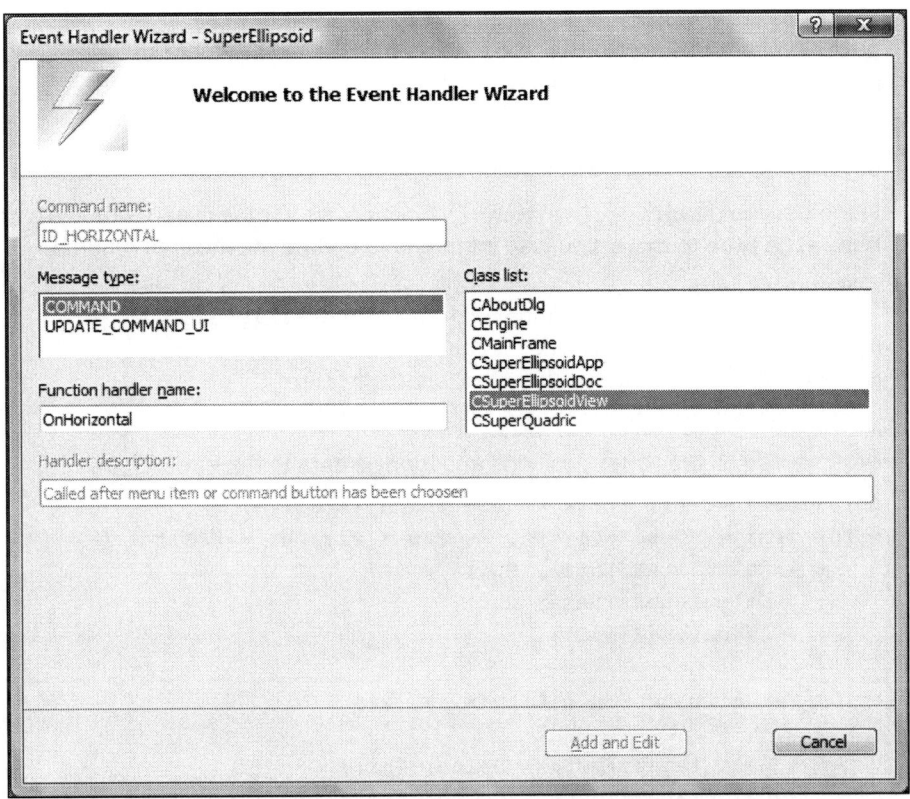

5. In the **Event Handler Wizard** that opens, select the **COMMAND** as the **Message type** and **CSupperEllipsoidView** from the **Class list**. Click on **Add and Edit**, and the wizard will generate the event handler function.

In each event handler function, we read the input value, set the appropriate m_ SuperQuadric property, and then call m_SuperQuadric.UpdateMesh().

For example, the CSuperEllipsoidView::OnHorizontal() function reads the slider position, and then sets the m_SuperQuadric.m_HorFactor.

```
CMainFrame *MainFrame = (CMainFrame *)(
  (CSuperEllipsoidApp*)AfxGetApp())->GetMainWnd();
CMFCRibbonBar* RibbonBar = MainFrame->GetRibbonBar();

CMFCRibbonSlider* Slider = DYNAMIC_DOWNCAST(CMFCRibbonSlider,
  RibbonBar->FindByID(ID_HORIZONTAL));
CMFCRibbonEdit* Edit = DYNAMIC_DOWNCAST(CMFCRibbonEdit,
  RibbonBar->FindByID(ID_HORIZONTAL_EDIT));

m_SuperQuadric.m_HorFactor = (double)Slider->GetPos() / 10.0;
CString Text;
```

```
Text.Format("%.2f", m_SuperQuadric.m_HorFactor);
Edit->SetEditText(Text);
m_SuperQuadric.UpdateMesh();
```

6. To create the superellipsoid `ManualObject` initially, we add a call to `m_SuperQuadric.DrawMesh()` inside `CSuperEllipsoidView::EngineSetup()`.

7. In the `CSuperQuadric::DrawMesh()` function, we set the dynamic property of the `ManualObject` to `true`, because we intend to update the mesh at runtime.

```
m_ManualObject =
  SceneManager->createManualObject("Superellipsoid");
m_ManualObject->setDynamic(true);
m_ManualObject->begin("BaseWhiteNoLighting",
  Ogre::RenderOperation::OT_TRIANGLE_LIST);
```

8. Next, we add all the vertex positions and triangle data to the `ManualObject`.

```
for (Theta = -Pi; Theta <= Pi; Theta += Delta) {
  for (Phi = -0.5 * Pi; Phi <= 0.5 * Pi; Phi += Delta) {
    x = CalculateX(Theta, Phi);
    y = CalculateY(Theta, Phi);
    z = CalculateZ(Phi);

    m_ManualObject->position(x, y, z);

    x = CalculateX(Theta + Delta, Phi);
    y = CalculateY(Theta + Delta, Phi);
    z = CalculateZ(Phi);

    m_ManualObject->position(x, y, z);

    x = CalculateX(Theta + Delta, Phi + Delta);
    y = CalculateY(Theta + Delta, Phi + Delta);
    z = CalculateZ(Phi + Delta);

    m_ManualObject->position(x, y, z);

    m_ManualObject->triangle(TriangleIndex * 3 + 0, TriangleIndex
      * 3 + 1, TriangleIndex * 3 + 2);
    TriangleIndex++;

    x = CalculateX(Theta, Phi);
    y = CalculateY(Theta, Phi);
    z = CalculateZ(Phi);

    m_ManualObject->position(x, y, z);
```

```
        x = CalculateX(Theta + Delta, Phi + Delta);
        y = CalculateY(Theta + Delta, Phi + Delta);
        z = CalculateZ(Phi + Delta);

        m_ManualObject->position(x, y, z);

        x = CalculateX(Theta, Phi + Delta);
        y = CalculateY(Theta, Phi + Delta);
        z = CalculateZ(Phi + Delta);

        m_ManualObject->position(x, y, z);

        m_ManualObject->triangle(TriangleIndex * 3 + 0, TriangleIndex
          * 3 + 1, TriangleIndex * 3 + 2);
        TriangleIndex++;
    }
}
```

9. When we're done, we call `ManualObject::end()` to indicate that we have finished entering data.

```
m_ManualObject->end();
```

10. Now, when the user moves a slider or enters in new values for the superellipsoid, the `CSuperQuadric::UpdateMesh()` function is called and the positions for the mesh are updated, based on the new horizontal and vertical superellipsoid values.

```
m_ManualObject->beginUpdate(0);

for (Theta = -Pi; Theta <= Pi; Theta += Delta) {
  for (Phi = -0.5 * Pi; Phi <= 0.5 * Pi; Phi += Delta) {
      x = CalculateX(Theta, Phi);
      y = CalculateY(Theta, Phi);
      z = CalculateZ(Phi);

      m_ManualObject->position(x, y, z);

      x = CalculateX(Theta + Delta, Phi);
      y = CalculateY(Theta + Delta, Phi);
      z = CalculateZ(Phi);

      m_ManualObject->position(x, y, z);

      x = CalculateX(Theta + Delta, Phi + Delta);
      y = CalculateY(Theta + Delta, Phi + Delta);
      z = CalculateZ(Phi + Delta);
```

```
        m_ManualObject->position(x, y, z);

    x = CalculateX(Theta, Phi);
    y = CalculateY(Theta, Phi);
    z = CalculateZ(Phi);

        m_ManualObject->position(x, y, z);

    x = CalculateX(Theta + Delta, Phi + Delta);
    y = CalculateY(Theta + Delta, Phi + Delta);
    z = CalculateZ(Phi + Delta);

        m_ManualObject->position(x, y, z);

    x = CalculateX(Theta, Phi + Delta);
    y = CalculateY(Theta, Phi + Delta);
    z = CalculateZ(Phi + Delta);

        m_ManualObject->position(x, y, z);
      }
    }
    m_ManualObject->end();
```

The final bits of code that we add to our application are for the mouse and the keyboard input. See the first two recipes of *Chapter 2, Let Us Be Multimodal* for the details on how to add a mouse and a keyboard input to an application.

How it works...

Superellipsoids come from the graphical primitive family of **superquadrics**. By manipulating a small number of controlling parameters in the quadric equations used to generate the shape, we get a wide variety of forms including spheres, cylinders, pinched stars, and rectangles with rounded edges. A superellipsoid surface is defined by the following formula:

$$\underline{x}(\eta,\omega) = \begin{bmatrix} a_1 \cos^{\varepsilon_1} \eta \; \cos^{\varepsilon_2} \omega \\ a_2 \cos^{\varepsilon_1} \eta \; \sin^{\varepsilon_2} \omega \\ a_3 \sin^{\varepsilon_1} \eta \end{bmatrix} \quad \begin{array}{l} -\pi/2 \le \eta \le \pi/2 \\ -\pi \le \omega \le \pi \end{array}$$

The vector x sweeps out a closed surface as the two independent parameters, angles h and w change in the given intervals. Parameters a1, a2, and a3 define the superquadric scaling in the x, y and z directions, respectively. e1 is the squareness parameter in the north-south direction, while e2 is the squareness parameter in the east-west direction. The following figure illustrates some of the shapes that can be generated by varying the value of each of the squareness parameters.

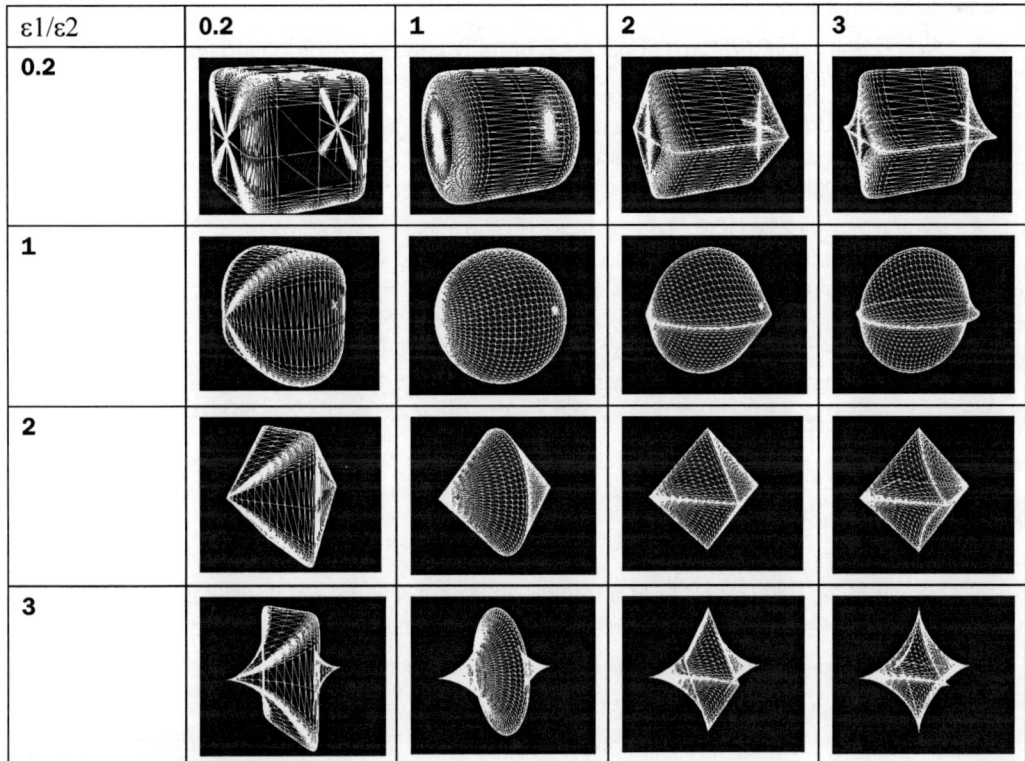

$\varepsilon1/\varepsilon2$	0.2	1	2	3
0.2				
1				
2				
3				

See also

If you would like more information on superellipsoids and superquadrics, see the Wikipedia article at http://en.wikipedia.org/wiki/Superquadrics.

Adding meshes on terrain

Now that we have a terrain mesh, we need to place objects precisely on top of the terrain. In this recipe, we will show you how to use Delaunay triangulation edge data for a terrain mesh to find the elevation of specific point on the terrain. Using this information, we will place an object precisely on the terrain.

Getting ready

To follow along with this recipe, open the solution located in the `Recipes/Chapter03/InsertMesh` folder in the code bundle available on the Packt website.

How to do it...

1. First, create an MFC Ogre application named `InsertMesh`, based on the *Create Delaunay triangulation* recipe.

2. Next, we add code to the `CInsertMeshView::EngineSetup()` function, to find the triangle that contains a point over the terrain. For our application, we are looking for the height of the terrain at the middle of the terrain mesh.

```
Vertex.m_Coordinate[0] = 0.5 *
    (m_Triangulation.m_VertexCollection.m_Max.m_Coordinate[0] +
    m_Triangulation.m_VertexCollection.m_Min.m_Coordinate[0]);

Vertex.m_Coordinate[1] = 0.5 *
    (m_Triangulation.m_VertexCollection.m_Max.m_Coordinate[1] +
    m_Triangulation.m_VertexCollection.m_Min.m_Coordinate[1]);

Vertex.m_Coordinate[2] = 0.0;

Edge = m_Triangulation.LocateTriangle(&Vertex, OnEdge);
```

3. Now that we have an edge of a triangle that contains the point, we can interpolate the positions of the three vertices that make up this triangle, and use the resulting position to place a robot entity.

```
m_Triangulation.TriangleInterpolate(Edge->m_Origin,
    Edge->m_Destination, Edge->m_Left->m_Destination, &Vertex);

Ogre::SceneNode *RobotNode = SceneManager->getRootSceneNode()->
    createChildSceneNode(
    Ogre::Vector3(Vertex.m_Coordinate[0],
    Vertex.m_Coordinate[1],
    Vertex.m_Coordinate[2]));
```

How it works...

In order to accurately place a mesh on top of the terrain, we need to get the height of the terrain at the x and z coordinates, where we intend to place the mesh. We use the Delaunay triangulation functionality to find the triangle under the 2d coordinates, and then interpolate the positions of the three vertices that make up that triangle to get a 3d point on the terrain.

The `CTriangulation::LocateTriangle()` method searches for the nearest edge to a point, or returns the existing edge a point is on. Using the found edge, we are then able to interpolate the vertex positions of the vertices for the triangle the edge belongs to.

Adding trees as billboards

Many objects on the terrain are displayed as 2D sprites or billboards when viewed from far away, or even from close up in the case of grass and small plants. In this recipe, we will show you how to use billboards to display trees on top of a terrain.

Getting ready

For this recipe we use a custom material named `Trees`. The `Trees` material is made up of two files: the `trees.material` file found in `media/materials/scripts` and the texture `trees.png` in `media/materials/textures`.

To follow along with this recipe, open the solution located in the `Recipes/Chapter03/ AddingTrees` folder in the code bundle available on the Packt website.

How to do it...

1. First, create an MFC Ogre application named `AddingTrees`.

2. Next, in `EngineSetup()`, define an array that contains all the texture coordinates for the various plant and tree images that are combined in the `trees.png` image.

```
Ogre::FloatRect TextureCoordinates[]={
  Ogre::FloatRect(113.0/5000.0,121.0/5000.0,851.0/5000.0,1073.0/
    5000.0),
  Ogre::FloatRect(1021.0/5000.0,114.0/5000.0,3386.0/5000.0,1984.0/
    5000.0),
  Ogre::FloatRect(3825.0/5000.0,1049.0/5000.0,4871.0/
    5000.0,3588.0/5000.0),
  Ogre::FloatRect(1739.0/5000.0,2418.0/5000.0,2796.0/
    5000.0,4774.0/5000.0),
  Ogre::FloatRect(221.0/5000.0,2723.0/5000.0,1464.0/
    5000.0,3795.0/5000.0),
  Ogre::FloatRect(505.0/5000.0,4391.0/5000.0,805.0/
    5000.0,4662.0/5000.0),
  Ogre::FloatRect(339.0/5000.0,2085.0/5000.0,482.0/
    5000.0,2216.0/5000.0),
  Ogre::FloatRect(2803.0/5000.0,3355.0/5000.0,3891.0/
    5000.0,4912.0/5000.0)
};
```

3. Next, we create a `BillboardSet` to manage all of our tree billboards. We indicate that we want to use our `Trees` material, and that we want to use the `TextureCoordinates` we just defined.

```
Ogre::BillboardSet *Trees =
  SceneManager->createBillboardSet("Trees");

Trees->setTextureCoords(TextureCoordinates, 8);
Trees->setMaterialName("Trees");
Trees->setCastShadows(true);
Trees->setSortingEnabled(true);
Trees->setBillboardType(Ogre::BBT_ORIENTED_COMMON);
```

4. Finally, we create our tree billboards, and position them in a grid with different texture indexes. Each texture index corresponds to a different plant or tree graphic in our `trees.png` texture.

```
double x = 0.0;
double y = 0.0;
double z = 0.0;

double TreeWidth;
double TreeHeight;
int TextureIndex;

for (int i = 0; i < 40; i++) {
for (int j = 0; j < 40; j++) {
  x = i * 5;
  y = j * 5;
  z = 0;

  TextureIndex = (i + j) / 10;
  TreeWidth = (i + j + 10) / 10;
  TreeHeight = (i + j + 10) / 5;

  Ogre::Vector3 TreePosition(x, y, z);
  Ogre::Billboard* Tree = Trees->createBillboard(TreePosition);
  Tree->setDimensions(TreeWidth, TreeHeight);
  Tree->setTexcoordIndex(TextureIndex);
}
```

How it works...

A billboard is a flat rectangular primitive, which, in our application, faces the camera. In Ogre, billboards are managed by `BillboardSets`, because they provide many useful set operations, as well as performance enhancements.

In our application, we use a single texture to hold all of our plant and tree images, and then indicate which image to use, by providing a texture coordinate index when we create the billboard. The actual texture graphic looks like this:

The `Trees` material that we use for our billboards references the `trees.png` texture, takes transparency into account for shadows, and allows shadows cast from other objects to fall on the tree billboards.

```
material Trees {
   transparency_casts_shadows on
   receive_shadows on

     technique {
   pass {
     ambient 1.0 1.0 1.0 1
     diffuse 1.0 1.0 1.0 1
        depth_check on
        depth_write off
     depth_func less_equal
        depth_bias 0.4
        scene_blend src_alpha one_minus_src_alpha
        texture_unit {
      texture_alias 0
      texture Trees.png
   }
     }
   }
     technique {
   pass {
     diffuse 0.0 1.0 0.0
     depth_check off
      }
  }
}
```

There's more...

Instead of using a texture coordinates array, we could just specify the texture coordinates directly just after creating each billboard, as follows:

```
Ogre::FloatRectTree1(113.0/5000.0,121.0/5000.0,851.0/5000.0,1073.0/
   5000.0);
Tree->setTexcoordIndex(Tree1);
```

Also, it is best to create billboard sets based on the dimensions of the billboard. By using the same dimension for each billboard in a set, Ogre can perform calculations more efficiently when rendering.

Creating and editing a scene

Most professional game studios use applications to build scenes for each level in their games. In this recipe, we will show you how to build an application with an interface for creating scene nodes and entities—the basis for your first scene editor!

Getting ready

To follow along with this recipe, open the solution located in the `Recipes/Chapter03/SceneEditor` folder in the code bundle available on the Packt website.

How to do it...

1. First, create a new MFC Ogre application named `SceneEditor`.

2. Next, edit the main menu and add a submenu named `Edit Scene`. Add a submenu item named `Scene Manager`, which we will use to launch a dialog-box that displays the scene graph in a tree control. Next, for each type of Ogre object that we wish to create, add a sub-item, such as `Add Entity` or `Add Node`. Lastly, add two submenu items for destroying all cameras and entities.

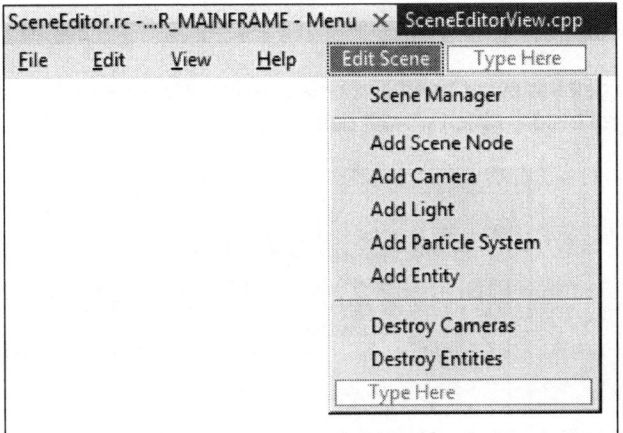

3. Next, add event handlers for each submenu item, by right-clicking on each submenu item and selecting **Add Event Handler**.

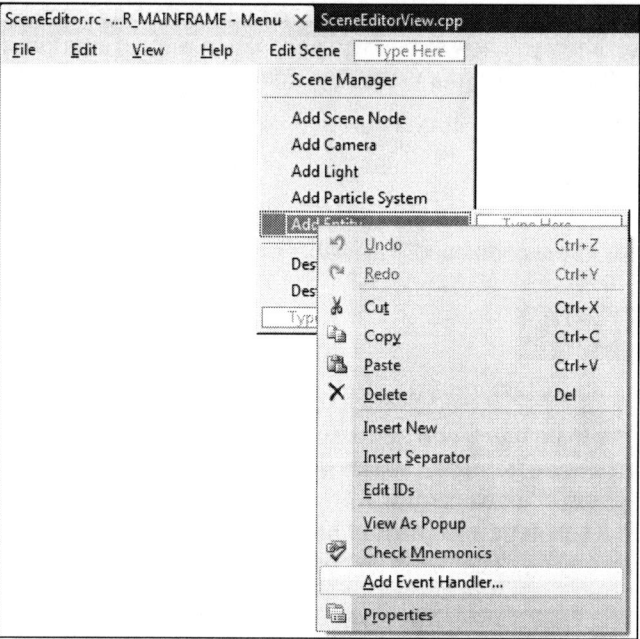

4. After adding all the event handlers, create a dialog-box named `Scene Manager` with a tree control inside, which we will use for managing the scene graph.

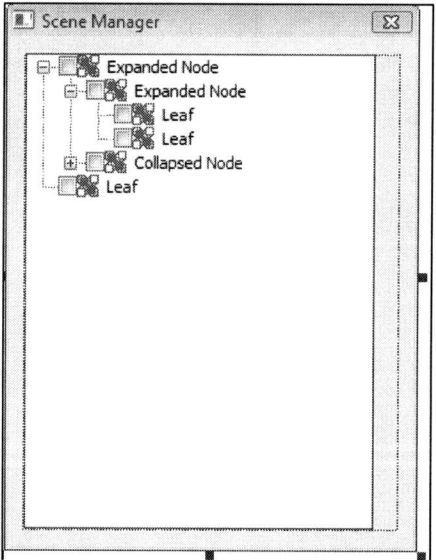

The handler for the `Scene Manager` submenu item that brings up the `Scene Manager` dialog-box looks like this:

```
voidCSceneEditorView::OnEditSceneManager() {
  if (this->m_SceneManagerDlg == NULL) {
    m_SceneManagerDlg = newCSceneManagerDlg();
    m_SceneManagerDlg->Create(IDD_SCENE_MANAGER);
  }

  m_SceneManagerDlg->ShowWindow(SW_SHOW);
}
```

5. In the same way, create a dialog-box for adding a child scene node.

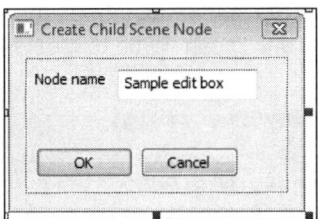

This dialog-box will appear when the user clicks on a node in the tree control and then clicks on the **Add Scene Node** submenu item. The handler function for the **Add Scene Node** submenu item looks like this:

```
voidCSceneEditorView::OnEditsceneAddscenenode() {
  CChildSceneNodeDlgChildSceneNodeDlg;

  if (IDOK == ChildSceneNodeDlg.DoModal()) {
    HTREEITEM Selected =
      m_SceneManagerDlg->m_SceneTree.GetSelectedItem();
    m_SceneManagerDlg->m_SceneTree.
      InsertItem(ChildSceneNodeDlg.m_NodeName, Selected);
    m_SceneManagerDlg->m_SceneTree.Expand(Selected, TVE_EXPAND);
    m_SceneManager->getRootSceneNode()->createChildSceneNode(
      Ogre::String(ChildSceneNodeDlg.m_NodeName));

    if (m_Root != NULL) {
      m_Root->renderOneFrame();
    }
  }
}
```

The handler code finds the selected tree element and creates a new node with the name from the **Create Child Scene Node** dialog-box. It also creates the scene node in the scene graph.

6. Next, create an entity creator dialog-box with **Entity Name** and **Mesh Name** fields. This dialog-box will be activated when the user clicks on the **Add Entity** submenu item.

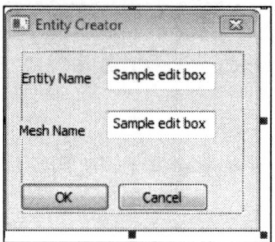

The handler for the **Add Entity** submenu item opens the **Entity Creator** dialog-box, then uses the entity name and mesh name to create a new entity, and adds it to the selected scene node.

```cpp
CEntityCreatorDlgEntityCreatorDlg;

if (IDOK == EntityCreatorDlg.DoModal()) {
  HTREEITEM Selected = m_SceneManagerDlg->
    m_SceneTree.GetSelectedItem();
  m_SceneManagerDlg->m_SceneTree.InsertItem(
    EntityCreatorDlg.m_EntityName, Selected);

  Ogre::String SceneNodeName = m_SceneManagerDlg->
    m_SceneTree.GetItemText(Selected);
  Ogre::Entity *Entity = m_SceneManager->createEntity
    (Ogre::String(EntityCreatorDlg.m_EntityName),
    Ogre::String(EntityCreatorDlg.m_MeshName));
  Ogre::SceneNode *SceneNode = m_SceneManager->
    getSceneNode(SceneNodeName);
  SceneNode->attachObject(Entity);

  Ogre::AxisAlignedBox Box = Entity->getBoundingBox();
  Ogre::Vector3 Center = Box.getCenter();
  m_Camera->lookAt(Center);

  m_SceneManagerDlg->m_SceneTree.Expand(Selected, TVE_EXPAND);

  if (m_Root != NULL) {
    m_Root->renderOneFrame();
  }
}
```

How it works...

Each event handler for the submenu items that we added, creates nodes, entities, lights, and cameras, or removes them. As entities and nodes are added to the scene, they appear in the **Scene Manager** tree structure as well as in the 3D viewport.

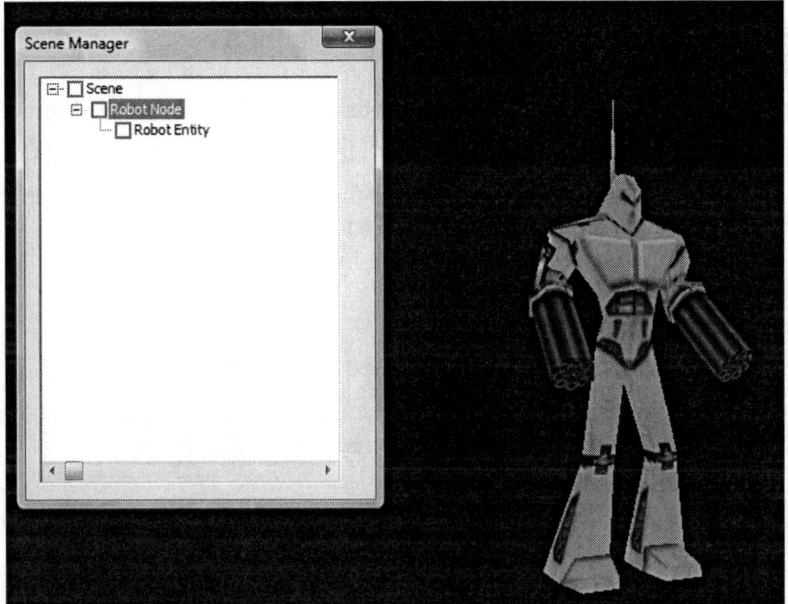

There's more...

You can right-click on the tree control to open a pop-up menu with functionality to add a scene node, add an entity, or delete the scene node.

In addition to the **Edit Scene** menu item, it might be helpful to create a floating toolbar version of the **Edit Scene** menu.

See also

In this chapter:

- ▸ *Saving a scene to an XML file*
- ▸ *Loading a scene from an XML file*

Saving a scene to an XML file

No scene editor would be complete without the ability to save a scene to file. It is also possible that you may want to save the state of your game's scene in an XML file. In this recipe, we will show you how to do just that.

Getting ready

To follow along with this recipe, open the solution located in the `Recipes/Chapter03/SaveScene` folder in the code bundle available on the Packt website.

In this recipe, we will be using the `libxml2` library, which you should download from `http://xmlsoft.org`, and put in your `Recipes` folder.

How to do it...

1. First, create a MFC Ogre application named `SaveScene`.

2. Next, in the `CSaveSceneView::EngineSetup()` function, we instantiate an `Xmlm_XmlWriter` object, and use it to create our XML document.

   ```
   xmlDocPtr doc;
   // Create a new Xmlm_XmlWriter for DOM, with no compression.
   m_XmlWriter = xmlNewTextWriterDoc(&doc, 0);
   // Start the document with the xml default for the version,
   // encoding ISO 8859-1 and the default for the standalone
   // declaration.
   xmlTextWriterStartDocument(m_XmlWriter, NULL, MY_ENCODING, NULL);

   SceneExplore(SceneManager);

   xmlTextWriterEndDocument(m_XmlWriter);
   xmlFreeTextWriter(m_XmlWriter);
   xmlSaveFileEnc("1.scene", doc, MY_ENCODING);
   xmlFreeDoc(doc);
   ```

3. We start writing the document in memory, by calling `xmlTextWriterStartDocument()`, then call the `CSaveSceneView::SceneExplore()` utility function to write all the scene information to memory, and then finally we save XML to a file called `1.scene`.

4. The `CSaveSceneView::SceneExplore()` function simply creates the XML root scene node and then calls `CSaveSceneView::SceneNodeExplore()` with the `RootSceneNode`.

```
Ogre::SceneNode *RootSceneNode = SceneManager->getRootSceneNode();

xmlTextWriterStartElement(m_XmlWriter, BAD_CAST
  "RootSceneNode");//start RootSceneNode

SceneNodeExplore(RootSceneNode);

xmlTextWriterEndElement(m_XmlWriter); //end RootSceneNode
```

5. The `CSaveSceneView::SceneNodeExplore` function writes information about the current scene node to memory, including all the entities attached to the node, then it iterates over each scene node child and calls `CSaveSceneView::SceneNodeExplore` with that child, as the current scene node.

```
Ogre::Entity *Entity = NULL;
Ogre::Camera *Camera = NULL;
Ogre::Light *Light = NULL;
Ogre::ParticleSystem *ParticleSystem = NULL;
Ogre::ManualObject *ManualObject = NULL;
Ogre::BillboardSet *BillboardSet = NULL;

Ogre::SceneNode::ObjectIterator obji =
  SceneNode->getAttachedObjectIterator();

xmlTextWriterStartElement(m_XmlWriter, BAD_CAST "SceneNode");

Ogre::String SceneNodeName = SceneNode->getName();

xmlTextWriterWriteAttribute(m_XmlWriter,
  BAD_CAST "SceneNodeName",
  BAD_CAST SceneNodeName.c_str());

while (obji.hasMoreElements()) {
  Ogre::MovableObject* mobj = obji.getNext();

  Ogre::String Type = mobj->getMovableType();

  if (Type == "Entity") {
    Entity = (Ogre::Entity *)(mobj);
    Ogre::String EntityName = Entity->getName();
    xmlTextWriterStartElement(m_XmlWriter, BAD_CAST "Entity");
```

```
    xmlTextWriterWriteAttribute(m_XmlWriter,
      BAD_CAST "EntityName",
      BAD_CAST EntityName.c_str());

    Ogre::MeshPtr Mesh = Entity->getMesh();
    Ogre::String MeshName = Mesh->getName();
    xmlTextWriterWriteAttribute(m_XmlWriter,
      BAD_CAST "MeshName",
      BAD_CAST MeshName.c_str());

    xmlTextWriterEndElement(m_XmlWriter);
  }

  if (Type == "Camera") {
    Camera = (Ogre::Camera *)(mobj);
    Ogre::String CameraName = Camera->getName();
    xmlTextWriterStartElement(m_XmlWriter, BAD_CAST "Camera");

    xmlTextWriterWriteAttribute(m_XmlWriter,
      BAD_CAST "CameraName",
      BAD_CAST CameraName.c_str());

    Ogre::Vector3 CameraPosition = Camera->getPosition();

    xmlTextWriterWriteFormatAttribute(m_XmlWriter,
      BAD_CAST "XPosition",
      "%f",CameraPosition.x);

    xmlTextWriterWriteFormatAttribute(m_XmlWriter,
      BAD_CAST "YPosition",
      "%f",CameraPosition.y);

    xmlTextWriterWriteFormatAttribute(m_XmlWriter,
      BAD_CAST "ZPosition",
      "%f",CameraPosition.z);

    Ogre::Vector3 CameraDirection = Camera->getDirection();

    xmlTextWriterWriteFormatAttribute(m_XmlWriter,
      BAD_CAST "XDirection",
      "%f",CameraDirection.x);

    xmlTextWriterWriteFormatAttribute(m_XmlWriter,
      BAD_CAST "YDirection",
      "%f",CameraDirection.y);
```

```
      xmlTextWriterWriteFormatAttribute(m_XmlWriter,
        BAD_CAST "ZDirection",
        "%f",CameraDirection.z);

      xmlTextWriterEndElement(m_XmlWriter);
    }

    if (Type == "Light") {
      Light = (Ogre::Light *)(mobj);
    }

    if (Type == "ParticleSystem") {
      ParticleSystem = (Ogre::ParticleSystem *)(mobj);
    }

    if (Type == "ManualObject") {
      ManualObject = (Ogre::ManualObject *)(mobj);
    }

    if (Type == "BillboardSet") {
      BillboardSet = (Ogre::BillboardSet *)(mobj);
    }

  }

  Ogre::Node::ChildNodeIterator nodei =
    SceneNode->getChildIterator();

  while (nodei.hasMoreElements()) {
    Ogre::SceneNode* node = (Ogre::SceneNode*)(nodei.getNext());
    // Add this subnode and its children...
    SceneNodeExplore(node);
  }

  xmlTextWriterEndElement(m_XmlWriter); //end SceneNode
```

You may notice that not all the code for writing all the object types is included here, but the section for writing an entity gives the general idea.

How it works...

We iterate over all nodes in the scene graph, and write information about each node and the entities attached to that node into a simple XML file.

The resulting file will look something like this:

```
<?xml version="1.0" encoding="ISO-8859-1"?>
<RootSceneNode>
  <SceneNode SceneNodeName="Ogre/SceneRoot">
    <SceneNode SceneNodeName="CameraNode">
      <Camera CameraName="Camera" XPosition="200.000000"
        YPosition="50.000000" ZPosition="100.000000" XDirection="-
        0.888767" YDirection="-0.006624" ZDirection="-0.458312"/>
    </SceneNode>
    <SceneNode SceneNodeName="Unnamed_1">
      <Entity EntityName="Robot" MeshName="robot.mesh"/>
    </SceneNode>
  </SceneNode>
</RootSceneNode>
```

See also

In this chapter:

▶ *Creating and editing a scene*

▶ *Loading a scene from an XML file*

Loading a scene from an XML file

In the previous recipe, we showed you how to write information about a 3D scene to an XML file, and in this recipe we will show you how to read that data back in to re-create the scene.

Getting ready

To follow along with this recipe, open the solution located in the `Recipes/Chapter03/LoadScene` folder in the code bundle available on the Packt website.

In this recipe, we will be using the `libxml2` library, which you should download from `http://xmlsoft.org`, and put in your `Recipes` folder.

How to do it...

1. First, create a MFC Ogre application named `LoadScene`.
2. Next, in the `CSaveSceneView::EngineSetup()` function, we use the `xmlReadFile()` API method to load the XML file into memory, and then get a pointer to the root XML node.

```
xmlDocPtr doc;
xmlNode *root_element = NULL;

LIBXML_TEST_VERSION

doc = xmlReadFile(ScenePath, MY_ENCODING, 0);
root_element = xmlDocGetRootElement(doc);
```

3. Next, we call a function named `Traverse()`, and pass it the root XML node and the root scene node.

```
Traverse(root_element, m_SceneManager->getRootSceneNode());
```

The `CLoadSceneView::Traverse()` function will loop through all nodes on the level of the passed on XML node, and depending on each node's name, will recursively call itself. If it is a root scene node, create a new scene node and then recursively call itself. If it is a regular scene node, create an entity and attach it to the current scene node.

```
xmlNode *cur_node = NULL;
Ogre::SceneNode *ChildNode = NULL;
Ogre::Camera * Camera = NULL;

for (cur_node = XmlNode; cur_node; cur_node = cur_node->next) {
  if (cur_node->type == XML_ELEMENT_NODE) {
    if (_mbscmp(cur_node->name, BAD_CAST "RootSceneNode") == 0) {
      Traverse(cur_node->children, SceneNode);
    }

    if (_mbscmp(cur_node->name, BAD_CAST "SceneNode") == 0) {
      ChildNode = SceneNode->createChildSceneNode();
      Traverse(cur_node->children, ChildNode);
    }

    if (_mbscmp(cur_node->name, BAD_CAST "Entity") == 0) {
      Ogre::String EntityName((char *)cur_node->properties->
        children->content);
      Ogre::String MeshName((char *)cur_node->properties->
        next->children->content);

      Ogre::Entity *Entity = m_SceneManager->
        createEntity(EntityName, MeshName);
      SceneNode->attachObject(Entity);
    }
  }
}
```

How it works...

The XML scene file we are loading looks something like the following:

```xml
<?xml version="1.0" encoding="ISO-8859-1"?>
<RootSceneNode>
  <SceneNode SceneNodeName="Ogre/SceneRoot">
    <SceneNode SceneNodeName="CameraNode">
      <Camera CameraName="Camera" XPosition="200.000000"
        YPosition="50.000000" ZPosition="100.000000" XDirection="-
        0.888767" YDirection="-0.006624" ZDirection="-0.458312"/>
    </SceneNode>
    <SceneNode SceneNodeName="Unnamed_1">
      <Entity EntityName="Robot" MeshName="robot.mesh"/>
    </SceneNode>
  </SceneNode>
</RootSceneNode>
```

Each scene node is represented in the XML by a `SceneNode` element, and all the entities attached to that scene node are children of each `SceneNode` element.

There's more...

The functionality to create lights, cameras, and other types of objects is not included, but is very similar to and can be based off of the code used to create an entity.

See also

In this chapter:

- ▶ *Creating and editing a scene*
- ▶ *Saving a scene to an XML file*

4
Let There Be Light

In this chapter, we will cover the following recipes:

- ▸ Creating weather controls
- ▸ Creating lights
- ▸ Creating dynamic effects
- ▸ Managing particle systems
- ▸ Managing shadows

Introduction

In this chapter, we'll explore some of the dynamic features of Ogre, such as particle systems, lights, and shadows. All of the dynamic features that we show you in this chapter can be manipulated with code to increase the realism of the effects or the artistic quality. Particle systems, in particular, are designed to change dynamically over time to achieve effects, such as sparks, explosions, or even a waterfall. Similarly, we can manipulate a light dynamically if we want to simulate the flickering of a fire.

Creating weather controls

When building Ogre applications that simulate an outdoor environment, we often need to control weather conditions. In this recipe, we'll build an application with controls that change the parameters of a particle system to simulate different rain-like conditions. We'll also use sound in our application to enhance the rain effect.

Getting ready

Add the `sounds` folder, which contains nature sounds, such as rain and thunder, in your `media` folder.

To follow along with this recipe, open the solution located in the `Recipes/Chapter04` folder in the code bundle available on the Packt website.

How to do it...

1. First, create a new Ogre MFC application named `WeatherConditions`, by following the *Creating an MFC Ogre application* recipe, in *Chapter 1, Delving Deep into Application Design*.

2. Next, create a SAPI voice.

   ```
   m_cpVoice.CoCreateInstance(CLSID_SpVoice);
   ```

3. Create a submenu named **Weather Control** in the main menu. Then, add commands: **Rain**, **Snow**, **Fog**, **Sky**, and **Sun** to the submenu. For this recipe, we will only be implementing the rain functionality, but it will be easy to complete the other controls, once you see how the rain is implemented.

   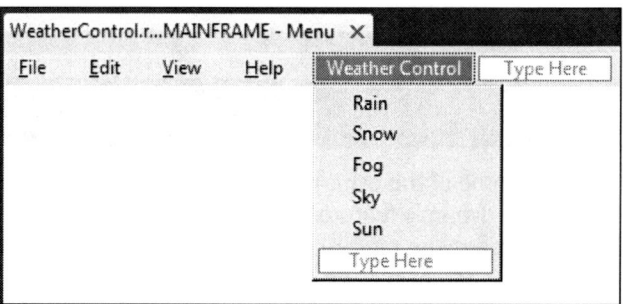

4. Next, add an event handler to the **Rain** submenu item using the **Event Handler Wizard**.

   ```
   void CWeatherControlView::OnWeatherControlRain() {
     Ogre::SceneNode *RainNode = NULL;

     if (!m_SceneManager->hasParticleSystem("Rain")) {
       m_Rain = m_SceneManager->createParticleSystem("Rain",
         "Examples/Rain");

       if (m_Rain != NULL) {
         RainNode = m_SceneManager->
   ```

```
          getRootSceneNode()->createChildSceneNode("RainNode");
        RainNode->attachObject(m_Rain);
      m_Rain->setVisible(false);
    }
  }

  if (m_RainControlDlg == NULL) {
    m_RainControlDlg = new CRainControlDlg();
    m_RainControlDlg->Create(IDD_RAIN_CONTROL);
  }

  m_RainControlDlg->ShowWindow(SW_SHOW);
}
```

5. In the **Rain** submenu event handler, we create the rain particle system and the **Rain Control** dialog-box, and then show it.

6. Create the **Rain Control** dialog-box using the **Dialog Editor**.

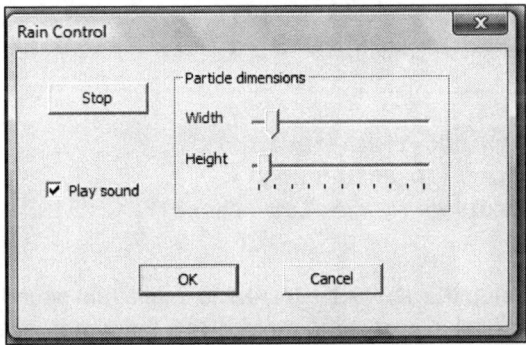

Using this dialog-box, we can start and stop the rain, control particle dimensions, and enable or disable rain sounds.

6. Now that we've created the dialog-box, we need to add the event handler code for the dialog-box controls. Add a message handler to the **Rain Control** dialog-box called OnHScroll that handles the WM_HSCROLL message. The WM_HSCROLL message is sent when a click is detected in a horizontal scroll bar. Inside the OnHScroll, we simply check the position of the particle width and height controls, and modify the particle system with the updated values.

```
void CRainControlDlg::OnHScroll(UINT nSBCode, UINT nPos,
  CScrollBar* pScrollBar) {
  CMainFrame *MainFrame = (CMainFrame *)((
    CWeatherControlApp*)AfxGetApp())->GetMainWnd();
```

```
CWeatherControlView *View =
  (CWeatherControlView *)MainFrame->GetActiveView();

int ParticleWidth = m_ParticleWidth.GetPos();
int ParticleHeight = m_ParticleHeight.GetPos();

View->m_Rain->setDefaultDimensions(ParticleWidth,
  ParticleHeight);

CDialogEx::OnHScroll(nSBCode, nPos, pScrollBar);
}
```

7. Next, add an event handler named `OnClickAction` to the **Start/Stop** button to handle the click event. Inside `OnClickAction`, we toggle the rain visibility and rain sounds.

```
View->m_Rain->setVisible(!View->m_Rain->getVisible());

if (View->m_Rain->getVisible()) {
  m_Action.SetWindowTextA("Stop");
  View->SetTimer(ID_RAIN_TIMER, 1, 0);
}
else {
  m_Action.SetWindowTextA("Start");
  View->KillTimer(ID_RAIN_TIMER);
  WeatherControlApp->m_cpVoice->Pause();
}
```

We also start or stop the `ID_RAIN_TIMER` to toggle rain sounds in our `OnTimer()` function that gets called every time we receive a timer message.

8. To handle the timer messages, add an `ON_WM_TIMER` message handler to `CWeatherControlView`, and name it `OnTimer`. In the `OnTimer` member function, we will play rain sounds and render the scene when we receive the `ID_RAIN_TIMER` timer event.

```
SoundPath += L"\\..\\..\\media\\sounds\\rain\\rain storm.wav";
CWeatherControlApp* WeatherControlApp = (CWeatherControlApp*)
AfxGetApp();
CComPtr<ISpVoice> Voice = WeatherControlApp->m_cpVoice;
CComPtr<ISpStream> cpWavStream;

switch (nIDEvent) {
  case ID_RAIN_TIMER:

    if (m_RainControlDlg != NULL){
      if (m_RainControlDlg->m_PlaySound && m_Rain->getVisible()) {
```

```
        SPBindToFile(SoundPath, SPFM_OPEN_READONLY, &cpWavStream);
        Voice->Resume();
        Voice->SpeakStream(cpWavStream, SPF_ASYNC, NULL);
      }
      else {
        Voice->Pause();
      }
    }
    Root->renderOneFrame();
```

The SPBindToFile function binds the audio stream to the specified file, and SpeakStream plays the contents of the stream. In our case, when we receive an ID_RAIN_TIMER event, we play the rain sound.

How it works...

The settings for our Examples/Rain particle system reside in the media/particle/ Examples.particle file. The .particle file is just a text file and the settings are detailed in the Ogre online manual:

```
particle_system Examples/Rain
{
    material        Examples/Droplet
    particle_width  20
    particle_height 100
    cull_each       true
    quota           10000
    // Make common direction straight down (faster than self oriented)
    billboard_type  oriented_common
    common_direction 0 -1 0

    // Area emitter
    emitter Box
    {
        angle           0
        emission_rate   100
        time_to_live    5
        direction       0 -1 0
        velocity        50
        width           1000
        height          1000
        depth           0
    }

    // Gravity
```

```
        affector LinearForce
        {
                force_vector        0 -200 0
                force_application add
        }

    }
```

The rain particle effect uses a box emitter, so all the particles originate from a flat `1000x1000` box. Note that we use the `Y`-axis as the up and down axis in our example, and our material is the `Examples/Droplet` material found in the `media/materials/scripts/Examples.material` file.

```
    material Examples/Droplet{
      technique {
        pass {
          emissive 0.3 0.3 0.3
              scene_blend colour_blend
              depth_write off
              diffuse vertexcolour

              texture_unit {
          texture basic_droplet.png
              }
            }
          }
        }
```

When you run the program and turn on the rain effect, you can see the rain particles falling on our robot overlord.

There's more...

You can add additional elements to the **Rain Control** dialog-box to control other parameters of the rain particle system, such as the speed or the color. By adding dialog-boxes for each weather control, we can create a full-scale weather editor.

Creating lights

In Ogre, when you create a light, you are defining the origin and color for a light, but there is no visible representation of an object casting light in the scene, such as a light bulb, or a window, or TV screen. In this recipe, we'll show you how to create those illuminated objects that represent the light source object in a 3D scene.

Getting ready

First, add `Wall.material` to `media\materials\scripts`, and then add the `White.jpg`, `Grey.jpg`, `Yellow.jpg`, and `Black.jpg` textures to the `media\materials\textures` folder.

To follow along with this recipe, open the solution located in the `Recipes/Chapter04` folder in the code bundle available on the Packt website.

How to do it...

1. First, create an MFC Ogre application named `Lights`.

2. Next, in `LightsView::EngineSetup()`, add a spotlight can and a light beam, to represent the light from the spotlight, hitting particles in the air.

```
// spotlight can
CCone ConeObject;
ConeObject.m_Height = 20.0;
ConeObject.m_Radius = 10.0;
Ogre::ManualObject *Can =
    ConeObject.CreateCone(0,"SpotLightLight","Wall/Black");
Ogre::SceneNode *CanNode = SceneManager->getRootSceneNode()->
    createChildSceneNode(Ogre::Vector3(100.0, 181.0, 0.0));
//Can->setCastShadows(true);
CanNode->attachObject(Can);

// spotlight beam
ConeObject.m_Height = 200.0;
ConeObject.m_Radius = 80.0;
Ogre::ManualObject *Beam =
    ConeObject.CreateCone(0.99,"SpotLightBeam","LightBeam",0.5);
```

```
Ogre::SceneNode *BeamNode = SceneManager->getRootSceneNode()->
  createChildSceneNode(Ogre::Vector3(100.0, 0.0, 0.0));
Beam->setCastShadows(false);
BeamNode->attachObject(Beam);

// spotlight light
Ogre::Light* SpotLight = SceneManager->createLight("SpotLight");
SpotLight->setDirection((Ogre::Vector3(0.0, 0.0, 0.0) -
  Ogre::Vector3(0.0, 100.0, 0.0)).normalisedCopy());
SpotLight->setType(Ogre::Light::LT_SPOTLIGHT);
SpotLight->setDiffuseColour(1.0, 1.0, 0.0);
SpotLight->setSpecularColour(1.0, 1.0, 0.0);
//SpotLight->setAttenuation(150, 1.0, 0.005, 0.0);
SpotLight->setSpotlightRange(
  Ogre::Radian(0.5),Ogre::Radian(0.9),2.0f);
SpotLight->setVisible(true);
Ogre::SceneNode *LightNode = SceneManager->getRootSceneNode()->
  createChildSceneNode("SpotLight");

LightNode->attachObject(SpotLight);
LightNode->setPosition(Ogre::Vector3(100.0,199,0.0));
```

We position the light beam cone and the spotlight, just under the can.

3. Next, create a point light and a flare billboard sprite as its visual representation.

```
// point light
Ogre::Light* PointLight = SceneManager->createLight("PointLight");
PointLight->setType(Ogre::Light::LT_POINT);
PointLight->setDiffuseColour(1.0, 0.0, 0.0);
PointLight->setSpecularColour(1.0, 0.0, 0.0);
PointLight->setVisible(true);
PointLight->setAttenuation(3250.0,1.0,0.0014,0.000007);
Ogre::SceneNode *PointLightNode = SceneManager->
  getRootSceneNode()->createChildSceneNode("PointLight");

PointLightNode->attachObject(PointLight);
PointLightNode->setPosition(Ogre::Vector3(-100.0,150,30.0));

// attach a flare to the point light node
Ogre::BillboardSet* FlareSet = SceneManager->
  createBillboardSet("FlareSet");
FlareSet->setMaterialName("Examples/FlarePointSprite");
FlareSet->setDefaultDimensions(50.0,50.0);
Ogre::Billboard* Flare = FlareSet->createBillboard(
  Ogre::Vector3(0,0,0),Ogre::ColourValue(1.0,0.0,0.0,0.5));
PointLightNode->attachObject(FlareSet);
```

4. Finally, add a couple dangerous robots under each light and a ground plane.

```
// floor mesh
Ogre::Plane Floor(Ogre::Vector3::UNIT_Y, 0);
Ogre::MeshPtr WallMesh =
  Ogre::MeshManager::getSingleton().createPlane("Floor",
  Ogre::ResourceGroupManager::DEFAULT_RESOURCE_GROUP_NAME, Floor,
  1000,1000,100,100,true,1,5,5, Ogre::Vector3::UNIT_Z);

Ogre::Entity *FloorEntity = SceneManager->createEntity("Floor",
  "Floor");
FloorEntity->setCastShadows(false);
Ogre::SceneNode *FloorNode = SceneManager->getRootSceneNode()->
  createChildSceneNode("Floor");
FloorNode->attachObject(FloorEntity);

Ogre::Entity *RobotEntity = SceneManager->createEntity("Robot",
  "robot.mesh");
Ogre::SceneNode *RobotNode = SceneManager->getRootSceneNode()->
  createChildSceneNode(Ogre::Vector3(100.0,00.0,0.0));
RobotNode->yaw(-Ogre::Radian(Ogre::Math::HALF_PI));
RobotEntity->setCastShadows(true);
RobotNode->attachObject(RobotEntity);

Ogre::Entity *RobotEntity2 = SceneManager->createEntity("Robot2",
  "robot.mesh");
Ogre::SceneNode *RobotNode2 = SceneManager->getRootSceneNode()->
  createChildSceneNode(Ogre::Vector3(-100.0,00.0,0.0));
RobotNode2->yaw(-Ogre::Radian(Ogre::Math::HALF_PI));
RobotEntity2->setCastShadows(true);
RobotNode2->attachObject(RobotEntity2);
```

How it works...

In Ogre 3D, there are three types of lights: **point lights**, **spot lights**, and **directional lights**. In this recipe, we use a transparent cone to represent the light from the spot light, hitting air particles. To accomplish this, we create a cone mesh using an `Ogre::ManualObject` with each vertex having an alpha value based on the height of the vertex. This way, the vertices at the bottom of the spot light cone are fully transparent, and vertices at the top of the cone are less transparent.

```
Cone->colour(Intensity, Intensity, 0.0, ((Ogre::Real)
  HeightSegmentIndex / (Ogre::Real)m_HeightSegments) * fadeAmount);
```

The alpha value for each vertex in the cone is also multiplied by some variable `fadeAmount`. For this recipe, we set the `fadeAmount` to `0.5`, so that the top of the cone is not opaque.

For the point light, we use a flare sprite tinted red that always faces the camera. This is the most common approach for making light sources visible. We make use of the `Ogre::BillboardSet` and the `Ogre::Billboard` classes to create flares that will always face the camera, because Ogre will adjust the billboard positions for every frame for us. The `Ogre::BillboardSet` class is also very efficient at managing and rendering many billboards at once.

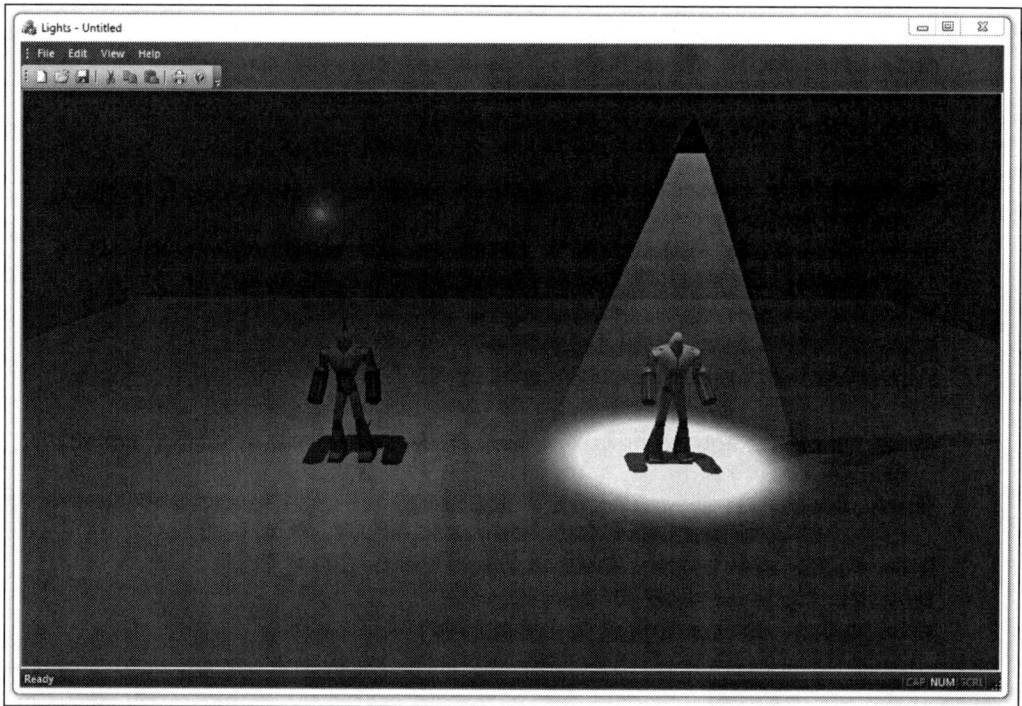

Our robot overlords sure know how to get their mood on!

There's more...

Our recipe does not have a flare for the spotlight. Create another flare for the spotlight, then make the transparency of each flare dependent on the view angle from the camera to the flare, so that, when looking directly at the flare, it is most visible, but as the camera looks away from the flare, it becomes less visible. Ideally, the flare for the spotlight should only be visible from under the spotlight.

The directional light, not shown in this recipe, is a good choice for representing the sun or moon, which also can be represented with a billboard sprite that always faces the camera.

See also

In this chapter:

▶ *Creating dynamic effects*

Creating dynamic effects

In this recipe, we'll show you how to dynamically adjust the intensity of a spotlight beam, based on the camera's view angle. Our goal is to render a spotlight beam that is barely visible when the camera angle is perpendicular to the angle of the spotlight beam, and we want the spotlight beam to be most visible when the camera is directly in the spotlight beam, looking at it.

Getting ready

To follow along with this recipe, open the solution located in the `Recipes/Chapter04` folder in the code bundle available on the Packt website.

How to do it...

1. First, create an MFC Ogre application named `DynamicEffects`.

2. Next, add an `Ogre::Light` member variable to the `CDynamicEffectsView` class, and then initialize it in `CDynamicEffectsView::EngineSetup()`.

```
Ogre::AxisAlignedBox Box(-1000, -1000, -1000, 1000, 1000, 1000);
Ogre::Vector3 Center = Box.getCenter();

Light = SceneManager->createLight();

m_Camera->setPosition(Ogre::Vector3(25.0, 25.0, 25.0));
m_Camera->setDirection((Ogre::Vector3(0.0, 100.0, 0.0) -
  m_Camera->getPosition()).normalisedCopy());
Light->setDirection((Ogre::Vector3(0.0, 100.0, 0.0) -
  Ogre::Vector3(0.0, 0.0, 0.0)).normalisedCopy());

Ogre::Real Intensity = m_Camera->getDirection().dotProduct(
  Light->getDirection());

Ogre::SceneNode* lightNode = SceneManager->getRootSceneNode()->
  createChildSceneNode(Center);

Light->setType(Ogre::Light::LT_SPOTLIGHT);
Light->setVisible(true);
```

```
Light->setPosition(Ogre::Vector3(0.0, 100.0, 0.0));
Light->setSpotlightOuterAngle(Ogre::Radian(0.4));
Light->setDiffuseColour(Intensity, Intensity, 0.0);
Light->setSpecularColour(Intensity, Intensity, 0.0);

lightNode->attachObject(Light);
```

3. After creating the light, we set its type to `Ogre::Light::LT_SPOTLIGHT`, and attach it to the scene graph.

4. Next, add the `Cone.cpp` and the `Cone.h` files from the example project, and then create a new `CCone` object in `CDynamicEffectsView::EngineSetup()`.

```
CCone ConeObject;
Cone = ConeObject.CreateCone(Intensity);
Ogre::SceneNode *ConeNode = SceneManager->getRootSceneNode()->
    createChildSceneNode(Ogre::Vector3(0.0, 100.0, 0.0));
ConeNode->attachObject(Cone);
```

The cone mesh object will represent our spotlight beam in the scene.

5. Now that we have all the graphical elements we need in the scene, it's time to add controls, so that we can move the camera. Add an integer member variable named `m_WorkingTimer` to `CDynamicEffectsView`.

6. Next, add a handler for the `ON_WM_KEYDOWN` message named `CDynamicEffectsView::OnKeyDown()`.

```
m_WorkingTimer = 0;

switch (nChar) {
  case VK_LEFT: //left
  case 65: //A
  case 97: //a

    m_WorkingTimer = 1;

  break;

  case VK_UP:  //up
  case 87:  //W
  case 119: //w

    m_WorkingTimer = 2;

  break;

  case VK_RIGHT: //right
```

```
case 68: //D
case 100: //d

  m_WorkingTimer = 3;

break;

case VK_DOWN: //down
case 83: //S
case 115://s

  m_WorkingTimer = 4;

break;
}

if (m_WorkingTimer != 0)
  SetTimer(m_WorkingTimer, 10, NULL);
```

In OnKeyDown, we set a different working timer value, depending on which key is down.

7. Next, add a handler for the ON_WM_KEYUP message named CDynamicEffectsView::OnKeyUP().

```
KillTimer(m_WorkingTimer);

CView::OnKeyUp(nChar, nRepCnt, nFlags);
```

Here' we kill the m_WorkingTimer, so we stop generating WM_TIMER messages.

8. Next, add a handler for the ON_WM_TIMER message named CDynamicEffectsView::OnTimer().

```
CEngine *Engine = ((CDynamicEffectsApp*)AfxGetApp())->m_Engine;

if (Engine == NULL)
  return;

Ogre::Root *Root = Engine->GetRoot();

if (Root == NULL) {
  return;
}

Ogre::Vector3 CameraMove;

switch (nIDEvent) {
```

```
case 1:

    CameraMove[0] = -1;
    CameraMove[1] = 0;
    CameraMove[2] = 0;

break;

case 2:

    CameraMove[0] = 0;
    CameraMove[1] = 1;
    CameraMove[2] = 0;

break;

case 3:

    CameraMove[0] = 1;
    CameraMove[1] = 0;
    CameraMove[2] = 0;

break;

case 4:

    CameraMove[0] = 0;
    CameraMove[1] = -1;
    CameraMove[2] = 0;

break;
}
```

9. First, we check the timer event ID, and set the `CameraMove` variable appropriately, to move the camera in the right direction.

10. Next, we calculate the dot product between camera direction and the spotlight direction. The spotlight intensity is proportional to this dot product.

```
m_Camera->moveRelative(CameraMove);
m_Camera->setDirection((Light->getPosition() - m_Camera->
    getPosition()).normalisedCopy());

Ogre::Real Intensity = m_Camera->getDirection().dotProduct(Light->
    getDirection());

Light->setDiffuseColour(Intensity, Intensity, 0.0);
Light->setSpecularColour(Intensity, Intensity, 0.0);
```

11. Next, we update the vertex colors for the spotlight beam, so that their intensity matches the spotlight intensity.

```cpp
int numSegBase = 24;
int numSegHeight = 24;
Ogre::Real radius = 10.0;
Ogre::Real height = 20.0;

Cone->beginUpdate(0);

Ogre::Real deltaAngle = (Ogre::Math::TWO_PI / numSegBase);
Ogre::Real deltaHeight = height/(Ogre::Real)numSegHeight;

Ogre::Real uTile = 1.0;
Ogre::Real vTile = 1.0;

Ogre::Vector3 refNormal = Ogre::Vector3(radius, height,
  0.f).normalisedCopy();
Ogre::Quaternion q;
int offset = 0;

for (int i = 0; i <=numSegHeight; i++) {
  Ogre::Real r0 = radius * (1 - i / (Ogre::Real)numSegHeight);
  for (int j = 0; j<=numSegBase; j++) {
    Ogre::Real x0 = r0* cosf(j * deltaAngle);
    Ogre::Real z0 = r0 * sinf(j * deltaAngle);
    Cone->position(x0, i * deltaHeight, z0);
    Cone->colour(Intensity, Intensity, 0.0, 0.0);
    q.FromAngleAxis(Ogre::Radian(-j*deltaAngle),
      Ogre::Vector3::NEGATIVE_UNIT_Y);
    Cone->normal(q*refNormal);
    Cone->textureCoord(j / (Ogre::Real)numSegBase * uTile, i /
      (Ogre::Real)numSegHeight * vTile);

    if (i != numSegHeight&& j != numSegBase) {
      Cone->index(offset + numSegBase + 2);
      Cone->index(offset);
      Cone->index(offset + numSegBase + 1);
      Cone->index(offset + numSegBase + 2);
      Cone->index(offset + 1);
      Cone->index(offset);
    }

    offset ++;
  }
```

```
}
/**/
//low cap
int centerIndex = offset;

Cone->position(0,0,0);
Cone->normal(Ogre::Vector3::NEGATIVE_UNIT_Y);
Cone->textureCoord(0.0,vTile);
offset++;
for (int j=0; j<=numSegBase; j++) {
  Ogre::Real x0 = radius * cosf(j*deltaAngle);
  Ogre::Real z0 = radius * sinf(j*deltaAngle);

  Cone->position(x0, 0.0f, z0);
  Cone->colour(Intensity, Intensity, 0.0, 0.0);
  Cone->normal(Ogre::Vector3::NEGATIVE_UNIT_Y);
  Cone->textureCoord(j/(Ogre::Real)numSegBase*uTile,0.0);
  if (j!=numSegBase) {
    Cone->index(centerIndex);
    Cone->index(offset);
    Cone->index(offset+1);
  }
  offset++;
}
/**/
Cone->end();
```

How it works...

Each time we render a frame, we calculate the dot product of the spotlight direction vector and the camera view vector, and use that value to set the intensity for the spotlight beam. The dot product value is the cosine of the angle between the two vectors. So, when the vectors are parallel, this value will be 1 or -1, and when the vectors are perpendicular, the dot product will be 0. In this recipe, we set the Intensity variable value based on the dot product, so that if the camera is looking directly at the spotlight beam, the intensity will be magnified, but if the camera is looking away, the intensity will be less. The effect of changing the intensity of the light is meant to be similar to the way our eyes adjust to lights when we look directly at them or an angle.

If we were using a point light, which has no direction, we would take the dot product of a camera view vector, and a normalized vector from the light's origin to the camera's origin.

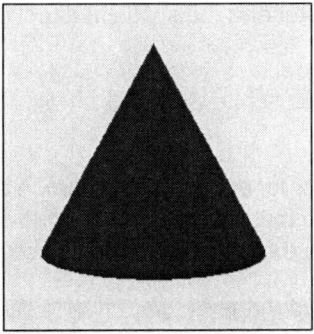

The intensity of the spotlight beam cone is very low when the camera direction vector is perpendicular to the spotlight direction vector.

As the camera has moved, and the angle between the camera view vector and the spotlight direction vector is smaller, the intensity has increased.

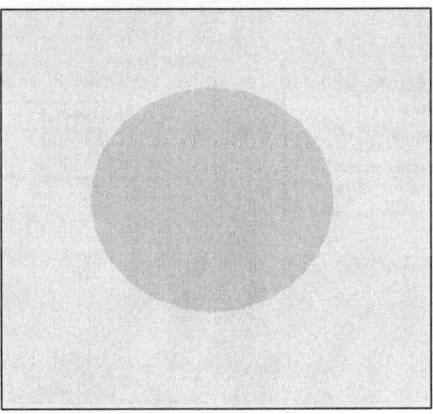

Finally, when the camera view vector and the spotlight direction vector are parallel, the intensity is at its maximum value.

There's more...

In this recipe, we used a solid color for our spotlight beam. A better looking spotlight beam should use a gradient texture; one that is bright and opaque at the spotlight source, then progressively fades out, relative to the distance to the source.

Managing particle system

In this recipe, we'll create a basic particle system editor. Using this editor, we will be able to try out various particle effects that we can then use in our 3D application.

Getting ready

To follow along with this recipe, open the solution located in the `Recipes/Chapter04` folder in the code bundle available on the Packt website.

How to do it...

1. First, create an MFC Ogre application named `ParticleSystem`.

2. Next, create a dialog-box named **Particle System Editor** using the **Visual Studio Dialog Editor**. Add two menus to the dialog-box—a menu to add various types of **emitters** and a menu to add **affecters**. Add event handles to each menu item. Next, add a tree control to manage the structure of the particle system, and controls for creating particle systems.

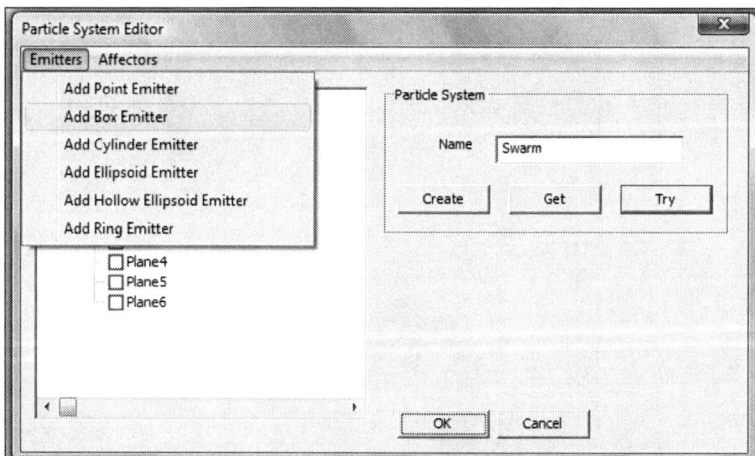

3. Add a click handler for the **Create** button named
   `OnBnClickCreateParticleSystem()`.

```
void CParticleSystemControlDlg::OnBnClickedCreateParticleSystem()
{
  CMainFrame *MainFrame = (CMainFrame *)((
    CParticleSystemApp*)AfxGetApp())->GetMainWnd();

  CEngine *Engine = ((CParticleSystemApp*)AfxGetApp())->m_Engine;
  Ogre::Root *Root = Engine->GetRoot();
  Ogre::SceneManager *SceneManager = Root->
    getSceneManager("ParticleSystem");

  m_ParticleSystem = SceneManager->createParticleSystem("Sun");

  m_ParticleSystem->setDefaultDimensions(12, 24);
  m_ParticleSystem->setSortingEnabled(true);
  m_ParticleSystem->setMaterialName("Examples/Flare2");
  m_ParticleSystem->setCullIndividually(true);
  m_ParticleSystem->setParticleQuota(3000);
  m_ParticleSystem->setRenderer("billboard");
  m_ParticleSystem->setKeepParticlesInLocalSpace(false);
}
```

When the **Create** button is pressed, we add a new particle system called `sun`, and set default dimensions, a material name, the particle type, and the maximum number of particles.

4. Next, create a handler for the **Try** button named
   `OnBnClickedTryParticleSystem()`.

```
void CParticleSystemControlDlg::OnBnClickedTryParticleSystem()
{
  CMainFrame *MainFrame = (CMainFrame *)((
    CParticleSystemApp*)AfxGetApp())->GetMainWnd();
  CEngine *Engine = ((CParticleSystemApp*)AfxGetApp())->m_Engine;
  Ogre::Root *Root = Engine->GetRoot();
  Ogre::SceneManager *SceneManager = Root->
    getSceneManager("ParticleSystem");

  Ogre::SceneNode *SceneNode = SceneManager->getRootSceneNode()->
    createChildSceneNode();
  SceneNode->attachObject(m_ParticleSystem);
  SceneNode->setPosition(0, 10, 0);
  m_ParticleSystem->setVisible(true);
  Root->renderOneFrame();
  MainFrame->GetActiveView()->SetTimer(1,1,0);
}
```

In `OnBnClickedTryParticleSystem()`, we attach the particle system to a scene node, and render the scene. We also activate a timer to render the scene and update the particle system at regular intervals.

5. Next, we need to implement the handlers for creating the emitters and affecters. In this recipe, we will show you how to implement the **Box Emitter** and the **Deflector plane affecter**. The implementation for the remaining emitters and affecters should be very similar.

   The message handler for **Add Box Emitter** should look like this:

```
void CParticleSystemControlDlg::OnEmittersAddBoxEmitter()
{
  CBoxEmitterDlg BoxEmitterDlg;

  if (IDOK == BoxEmitterDlg.DoModal()) {
    HTREEITEM EmitterItem =
      m_ParticleSystemTree.InsertItem(BoxEmitterDlg.m_EmitterName,
      m_EmittersItem);
    m_ParticleSystemTree.EnsureVisible(EmitterItem);

    Ogre::ParticleEmitter *BoxEmitter = m_ParticleSystem->
      addEmitter("Box");
```

   When the **Add Box Emitter** menu item is selected, the `BoxEmitterDlg` dialog-box is displayed, and a box emitter is added to the particle system.

6. Create a dialog-box named `CBoxEmitterDlg` with a single text field for the emitter name.

7. Now, let's implement the **Add Deflector Plane** menu item handler. Create a dialog-box named `CDeflectorPlaneAffectorDlg`, and add controls for naming the affecter, setting the plane origin, normal, and bounce value.

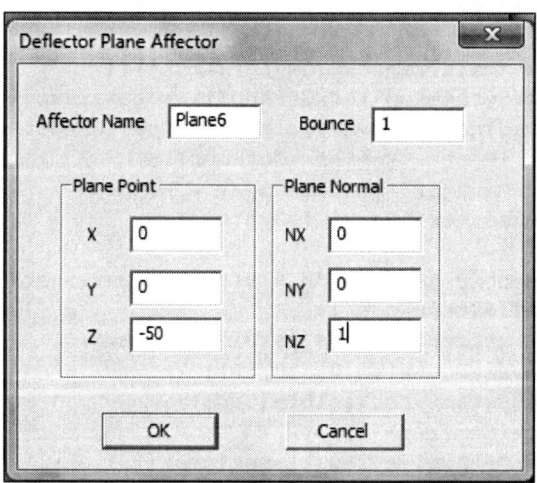

8. Next, we add code to the **Add Deflector Plane Affector** menu item that opens the **CDeflectorPlaneAffectorDlg**, then uses the dialog-box settings to create the affecter, and add it to the scene.

```
void CParticleSystemControlDlg::
  OnAffectorsAdddeflectorplaneaffector() {
  CDeflectorPlaneAffectorDlg DeflectorPlaneAffectorDlg;

  if (IDOK == DeflectorPlaneAffectorDlg.DoModal()) {
    m_ParticleSystemTree.InsertItem(
      DeflectorPlaneAffectorDlg.m_AffectorName, m_AffectorsItem);

    Ogre::ParticleAffector *Plane = m_ParticleSystem->
      addAffector("DeflectorPlane");

    Plane->setParameter("plane_point", "0 -50 0");
    Plane->setParameter("plane_normal", "0 1 0");
    Plane->setParameter("bounce", "1");
  }
}
```

How it works...

When you create the particle system, and add emitters and affecters, they are added to the tree control. When the **Try** button is pressed, the particle system activates and a timer is enabled that renders the scene at regular intervals.

```
void CParticleSystemView::OnTimer(UINT_PTR nIDEvent) {
  CEngine * Engine = ((CParticleSystemApp*)AfxGetApp())->m_Engine;
    Ogre::Root *Root = Engine->GetRoot();
    Root->renderOneFrame();

    CView::OnTimer(nIDEvent);
}
```

We also add a robot mesh to the scene to give a sense of scale, though you may wish to remove it, if the particle system you are testing is obscured by it.

There's more...

In this recipe, we only implemented one emitter and one affecter. You can implement the handlers and dialog-boxes for the remaining emitters and affecters.

You can also add functionality to the tree, to enable and disable emitters and affecters by adding and removing them from the particle system, when the check-box next to each tree item is checked.

Managing shadows

When architects design buildings, they must adhere to city building codes and be aware of the impact on the environment caused by the structures they design. A tall building erected near others might cast a shadow over them, thus decreasing the warming rays of the sun, and increasing the cost of heating them. In this recipe, we will assume the role of the architect, and our job is to determine if the building that we want to erect will cast a shadow on an existing, nearby building. To simulate shadows cast on buildings, we will create a scene with a house to represent the affected building, and then use a 3D box model to represent the building we want to construct. We will also move a point light representing the sun, to simulate shadows at different times of day.

Getting ready

To follow along with this recipe, open the solution located in the `Recipes/Chapter04` folder in the code bundle available on the Packt website.

How to do it...

1. First, create an MFC Ogre application with a ribbon named `Shadows`.

2. Next, create the simple scene with a ground plane, a house model, and a box model to represent the new building.

   ```
   Ogre::Plane Ground(Ogre::Vector3::UNIT_Y, 0);
   Ogre::MeshPtr GroundMesh =
     Ogre::MeshManager::getSingleton().createPlane("Ground",
     Ogre::ResourceGroupManager::DEFAULT_RESOURCE_GROUP_NAME,
     Ground, 10000, 10000,20,20,true,1,5,5, Ogre::Vector3::UNIT_Z);

   Ogre::Entity *GroundEntity = SceneManager->createEntity("Ground",
     "Ground");
   ```

```
Ogre::SceneNode *GroundNode = SceneManager->getRootSceneNode()->
  createChildSceneNode("Ground");
GroundNode->attachObject(GroundEntity);
GroundEntity->setCastShadows(false);

Ogre::Vector3 InsertionPoint;

Ogre::Entity *HouseEntity = SceneManager->createEntity("House",
  "tudorhouse.mesh");
Ogre::AxisAlignedBox HouseBox = HouseEntity->getBoundingBox();
InsertionPoint = - HouseBox.getCorner(
  Ogre::AxisAlignedBox::NEAR_LEFT_BOTTOM);
Ogre::SceneNode *HouseNode = SceneManager->getRootSceneNode()->
  createChildSceneNode(InsertionPoint);
HouseNode->attachObject(HouseEntity);
HouseEntity->setCastShadows(false);

Ogre::Entity *BoxEntity = SceneManager->createEntity("Box",
  Ogre::SceneManager::PrefabType::PT_CUBE);
BoxEntity->setMaterialName("Examples/BeachStones");
Ogre::AxisAlignedBox Box = BoxEntity->getBoundingBox();
Ogre::SceneNode *BoxNode = SceneManager->getRootSceneNode()->
  createChildSceneNode("Box");
BoxNode->attachObject(BoxEntity);
BoxNode->setScale(Ogre::Vector3(5, 20, 5));
BoxNode->setPosition(Ogre::Vector3(-1000, 0, 1000));
BoxEntity->setCastShadows(true);
```

3. Next, add a point light to represent the sun in our simulation.

```
SceneManager->
  setShadowTechnique(Ogre::SHADOWTYPE_STENCIL_ADDITIVE);
Sun = SceneManager->createLight("Sun");
Sun->setType(Ogre::Light::LT_POINT);
Sun->setPosition(2500 * Ogre::Math::Cos(0), 1000, 2500 *
  Ogre::Math::Sin(0));
Sun->setDiffuseColour(0.35, 0.35, 0);
Sun->setSpecularColour(0.9, 0.9, 0);
Sun->setVisible(true);
```

4. Next, add panels and sliders to the ribbon for controlling the height of the building and the time of day.

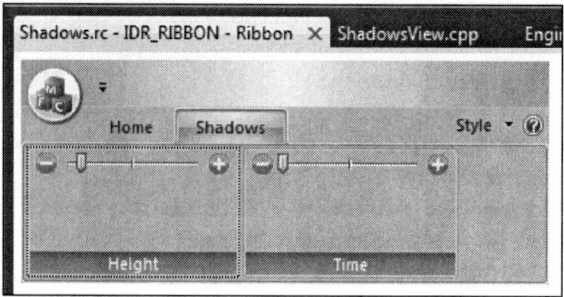

5. Now, it's time to create the event handlers for ribbon sliders.

```
void CShadowsView::OnTime() {
  CMainFrame *MainFrame = (CMainFrame *)((
    CShadowsApp*)AfxGetApp())->GetMainWnd();
  CMFCRibbonBar* RibbonBar = MainFrame->GetRibbonBar();

  CMFCRibbonSlider* Slider = DYNAMIC_DOWNCAST(CMFCRibbonSlider,
    RibbonBar->FindByID(ID_TIME));

  Ogre::Radian Angle = Ogre::Radian(Ogre::Math::TWO_PI * (
    double)Slider->GetPos() / 24);

  CEngine *Engine = ((CShadowsApp*)AfxGetApp())->m_Engine;
  Ogre::Root *Root = Engine->GetRoot();
  Ogre::SceneManager *SceneManager = Root->
    getSceneManager("Shadows");
  Ogre::Light *Sun = SceneManager->getLight("Sun");
  Sun->setPosition(2500 * Ogre::Math::Cos(Angle), 1000, 2500 *
    Ogre::Math::Sin(Angle));

  if (Root != NULL) {
    Root->renderOneFrame();
  }
}
```

6. For the `Time` slider, we convert the slider position to an angle, and use that value to set the sun position.

```
void CShadowsView::OnHeight() {
  CMainFrame *MainFrame = (CMainFrame *)((
    CShadowsApp*)AfxGetApp())->GetMainWnd();
  CMFCRibbonBar* RibbonBar = MainFrame->GetRibbonBar();
```

```
CMFCRibbonSlider* Slider = DYNAMIC_DOWNCAST(CMFCRibbonSlider,
  RibbonBar->FindByID(ID_HEIGHT));

CEngine *Engine = ((CShadowsApp*)AfxGetApp())->m_Engine;
Ogre::Root *Root = Engine->GetRoot();
Ogre::SceneManager *SceneManager = Root->
  getSceneManager("Shadows");
Ogre::SceneNode *BoxNode = SceneManager->getSceneNode("Box");
BoxNode->setScale(5, Slider->GetPos(), 5);

if (Root != NULL) {
  Root->renderOneFrame();
}
}
```

The `Height` slider simply scales the 3D box that represents the new building.

How it works...

When the `Time` slider is moved, we change the position of the sun point light, and render the scene again. Each time the scene is rendered, Ogre automatically updates the shadows in the scene, based on the light position, the shadow casters, and receivers in the scene. In this recipe, we specifically instructed Ogre to only cast shadows for the 3D box that represents our new building, so the shadow is clearly visible. We also set the shadow type to `SHADOWTYPE_STENCIL_ADDITIVE`, so the shadows are very crisp and defined.

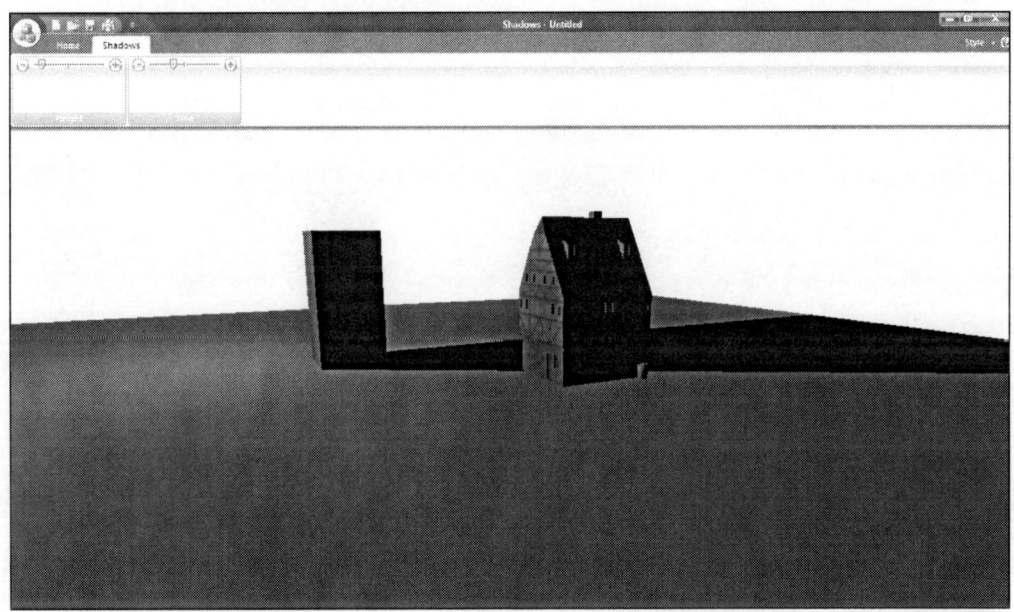

There's more...

To make a complete shadows analyzer, you should add a sun position calculator based on real locations in the world at various times of year. You can also add terrain to the scene, to more accurately represent the building location. Finally, using the *Creating and Editing a Scene* recipe, from the previous chapter, you can add functionality to add and remove objects in the scene.

See also

Chapter 3, *Managing Objects and Scenes*:

- ▸ *Creating a terrain from a LandXML file*
- ▸ *Creating Delaunay triangulation*
- ▸ *Creating and editing a scene*

5
Playing with Materials

In this chapter, we will cover:

- ► Using geoimages as terrain textures
- ► Creating transparent materials
- ► Creating dynamic textures
- ► Creating movable text
- ► 2D image manipulation

Introduction

In this chapter, we'll use advanced materials in Ogre applications to show you how to accomplish some common and some uncommon effects. The effects range from terrain texturing and transparent windows to animated textures and billboard textures.

We will also use a 3D anaglyph image example to show how you can manipulate 2D texture data in your Ogre 3D application.

Using geoimages as terrain textures

Creating realistic looking terrain is a necessity for most graphics programs. Often, the terrain is created by referencing a height map that an artist created, or that came from an aerial/ satellite image or map.

In this recipe, we'll use a DEM file for our terrain height data and an image in GeoTiff format with georeferencing information embedded in it, to get UV co-ordinates for each point on the mesh. **GeoTiff** is a public domain metadata standard, which allows georeferencing information to be embedded within a TIFF file. For more information see the GeoTiff website at `http://trac.osgeo.org/geotiff/`.

Getting ready

To follow along with this recipe:

1. Open the solution located in the `Recipes/Chapter05` folder in the code bundle available on the Packt website.

2. Next, download the `GeoTiff` library from `http://download.osgeo.org/geotiff/libgeotiff/`.

3. Finally, download the sample `GeoTiff` image `o41078a1.tif` from `ftp://ftp.remotesensing.org/pub/geotiff/samples/usgs/`, and the terrain DEM file `karthaus_pa.dem` from `http://dbwww.essc.psu.edu/geotree/dbtop/amer_n/us_ne/pa/n41w078/n41w078a1/data/dem/30m_utm17/karthaus_pa.dem.gz`.

How to do it...

1. First, create a new Ogre MFC application named `GeoImage`, by following the *Creating an MFC Ogre application* recipe, in *Chapter 1, Delving Deep into Application Design*.

2. Create a material script text file named `terrain.material` for the terrain texture in the `media/materials/scripts` folder, and put the following text in the file:

```
material Terrain
{
  technique
  {
    pass
    {
      ambient 1 1 1
      diffuse 1 1 1

      cull_hardware none
      cull_software none

      depth_bias 0

      texture_unit
      {

        // Following Tif file contains map image and geotiff tags.

        texture o41078a1.tif.tif
      }
    }
  }

  technique
  {
```

```
    pass
    {
      diffuse 1  0 0
    }
  }
}
```

3. Next, edit the `GeoImageView::EngineSetup()` function, and add code to read the geo information from the header of tiff file.

```
TIFF   *Tif = (TIFF*)0;  /* TIFF-level descriptor */
GTIF   *GTif = (GTIF*)0; /* GeoKey-level descriptor */
int ImageWidth;
int ImageHeight;

double LowerLeftX;
double LowerLeftY;

double UpperRightX;
double UpperRightY;

Tif = XTIFFOpen((LPCSTR)SourcePath, "r");

GTif = GTIFNew(Tif);

GTIFDefn Definition;
GTIFGetDefn(GTif, &Definition);

TIFFGetField( Tif, TIFFTAG_IMAGEWIDTH, &ImageWidth);
TIFFGetField( Tif, TIFFTAG_IMAGELENGTH, &ImageHeight);

LowerLeftX = 0.0;
LowerLeftY = ImageHeight;

GTIFImageToPCS(GTif, &LowerLeftX, &LowerLeftY);

UpperRightX = ImageWidth;
UpperRightY = 0.0;
GTIFImageToPCS(GTif, &UpperRightX, &UpperRightY);
```

We read the image height and width, and then use the `GTIFImageToPCS` function to convert the four corners of the image from image space to projected coordinate space.

4. Next, parse the `karthaus_pa.dem` file, and create an `Ogre::ManualObject` from the terrain information within it. In this recipe, we use the `OT_TRIANGLE_FAN` rendering operation type for our mesh. This means that we first input three vertices for the first triangle, and then one vertex per triangle after that.

```
Ogre::ManualObject *Terrain = SceneManager->
  createManualObject("Terrain");
```

```
Terrain->setDynamic(false);
Terrain->begin("Terrain", Ogre::RenderOperation::OT_TRIANGLE_FAN);

for (c = 1; c <= columnCount; c++) {

  for (r = firstRow; r <= lastRow; r += rowInt) {
    tempFloat = (float) base[r]  * verticalScale;
    Terrain->position(planCoords[0], tempFloat, planCoords[1]);

    Ogre::Real u = 0.0;
    Ogre::Real v = 0.0;

    if (planCoords[0] > LowerLeftX && planCoords[0] < UpperRightX)
    {
      u = (planCoords[0] - LowerLeftX) / (UpperRightX -
        LowerLeftX);
    }

    if (planCoords[1] > LowerLeftY && planCoords[1] < UpperRightY)
    {
      v = (planCoords[1] - LowerLeftY) / (UpperRightY -
        LowerLeftY);
    }

    Terrain->textureCoord(u, v);
    planCoords[1] += deltaY;
  }
}
```

We use the projection coordinates from the `geotiff` image to calculate texture coordinates for each vertex.

The result is a 3D Ogre mesh of the specific place with the tiff map as a texture.

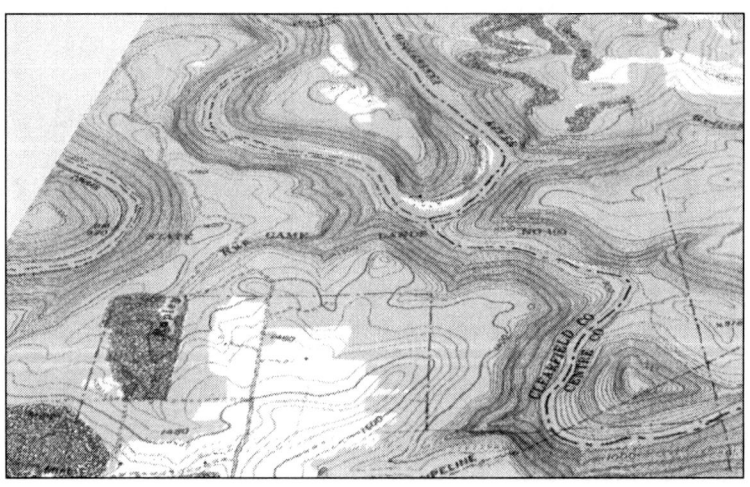

How it works...

In this recipe, we use two topographic information formats: **GeoTiff** for the terrain texture and **USGS DEM** for the terrain elevation.

The GeoTiff format provides the information necessary to convert a 2D image to a model space or map projection.

The USGS DEM format stores raster-based digital elevation models, and is a very popular open standard, used throughout the world.

There's more...

Instead of using a map TIFF, you can use one that has a satellite photo of the area for a more realistic terrain texture.

Creating transparent materials

In this recipe, we'll use a texture with an alpha channel to make a model of a window with colored glass in it. We use the same technique that is used to render the most flat and transparent objects, such as trees and plant billboards, in addition to applying a color to the transparent parts of the image.

Getting ready

To follow along with this recipe, open the solution located in the `Recipes/Chapter05` folder in the code bundle available on the Packt website.

Ensure that you have the `window.dds` texture in your `media/materials/textures` folder. This texture has the necessary transparency information, so that the glass parts of the image are transparent, and the wood parts are opaque.

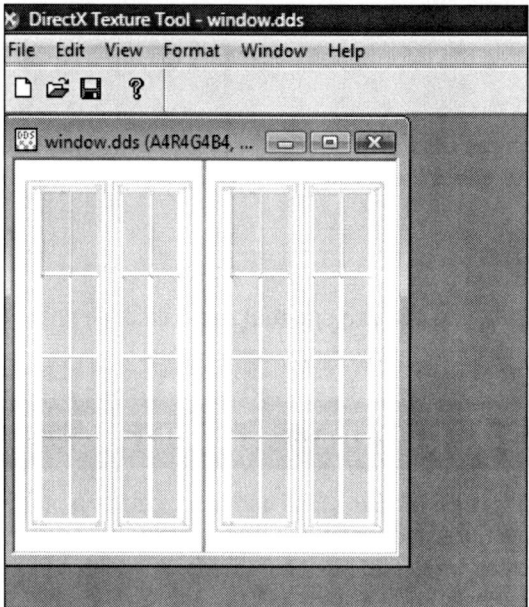

How to do it...

1. First, create a new Ogre MFC application named `TransparentMaterial` by following the *Creating an MFC Ogre application* recipe, in *Chapter 1, Delving Deep into Application Design*.

2. Create a material script text file named `window.material` in the `media/materials/scripts` folder, and add the following text in the file:

```
material window
{
  technique
  {

    // Make the glass in the first pass.

    pass
    {

      // Turn lighting off

      lighting off
```

```
            // Turn off culling so that the window will be two-sided

            cull_hardware none
            cull_software none

            // Use alpha blending to tint the object

            scene_blend alpha_blend

            // Do not write to the depth buffer so the window does not
            //obscure objects.

            depth_write off

            texture_unit
            {

               // Apply color.

               colour_op_ex source1 src_manual src_current 0.5 0.5 0

               // Apply opacity 0.2.

               alpha_op_ex source1 src_manual src_current 0.2
            }
         }
         // Make the window frame. Use image window.dds with
         //transparency.
         pass
         {
            lighting off
            cull_hardware none
            cull_software none
            scene_blend alpha_blend
            depth_write off

            texture_unit
            {
               alpha_rejection greater_equal 128
               texture window.dds
               tex_coord_set 0
            }
         }
      }
   }
}
```

We do not use the `colour_op` parameter to tell Ogre how to mix the second pass with the first one, because `modulate` is the default `colour_op`. We use the `alpha_rejection` parameter for the window frame, so the frame does not draw over the glass.

3. Next, add code to CTransparentMaterialView::EngineSetup(), to create a plane mesh with the window material, and add a robot mesh behind the window, so we have something to look at.

```
Ogre::ManualObject *Screen = SceneManager->
  createManualObject("Screen");
Screen->setDynamic(true);
Screen->begin("window", Ogre::RenderOperation::OT_TRIANGLE_LIST);

Screen->position(-100,-100,50);
Screen->textureCoord(0,0);

Screen->position(300,-100,50);
Screen->textureCoord(1,0);

Screen->position(300,300,50);
Screen->textureCoord(1,1);

Screen->triangle(0, 1, 2);

Screen->position(-100,-100,50);
Screen->textureCoord(0,0);

Screen->position(300,300,50);
Screen->textureCoord(1,1);

Screen->position(-100,300,50);
Screen->textureCoord(0,1);

Screen->triangle(3, 4, 5);

Screen->end();

Ogre::Entity *RobotEntity = SceneManager->createEntity("Robot",
  "robot.mesh");
Ogre::SceneNode *RobotNode = SceneManager->getRootSceneNode()->
  createChildSceneNode();
RobotNode->attachObject(RobotEntity);

Ogre::SceneNode *WindowNode = SceneManager->getRootSceneNode()->
  createChildSceneNode();
WindowNode->attachObject(Screen);
```

How it works...

The material we use for the window mesh, draws the glass in the first pass and the opaque window parts in the second pass. We use the `colour_op_ex` parameter to make the glass color yellow, and the `alpha_op_ex` parameter to define the glass opacity. We turn on `alpha_rejection` for the frame, so it doesn't draw over the glass.

When we're finished, we can see the robot through the glass window.

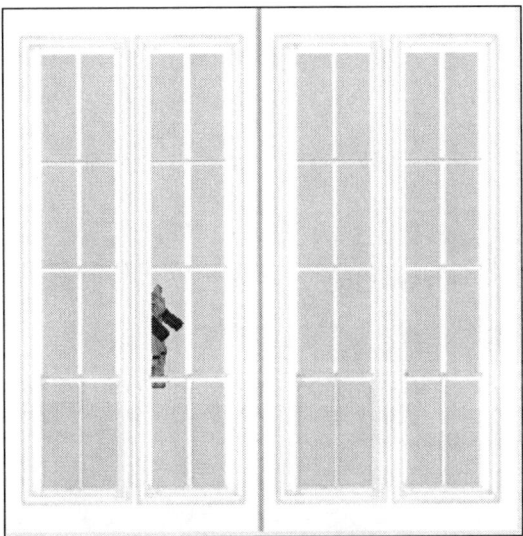

Creating dynamic textures

Many situations call for dynamic textures in graphics programs. Most running water, moving walkways, or animating screens in 3D applications use dynamic textures to make parts of the texture move, giving the illusion that the water is moving or a TV is playing. In this recipe, we will learn how to use a dynamic texture to display a video clip.

Getting ready

To follow along with this recipe, open the solution located in the `Recipes/Chapter05` folder in the code bundle available on the Packt website.

Also, we will be using a video clip in `.avi` format. So, download one from the code bundle, or use one of your own.

How to do it...

1. First, create a new Ogre MFC application named `DynamicTexture`, by following the *Creating an MFC Ogre Application* recipe, in *Chapter 1, Delving Deep into Application Design*.

2. Create a material script text file named `screen.material` in the `media/materials/scripts` folder, and put the following text in the file.

```
material Screen
{
  technique
  {

    pass
    {
      texture_unit
      {
        texture Screen.jpg
      }

      texture_unit
      {
        texture Screen
      }
    }
  }
}
```

The first `texture_unit` is going to be a blank white image, and the second `texture_unit`, will be the one we use to draw the dynamic texture.

3. Next, add a new menu item named `TV Control` to the main menu, and two sub-items – `Start` and `Stop`. Add event handlers for these sub-items:

```
void CDynamicTextureView::OnTvcontrolStart()
{
  SetTimer(1, 1, 0);
}


void CDynamicTextureView::OnTvcontrolStop()
{
  KillTimer(1);
}
```

The first event handler will start the timer, and the second one will stop it.

4. Add a public member variable named `PixelBuffer` that is an `Ogre::HardwareP ixelBufferSharedPtr`. We will use this pixel buffer to hold the pixel data for the dynamic texture.

5. In `CDynamicTextureView::EngineSetup()`, create the dynamic texture, and get a pointer to the pixel buffer.

```
Ogre::TexturePtr ScreenTexture =
   Ogre::TextureManager::getSingleton().createManual("Screen",
   Ogre::ResourceGroupManager::DEFAULT_RESOURCE_GROUP_NAME,
   Ogre::TEX_TYPE_2D, 640, 480, 0, Ogre::PF_R8G8B8A8,
   Ogre::TU_DYNAMIC_WRITE_ONLY_DISCARDABLE);

PixelBuffer = ScreenTexture->getBuffer();
```

6. Next, in `CDynamicTextureView::EngineSetup()`, create a plane on which we will display our dynamic texture.

```
Ogre::ManualObject *Screen = SceneManager->
   createManualObject("Screen");
Screen->setDynamic(true);
Screen->begin("Screen", Ogre::RenderOperation::OT_TRIANGLE_LIST);
```

7. Now that the texture has been created, and we have a 3D surface to draw it on, we must initialize the Microsoft `AVIFile` library, and get our AVI file stream set up.

```
AVIFileInit();

AVIFileOpen(&aviFile, <Path to your video clip>,OF_READ,NULL);

AVIFileGetStream(aviFile,&aviStream,streamtypeVIDEO,0);

AVIFileRelease(aviFile);

AVIStreamInfo(aviStream,&aviStreamInfo,sizeof(aviStreamInfo));
BITMAPINFOHEADER bmpInfo;

memset(&bmpInfo, 0, sizeof(BITMAPINFOHEADER));
bmpInfo.biSize = sizeof(BITMAPINFOHEADER) ;
bmpInfo.biBitCount = 32;
bmpInfo.biCompression = BI_RGB;
bmpInfo.biHeight = 480;
bmpInfo.biWidth = 640;
bmpInfo.biPlanes = 1;
bmpInfo.biSizeImage = 0;

Frame = AVIStreamGetFrameOpen(aviStream, &bmpInfo);
```

8. The last step is to create the `CDynamicTextureView::OnTimer` procedure.

   Add code to the `OnTimer` procedure to read the next frame of the video clip, and copy it into the buffer for the dynamic texture.

```
LPBITMAPINFOHEADER lpbi =
  (LPBITMAPINFOHEADER)AVIStreamGetFrame(Frame, ++m_FrameNumber);
LPVOID GetFrame = AVIStreamGetFrame(Frame, ++m_FrameNumber);

PixelBuffer->lock(Ogre::HardwareBuffer::HBL_DISCARD);
memcpy(PixelBuffer->getCurrentLock().data, lpbi +
  sizeof(LPBITMAPINFOHEADER) + 25, lpbi->biSizeImage);
PixelBuffer->unlock();
```

   After copying the video clip frame to the buffer, we render the scene again to draw the updated texture.

How it works...

We use the Microsoft `AVIFile` library to open an AVI file, and get a file stream object. Our timer calls the `OnTimer()` procedure, which uses the `AVIStreamGetFrame` function to get the pixel data for the current video clip frame, and then copies that data into the pixel buffer for the dynamic texture. The result is a movie playing on a 3D surface.

See also

This recipe can help you produce 3D video, by combining the effects in the *2D Image Manipulation* recipe.

Creating movable text

In this recipe, we will show you how to create billboard-style 3D text in your Ogre3D application. This text is often used to display player names, and stats over their in-game model or to label buildings in a simulation. Because the text is attached to a `SceneNode`, it will become smaller as the camera moves away from it.

Getting ready

To follow along with this recipe, open the solution located in the `Recipes/Chapter05` folder in the code bundle available on the Packt website.

Download files for the `MovableText` class from the Ogre3d site at `http://www.ogre3d.org/tikiwiki/MovableText`.

Prepare definitions for the fonts that you'd like to use in the file `sample.fontdef`, in the `media/fonts` folder.

How to do it...

1. First, create a new Ogre MFC application named `MovableText`, by following the *Creating an MFC Ogre application* recipe, in *Chapter 1, Delving Deep into Application Design*.

2. In `CMovableTextView::EngineSetup()`, add two robot meshes to the scene.

```
Ogre::Entity *RobotEntity1 = SceneManager->createEntity("Robot1",
    "robot.mesh");
Ogre::SceneNode *RobotNode1 = SceneManager->getRootSceneNode()->
    createChildSceneNode();
RobotNode1->attachObject(RobotEntity1);

Ogre::Entity *RobotEntity2 = SceneManager->createEntity("Robot2",
    "robot.mesh");
Ogre::SceneNode *RobotNode2 = SceneManager->getRootSceneNode()->
    createChildSceneNode(Ogre::Vector3(100, 100, 100));
RobotNode2->attachObject(RobotEntity2);
```

3. Create labels for each robot using `MovableText`.

```
Ogre::SceneNode *LabelNode1 = SceneManager->getRootSceneNode()->
  createChildSceneNode("Robot 1");
Ogre::MovableText *Label1 = new Ogre::MovableText("Label 1",
  "Robot 1", "BlueHighway", 1.0, Ogre::ColourValue::Black);

Label1->setTextAlignment(Ogre::MovableText::H_CENTER,
  Ogre::MovableText::V_ABOVE);

Label1->setColor(Ogre::ColourValue::Blue);
Label1->setAdditionalHeight(2.0);
Label1->setCastShadows(false);
LabelNode1->attachObject(Label1);
LabelNode1->setPosition(Center1);
```

The parameters for `Ogre::MovableText` are entity name, caption, font name, character height, and color.

We create our labels at the base of each robot, but for your application, it may make more sense for the labels to be above each model.

4. Next, create a line from one robot label using an `Ogre::ManualObject`, with the `render` operation set to `OT_LINE_LIST`.

```
Ogre::ManualObject *Measure = SceneManager->
  createManualObject("Measure");
Measure->begin("BumpyMetal", Ogre::RenderOperation::OT_LINE_LIST);
Measure->position(Center1);
Measure->position(Center2);
Measure->end();

Ogre::SceneNode *MeasureNode = SceneManager->getRootSceneNode()->
  createChildSceneNode("Measure");
MeasureNode->attachObject(Measure);
```

5. Finally, add a label at the mid-point of the line between the robots.

```
Ogre::Real Distance = Center2.distance(Center1);
char Dimension[20];
sprintf(Dimension ,"%.2f", Distance);
Ogre::SceneNode *MeasureTextNode = SceneManager->
  getRootSceneNode()->createChildSceneNode("MeasureText");

Ogre::MovableText *MeasureText = new Ogre::MovableText("Measure",
  Dimension, "BlueHighway", 1.0, Ogre::ColourValue::Black);
MeasureText->setTextAlignment(Ogre::MovableText::H_CENTER,
  Ogre::MovableText::V_ABOVE);
MeasureText->setColor(Ogre::ColourValue::Blue);
MeasureTextNode->attachObject(&MeasureText);

MeasureTextNode->setPosition(0.5 * (Center1 + Center2));
```

How it works...

We use the `Ogre::MovableText` class to create labels for each robot, and to label the mid-point of the line between the robots. We also set the font, color, and size of the labels as needed.

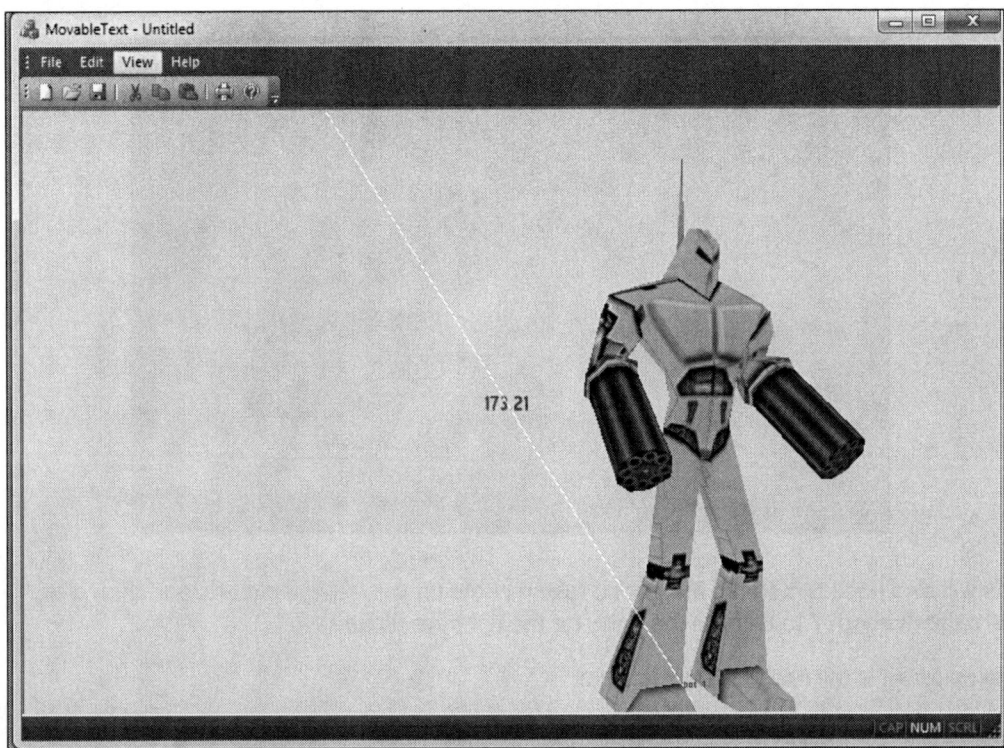

2D image manipulation

In this recipe, we will show you how to edit an image on the fly. We will create an anaglyph image from a pair of stereo images. Anaglyph images are used to provide a stereoscopic 3D effect, when viewed with red and blue.

Getting ready

To follow along with this recipe, open the solution located in the `Recipes/Chapter05` folder in the code bundle available on the Packt website.

Grab a pair of trendy 3D eyeglasses with red and blue plastic lenses.

You will also need two stereo images so take a photo for the left-eye picture, and then slide the camera about 7 to 8 cm to the right, for the right-eye picture.

The following is the image for the left eye:

The next image is for the right eye.

Name the files Left.jpg and Right.jpg, put the pictures in the media/stereo folder, and add the line FileSystem=../../media/stereo to resources.cfg.

How to do it...

1. First, create a new Ogre MFC application named ImageEditor, by following the *Creating an MFC Ogre application* recipe, in *Chapter 1, Delving Deep into Application Design*.

2. Create a material file named stereo.material in media/materials/scripts, and add the following text to it:

```
material stereo
{
  technique
  {
    pass
    {
      texture_unit
      {
        texture Screen.jpg
      }
      texture_unit
      {
        texture stereo
      }
    }
  }
}
```

The first texture unit is just a blank white image, and the second texture unit is the one we will edit.

3. Create a plane entity and a dynamic texture named stereo to display on it.

```
Ogre::TexturePtr StereoTexture =
  Ogre::TextureManager::getSingleton().createManual("stereo",
  Ogre::ResourceGroupManager::DEFAULT_RESOURCE_GROUP_NAME,
  Ogre::TEX_TYPE_2D, 825, 612, 0, Ogre::PF_R8G8B8,
  Ogre::TU_DYNAMIC_WRITE_ONLY_DISCARDABLE);


Ogre::HardwarePixelBufferSharedPtr PixelBuffer = StereoTexture->
  getBuffer();
```

We use the `Ogre::TU_DYNAMIC_WRITE_ONLY_DISCARDABLE` setting, because we intend to update this image dynamically.

4. Load the left eye and right eye images, so that we can combine them to produce the 3D anaglyph.

```
LoadImage.load("Left.jpg",
  Ogre::ResourceGroupManager::DEFAULT_RESOURCE_GROUP_NAME);
LeftImage = LoadImage.flipAroundX();
Ogre::PixelBox LeftBox = LeftImage.getPixelBox();


LoadImage.load("Right.jpg",
  Ogre::ResourceGroupManager::DEFAULT_RESOURCE_GROUP_NAME);
RightImage = LoadImage.flipAroundX();
Ogre::PixelBox RightBox = RightImage.getPixelBox();
```

5. Convert the left and right images to greyscale.

```
for (PixelIndex = 0; PixelIndex < LeftBox.getConsecutiveSize()/3;
  PixelIndex++) {
  Red = LeftData[PixelIndex * 3 + 0];
  Green = LeftData[PixelIndex * 3 + 1];
  Blue = LeftData[PixelIndex * 3 + 2];

  Grey = Red * 0.212671 + Green * 0.715160 + Blue * 0.072169;

  LeftData[PixelIndex * 3 + 0] = Grey;
  LeftData[PixelIndex * 3 + 1] = Grey;
  LeftData[PixelIndex * 3 + 2] = Grey;
}
```

6. Fill the pixel buffer of the dynamic stereo texture using the red channel from left image, and the blue channel from the right image. The `Ogre::PixelUtil::bulkPixelConversion()` function converts pixels from one format to another. In our case, the source and destination format match, so only a simple copy is done.

```
PixelBuffer->lock(Ogre::HardwareBuffer::HBL_DISCARD);
Ogre::PixelBox Destination = PixelBuffer->getCurrentLock();

BYTE *DestData;

DestData = (BYTE *)Destination.data;

for (PixelIndex = 0; PixelIndex < LeftBox.getConsecutiveSize()/3;
  PixelIndex++) {
  LeftData[PixelIndex * 3 + 1] = 0;
  LeftData[PixelIndex * 3 + 2] = RightData[PixelIndex * 3 + 2];
}

Ogre::PixelUtil::bulkPixelConversion(LeftBox, Destination);

//Releases the lock on the destination buffer.

PixelBuffer->unlock();
```

We lock the buffer for writing with the HBL_DISCARD option, which provides minor speed optimizations, because we don't need to preserve any of the content in the old buffer.

How it works...

When we look at an anaglyph with appropriately colored glasses, each eye sees a slightly different picture, and the result is that the image looks 3D. Our brains blend the images each eye receives, and interprets the differences as being the result of different distances. Of course, the downside is that the image loses the original coloring.

There's more...

It is best to avoid scenes with red or cyan objects. You may also try generating two views in Ogre with two cameras. You can even produce 3D video in this way, saving each frame to a video file using the Microsoft AVI library functions

See also

In this chapter:

▶ *Creating dynamic textures*: This recipe provides examples that explain how to work with the Microsoft AVI library functions

6
Learning to Move

In this chapter, we will cover the following recipes:

- ▸ Walking between points
- ▸ Walking along a path
- ▸ Collision detection
- ▸ Converting a 2D path into a 3D path
- ▸ Walking on terrain
- ▸ Linked movement

Introduction

Most graphics applications will have some kind of moving, animated objects, and Ogre3D has all the essential tools that you will need to translate, rotate, and animate 3D meshes. In this chapter, we will cover the basics of object movement and animation, by moving the familiar robot mesh along various paths. We will also show you how to find the collision point of a ray and a 3D mesh, and use that knowledge to create a path for our robot, to follow on top of terrain.

Walking between points

Moving a 3D mesh from point A to point B is very simple with Ogre3D. In this recipe, we'll cover the basics of moving a 3D mesh from one point to another, while animating the mesh along the way.

Getting ready

To follow this recipe, open the solution located in the `Recipes/Chapter06` folder in the code bundle available on the Packt website.

How to do it...

First, create a new Ogre MFC application named `Walking`, by following the *Creating an MFC Ogre Application* recipe from *Chapter 1, Delving Deep into Application Design*.

1. Create a sphere behind the robot as a background and a reference, so we can easily visualize the robot's movement.

   ```
   Ogre::SceneNode *SphereNode =
     SceneManager->getRootSceneNode()->createChildSceneNode("Sphere",
   Ogre::Vector3(0,0,0));
   Ogre::Entity *SphereEntity =
     SceneManager->createEntity("Sphere", "sphere.mesh");
   SphereEntity->setMaterialName("Wall/Screen");
   SphereNode->attachObject(SphereEntity);
   SphereEntity->getParentNode()->scale(0.5,0.5,0.5);
   ```

2. Next, create a robot entity using the `robot.mesh` file for the model.

   ```
   Ogre::SceneNode *RobotNode =
     SceneManager->getRootSceneNode()->createChildSceneNode(
     "Robot", Ogre::Vector3(50,0,0));
   Ogre::Entity *RobotEntity =
     SceneManager->createEntity("Robot", "robot.mesh");

   RobotNode->attachObject(RobotEntity);
   RobotEntity->getParentNode()->scale(0.2,0.2,0.2);

   Ogre::AxisAlignedBox Box = RobotEntity->getBoundingBox();
   Ogre::Vector3 Center = Box.getCenter();
   m_Camera->lookAt(Ogre::Vector3(0.0, 0.0, 0.0));
   ```

3. Enable the `Walk` animation state so our robot mesh will look as though it is walking when it animates. The robot mesh file also has an `Idle` animation, but we will not be using that for this recipe.

   ```
   m_Animation = RobotEntity->getAnimationState("Walk");
   m_Animation->setEnabled(true);
   ```

3. Next, add a new menu item named `Walking`, and two sub-items named `Start` and `Stop`. Add an event handler for the `Start` sub-item that creates a new timer, which we will use to make the robot move, and an event handler for the `Stop` sub-item that destroys this timer, thus stopping the robot from moving.

4. Now that we have a timer set up, we need a callback method for the timer to trigger periodically. Add a member function named `OnTimer` to the `CWalkingView` class, and add code within that function to increment the robot animation time.

```
m_Animation->addTime(0.01);
```

5. Finally, make the robot move, by calling the `SetPosition()` function with new x and y coordinates that we calculate for each frame. The coordinates we use for this recipe are points on a circle, based on an angle variable that we increment every frame.

```
const Ogre::Real Radius = 50.0;

Ogre::Real x = Radius * Ogre::Math::Cos(m_Angle);
Ogre::Real y = Radius * Ogre::Math::Sin(m_Angle);
m_Angle += 0.01;

RobotNode->setPosition(x, 0.0, y);
```

The resulting application will show a robot moving in a circle in front of a big yellow sphere.

How it works...

We set up a function named `OnTimer` that gets called at regular intervals. Each time the timer function is run, we increment the animation time, update the robot position, and re-render the 3D scene.

There's more...

You can create other user interface elements to move objects in the scene, and specify other parameters, such as the speed or the animation state to play.

See also

In this chapter:

The following recipes in this chapter cover the basics of moving the robot along a path:

- ▸ *Walking along a path*
- ▸ *Walking on terrain*

Walking along a path

In this recipe, we will show you how to move a robot mesh on a curved path, and draw the path in the scene. The method we use in this recipe for drawing the path is a useful technique when you want to visualize the projected movement in a 3D scene. It is often used in 3D editors for showing the movement paths of cameras and other objects in a scene.

Getting ready

To follow along with this recipe, open the solution located in the `Recipes/Chapter06` folder in the code bundle available on the Packt website.

How to do it...

First, create a new Ogre MFC application named `PathWalking`, by following the *Creating an MFC Ogre Application* recipe from *Chapter 1, Delving Deep into Application Design*.

1. The first step is to prepare an array of vectors that we will use to hold all the coordinates for the points in our path. Add a member variable named `m_Path` to the `CPathWalkingView` class.

    ```
    CArray<Ogre::Vector3, Ogre::Vector3> m_Path;
    ```

2. Next, create a member function named `CPathWalkingView::CreatePath()` in which we will add all our points to the `m_Path` member variable. The path coordinates will be calculated based on the function for a helix.

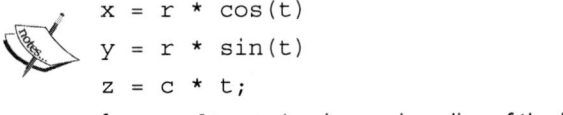 A helix is a curve with the following parametric equations:

```
x = r * cos(t)
y = r * sin(t)
z = c * t;
```

for t ∈ [0, 2π), where r is radius of the helix.

3. Inside the CreatePath() function, create a ManualObject, so that we can visualize the path. Next, create a loop that increments an angle variable, and calculates the points of the helix curve using that angle. The points we calculate are then added to the path, and also added as positions to the ManualObject.

```
Ogre::ManualObject *Path =
  SceneManager->createManualObject("Path");
Path->begin("BumpyMetal", Ogre::RenderOperation::OT_LINE_LIST);

const Ogre::Real Radius = 100.0;
const Ogre::Real Step = 10.0;

for (double Angle = 0.0; Angle < 2 * 3.14159265359; Angle += 0.01)
{
  Ogre::Vector3 Point;

  Point[0] = Radius * cos(Angle);
  Point[2] = Radius * sin(Angle);
  Point[1] = Step * Angle;

  m_Path.Add(Point);
  Path->position(Point);
}

Path->end();

Ogre::SceneNode *PathNode =
  SceneManager->getRootSceneNode()->createChildSceneNode("Path");
PathNode->attachObject(Path);
```

We set the `render` operation to `OT_LINE_LIST`, because we want the path to be rendered as a polyline. We also add the path to the scene graph, so that it will appear in the scene.

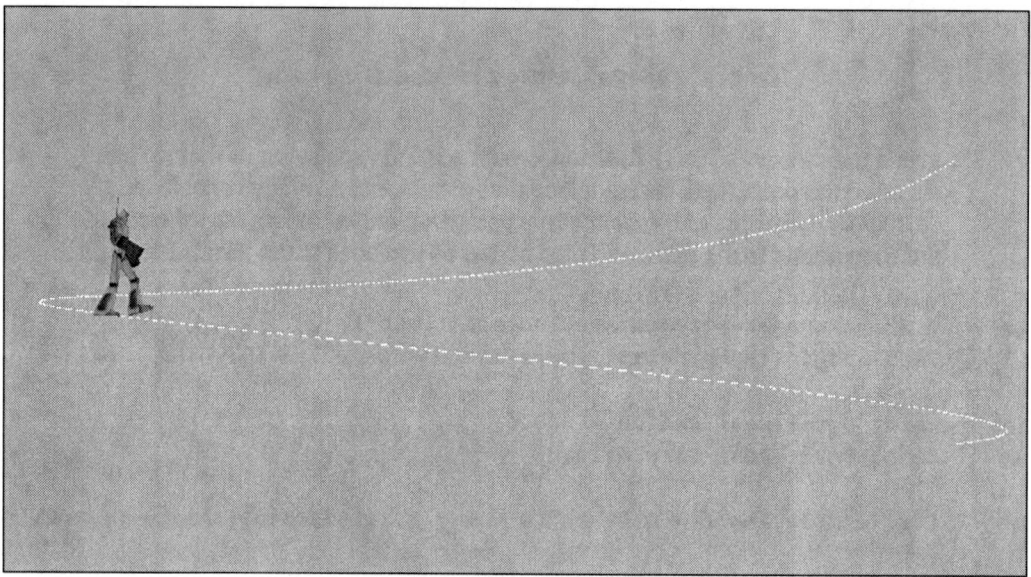

4. Now, add a new menu item named `Walking`, and two sub-items named `Start` and `Stop`. We will use these new menu items to start and stop the robot's movement. Add an event handler for the `Start` sub-item that creates a new timer, and an event handler for the `Stop` sub-item that destroys this timer.

```
void CPathWalkingView::OnWalkStart()
{
   SetTimer(1, 1, 0);
}
```

```
void CPathWalkingView::OnWalkStop()
{
   KillTimer(1);
}
```

5. Next, create a callback method for the timer to trigger periodically. Add a member function named `OnTimer` to the `CPathWalkingView` class, and add code within that function to update the robot's position along the path and re-render the scene.

```
RobotNode->setPosition(m_Path[m_PathIndex]);
m_PathIndex++

Root->renderOneFrame();
```

How it works...

Just as in the first recipe, here we set up a function named `OnTimer` that gets called at regular intervals. Each time the `OnTimer` function is called, we update the robot position to a new point on the path, and re-render the 3D scene.

There's more...

This simple path-following example can be improved by using a more useful path collection, such as a network of roads or an adjustable Bezier curve. You can also add controls to vary the movement speed of objects along the path using timers with different intervals, or smooth the movement by interpolating between points along the path.

See also

In this chapter:

▸ *Converting a 2D path into a 3D path*: This recipe shows how you can take a path like the one in this recipe, and conform it to the terrain using collision detection

Collision detection

The Ogre 3D graphics library provides collision detection tools that can find the intersection points between a ray cast into a scene and the meshes in that scene. In this recipe, we will show you how to use Ogre's collision tools.

Getting ready

To follow this recipe, open the solution located in the `Recipes/Chapter06` folder in the code bundle available on the Packt website.

We will be using the **Minimal Ogre Collision Tools** class, which is included in the example `CollisionDetection` project.

How to do it...

First, create a new Ogre MFC application named `CollisionDetection`, by following the *Creating an MFC Ogre application* recipe from *Chapter 1, Delving Deep into Application Design*.

1. Next, create a simple scene in `CCollisionDetectionView::EngineSetup()` that consists of three spheres, and a camera aimed at the spheres.

```
Ogre::Entity *SunEntity =
  SceneManager->createEntity("Sun", "sphere.mesh");
Ogre::Entity *EarthEntity =
  SceneManager->createEntity("Earth", "sphere.mesh");
Ogre::Entity *MoonEntity =
  SceneManager->createEntity("Moon", "sphere.mesh");

SunNode->attachObject(SunEntity);
SunEntity->getParentNode()->scale(0.1,0.1,0.1);

EarthNode->attachObject(EarthEntity);
EarthEntity->getParentNode()->scale(0.1,0.1,0.1);

MoonNode->attachObject(MoonEntity);
MoonEntity->getParentNode()->scale(0.1,0.1,0.1);
```

2. Include the Minimal Ogre Collision Tools class named `CollisionTools` in the project, and use it to find the collision point of a ray cast from the camera. Add a member variable named `m_CollisionTools` to `CCollisionDetectionView`, and initialize it in the `SetupEngine()` member function.

```
m_CollisionTools = new MOC::CollisionTools(SceneManager);
```

3. Next, use the `CollisionTools::collidesWithEntity()` function to check if a ray collides with one of the spheres in the scene. The ray that we will use is a vector that starts at the camera's position, and points in the direction the camera is facing.

```
Ogre::uint32 QueryMask = 0xFFFFFFFF;

if (m_CollisionTools->collidesWithEntity(m_Camera->getPosition(),
  Ogre::Vector3(50,0,0), 200.0f, 0.0f, QueryMask))

{
}
```

The parameters of the `collidesWithEntity()` method are the origin of the ray, the target of the ray, radius of collision, ray height, and a query mask, which we set to `0xFFFFFFFF` to enable collisions with any entities.

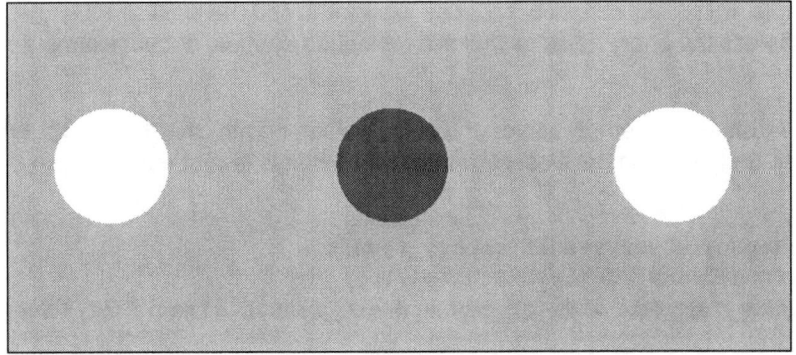

To demonstrate that the collision detection works, add code to `CollisionTools::collidesWithEntity()`, which changes the material of the object the ray collides with, so that the collided object appears red in the scene.

```
if (raycastFromPoint(fromPointAdj, normal, myResult, myObject,
  distToColl, queryMask))
  {
  distToColl -= collisionRadius;
  ((Ogre::Entity *)myObject)->setMaterialName("Wall/Red");
  return (distToColl <= distToDest);
}
```

How it works...

The `CollisionTools` class that we use in this recipe provides easy-to-use collision detection methods, but if you look at the code for this class, you will see that it is Ogre's `RaySceneQuery` class that does all the heavy lifting. `RaySceneQuery` can be used to get all entities that collide with a ray. Once you have the closest entity, you can iterate over the triangles in the mesh, and test for the closest ray-triangle collision.

A typical `RaySceneQuery` setup looks as follows:

```
mRaySceneQuery->setRay(ray);
    mRaySceneQuery->setSortByDistance(true);
    mRaySceneQuery->setQueryMask(queryMask);

// execute the query, returns a vector of hits
if (mRaySceneQuery->execute().size() <= 0)
{
  // raycast did not hit an objects bounding box
  return (false);
}
```

In this example, we sort by distance, because we want to find the closest entity that is hit. We could also use the query mask to filter out unneeded entities, but our example does not do that.

If the query returns a non-empty vector of results, we can iterate over the results, and find the closest entity, and then find the closest triangle that belongs to that entity's mesh that is hit by the ray.

```
Ogre::RaySceneQueryResult &query_result =
  mRaySceneQuery->getLastResults();
for (size_t qr_idx = 0; qr_idx < query_result.size(); qr_idx++)
{
  // stop checking if we have found a raycast hit that is closer
  // than all remaining entities
  if ((closest_distance >= 0.0f) &&
    (closest_distance < query_result[qr_idx].distance))
    {
      break;
  }

  // only check this result if its a hit against an entity
  if ((query_result[qr_idx].movable != NULL)  &&
    (query_result[qr_idx].movable->getMovableType().
    compare("Entity") == 0))
    {
    // get the entity to check
    Ogre::MovableObject *pentity =
      static_cast<Ogre::MovableObject*>(
      query_result[qr_idx].movable);

    // mesh data to retrieve
    size_t vertex_count;
    size_t index_count;
    Ogre::Vector3 *vertices;
    Ogre::uint32 *indices;

    // get the mesh information
      GetMeshInformation(((Ogre::Entity*)pentity)->getMesh(),
      vertex_count, vertices, index_count, indices,
      pentity->getParentNode()->_getDerivedPosition(),
      pentity->getParentNode()->_getDerivedOrientation(),
      pentity->getParentNode()->_getDerivedScale());

    // test for hitting individual triangles on the mesh
    //bool new_closest_found = false;
```

```
for (size_t i = 0; i < index_count; i += 3)
{
  // check for a hit against this triangle
  std::pair<bool, Ogre::Real> hit =
   Ogre::Math::intersects(ray, vertices[indices[i]],
   vertices[indices[i+1]], vertices[indices[i+2]], true,
   true);

  // if it was a hit check if its the closest
  if (hit.first)
  {
    if ((closest_distance < 0.0f) ||
      (hit.second < closest_distance))
      {
        // this is the closest so far, save it off
        closest_distance = hit.second;
        new_closest_found = true;
      }
  }
}

    // free the verticies and indicies memory
delete[] vertices;
delete[] indices;

// if we found a new closest raycast for this object, update
//the closest_result before moving on to the next object.
if (new_closest_found)
{
  target = pentity;
  closest_result = ray.getPoint(closest_distance);
}
  }
}
```

See also

In this chapter:

▸ *Converting a 2D path into a 3D path*: This recipe shows how to put collision detection to use, by dropping a 2D path down onto 3D terrain

Converting a 2D path into a 3D path

In this recipe, we will show you how to take a 2D path and drop it down onto a 3D terrain mesh, so that we can make our robot walk on top of the terrain. To calculate the height value for each point in the path, we will use the collision detection from the *Collision Detection* recipe.

Getting ready

To follow this recipe, open the solution located in the `Recipes/Chapter06` folder in the code bundle available on the Packt website.

We will also be using a terrain mesh file for this recipe. To create a terrain mesh file, you can add the following code to the `EngineSetup()` function in the `LandXML` project from *Chapter 3, Managing Objects and Scenes*, to export a mesh file.

```
Ogre::MeshPtr TopographyMesh =
   Topography->convertToMesh("Topography");
Ogre::MeshSerializer MeshSerializer;
MeshSerializer.exportMesh(TopographyMesh.getPointer(),
   "Topography.mesh");
```

Place the exported `Topography.mesh` file in the `media/models` folder, so that we can use it for this and other recipes.

How to do it...

Create a new Ogre MFC application named `PathDropping`, by following the *Creating an MFC Ogre application* recipe from *Chapter 1, Delving Deep into Application Design*.

1. We will be using the same collision detection tools class that we used in the *Collision Detection* recipe. In `CPathDroppingView::EngineSetup()`, create an instance of the `CollisionTools` class.

   ```
   m_CollisionTools = new MOC::CollisionTools(SceneManager);
   ```

2. Next, create a menu named `Walking`, and a menu item named `Drop`. Add an event handler to the menu item called `OnWalkingDrop()`.

   ```
   void CPathDroppingView::OnWalkingDrop()
   {
     CEngine *Engine = ((CPathDroppingApp*)AfxGetApp())->m_Engine;

     Ogre::Root *Root = Engine->GetRoot();
     DropPath();
     Root->renderOneFrame();
   }
   ```

In this function, we call `DropPath()`, and then render the scene.

3. Create a function named `DropPath()`, and add code to it to drop points along a line starting at one corner of the terrain mesh, and ending at the opposite corner. So that we can actually see the path, create a `ManualObject` whose vertices are the points along the path.

```
Ogre::ManualObject *Path =
  SceneManager->createManualObject("Path");
Path->begin("BumpyMetal", Ogre::RenderOperation::OT_LINE_LIST);
```

We set the `RenderOperation` to `OT_LINE_LIST`, so that the `ManualObject` mesh is rendered as a polyline.

4. Now, divide the line into segments, and iterate over these segments, calculating the height of each segment end point. We add the resulting 3D point to our `m_Path` vector, and also to the `ManualObject` path mesh.

```
Ogre::AxisAlignedBox TopographyBox =
  TopographyEntity->getBoundingBox();

Ogre::Vector3 Start = TopographyBox.getMinimum();
Ogre::Vector3 Finish = TopographyBox.getMaximum();

for (double Distance = 0; Distance < 1.0; Distance += 0.001)
{
  Ogre::Vector3 Position = Start + ((Finish - Start) * Distance);
  float x = Position[0];
  float y = Position[1];
  float z = Position[2];
```

5. We calculate intersection between the vertical ray that is cast down from each segment end point and the terrain, using the `CollisionTools::collidesWithE ntity()` function.

```
  m_CollisionTools->collidesWithEntity(Position,
    Ogre::Vector3(x,y-1,z), Ogre::Vector3(x,y+1,z), 100.0f, 0.0f,
    4294967295);
  m_Path.Add(Position);

  Path->position(Position);
}

Path->end();
```

```
Ogre::SceneNode *PathNode =
  SceneManager->getRootSceneNode()->createChildSceneNode("Path");
PathNode->attachObject(Path);
```

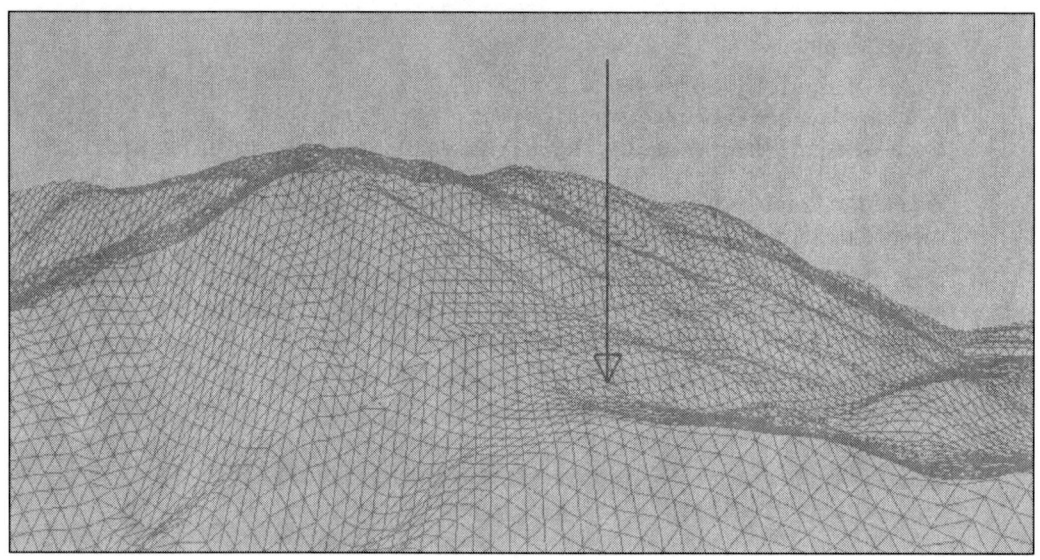

You can see the resulting white path on the brown terrain in the following image:

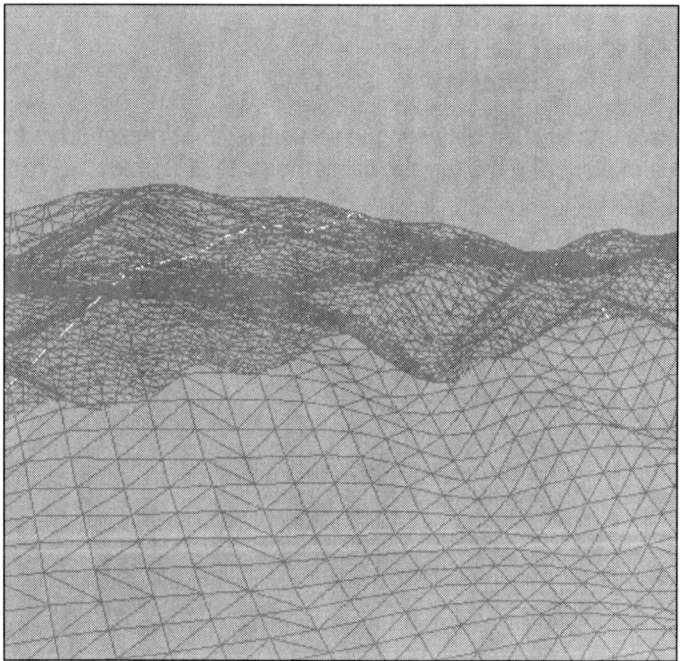

6. To make the path easier to see, create a menu named `Terrain`, and menu items named `Visible` and `Invisible`. Add event handlers to each menu item to show and hide the terrain. The code for the `Invisible` handler is as follows:

```
Ogre::Entity *TopographyEntity =
    SceneManager->getEntity("Topography");
TopographyEntity->setVisible(false);
Root->renderOneFrame();
```

The result of hiding the terrain, so that only the path mesh is visible, is shown in the following image:

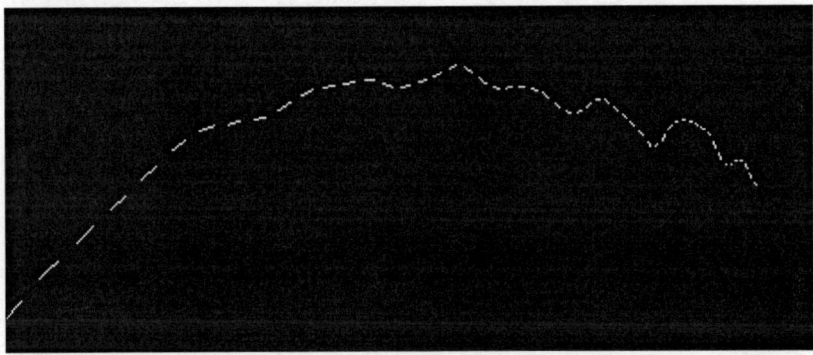

7. The last step is to make a robot mesh walk along the path we just created. To do this, create a robot entity, and use a timer to move the robot along the path, just as we did in the *Walking between points* recipe.

How it works...

The Ogre 3D library has mesh collision detection tools that are sufficient for finding the height of any point on the terrain mesh. The `CollisionTools` class simply builds on the existing Ogre 3D `RaySceneQuery` class, and provides easy-to-use functions. After we find the height of each point along the path, we create a mesh from those 3D points, so that we can visualize it. Finally, we move a robot along the path, using the same method described in the *Walking between points* recipe.

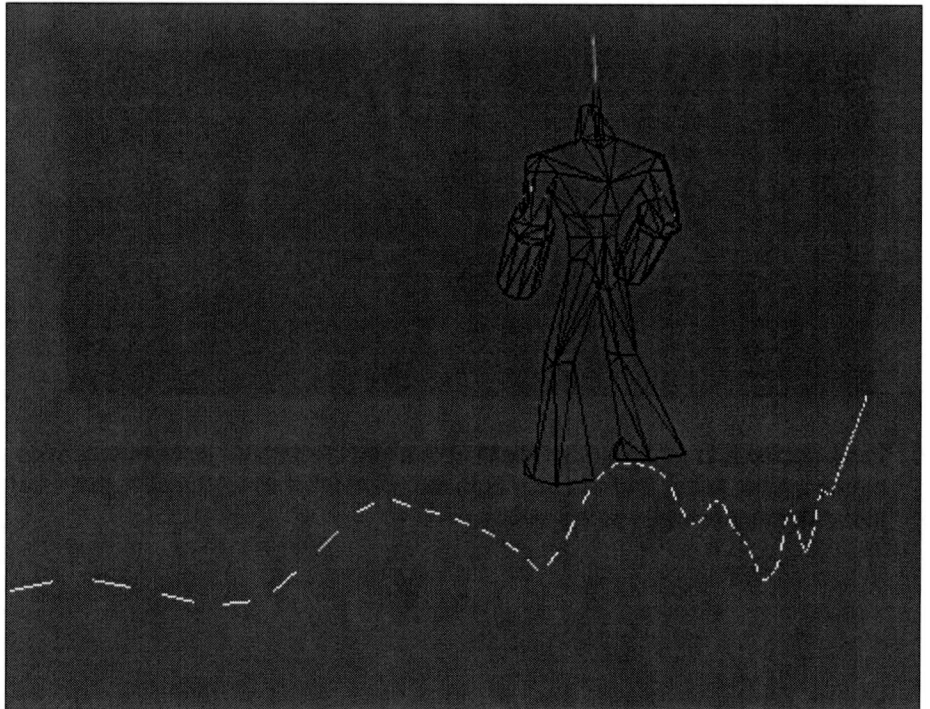

See also

In this chapter:

▶ *Collision Detection*: This recipe provides a more in-depth explanation of the `CollisionTools` class

Walking on terrain

In this recipe, we will show you how to make a robot walk on terrain, using collision detection to keep our robot's feet planted on the ground.

Getting ready

To follow this recipe, open the solution located in the `Recipes/Chapter05` folder in the code bundle available on the Packt website.

We will also be using the same `Topography.mesh` file that we created for the *Converting a 2D path into a 3D path* recipe.

How to do it...

First, create a new Ogre MFC application named `TerrainWalking`, by following the *Creating an MFC Ogre application* recipe from *Chapter 1, Delving Deep into Application Design*.

1. In `CTerrainWalkingView::EngineSetup()`, load the `Topography.mesh` file and the robot mesh, and create entities for each.

   ```
   Ogre::SceneNode *TopographyNode = SceneManager->
     getRootSceneNode()->createChildSceneNode("Topography");
   Ogre::Entity *TopographyEntity = SceneManager->
     createEntity("Topography", "Topography.mesh");
   TopographyNode->attachObject(TopographyEntity);

   Ogre::SceneNode *RobotNode = SceneManager->
     getRootSceneNode()->createChildSceneNode("Robot");
   Ogre::Entity *RobotEntity = SceneManager->
     createEntity("Robot", "robot.mesh");
   RobotNode->attachObject(RobotEntity);
   Ogre::AxisAlignedBox RobotBox = RobotEntity->getBoundingBox();
   ```

2. Next, add a member variable of type `CollisionTools` named `m_CollisionTools` to the `CTerrainWalkingView` class, and create an instance of it in `EngineSetup()`.

   ```
   m_CollisionTools = new MOC::CollisionTools(SceneManager);
   ```

3. Add a timer event handler named `OnTimer`, and add code to it to move the robot. For this recipe, we will move the robot from one corner of the terrain mesh to the opposite corner.

```
void CTerrainWalkingView::OnTimer(UINT_PTR nIDEvent)
{
  Ogre::AxisAlignedBox TopographyBox =
    TopographyEntity->getBoundingBox();

  Ogre::Vector3 Start = TopographyBox.getMinimum();
  Ogre::Vector3 Finish = TopographyBox.getMaximum();

  double x = Start[0] + (Finish[0] - Start[0]) *
    m_RelativeDistance;
  double y = Start[1] + (Finish[1] - Start[1]) *
    m_RelativeDistance;
  double z = Start[2] + (Finish[2] - Start[2]) *
    m_RelativeDistance;

  m_Animation->addTime(0.01);
  m_RelativeDistance += 0.01;

  if (m_CollisionTools->collidesWithEntity(Elevation,
    Ogre::Vector3(x,y - 1,z), Ogre::Vector3(x,y + 1,z), 100.0f,
    0.0f, 4294967295))
    {
      x = Elevation[0];
      y = Elevation[1] + RobotBox.getSize()[1];
      z = Elevation[2];
  }

  RobotNode->setPosition(x, y, z);
  m_Camera->lookAt(x, y, z);
  Root->renderOneFrame();
}
```

We take the line from one corner of the terrain to the opposite corner, and divide it up into small segments. Each time the timer function runs, we increment the robots movement along the line, using the `m_RelativeDistance` member variable. When the robot is at the beginning of the line, the relative distance is 0, when the robot reaches the end, the relative distance is 1, and we stop the timer so the robot stops moving. At each step along the line, we calculate the height of the terrain at the robots position, so that we can keep his feet planted on the ground. We use the same collision detection methods as in the previous recipe to get the terrain height.

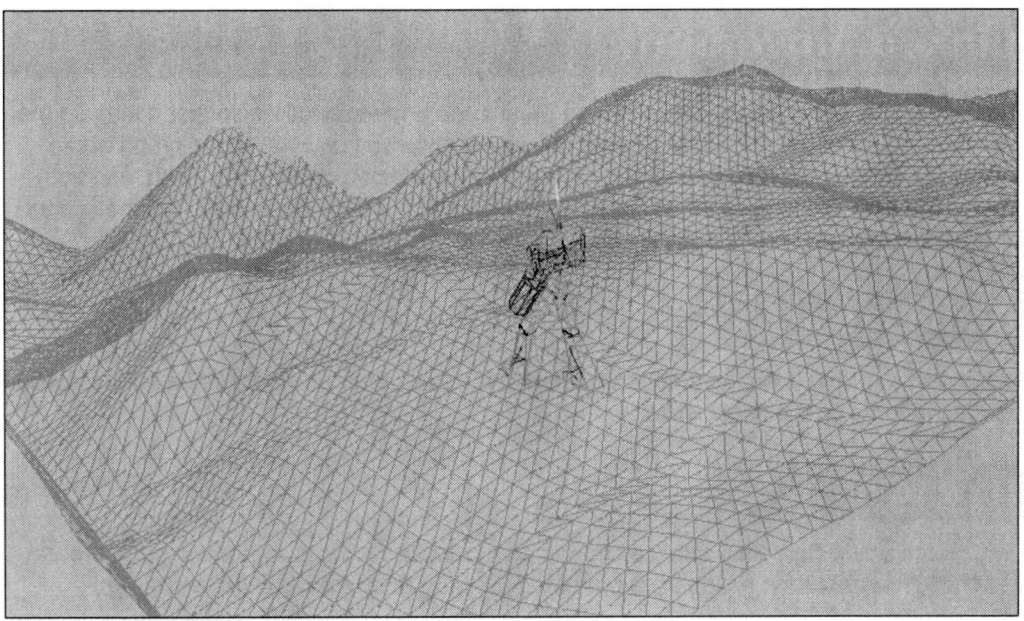

How it works...

In this recipe, we used a timer to periodically update the position of the robot. Each time our timer function was called, we moved the robot further along the terrain, and used the CollisionTools to get the height of the terrain at the robot's position. Once we knew the terrain height, we moved the robot, so that his feet lined up with the terrain.

There's more...

You can use this technique to move or insert objects anywhere on a terrain mesh.

See also

In this chapter:

▶   _Collision Tools_: See this recipe for more details on how the CollisionTools collision detection works

Linked movement

The beauty of a scene graph is that we can parent one node to another, so that it inherits the transform matrix of the parent. In this recipe, we will show you how the scene graph works in Ogre 3D, by creating a miniature solar system with the moon orbiting the Earth, and both orbiting the sun. The way we make the `Moon` node a child of the `Earth` node, will make it easy for us to rotate them both about the sun.

Getting ready

To follow this recipe, open the solution located in the `Recipes/Chapter06` folder in the code bundle available on the Packt website.

How to do it...

First, create a new Ogre MFC application named `LinkedMovement`, by following the *Creating an MFC Ogre application* recipe from *Chapter 1, Delving Deep into Application Design*.

1. In `EngineSetup()`, get the root scene node from the `SceneManager`, so that we can add child nodes to it for our solar system bodies.

   ```
   m_SystemNode = SceneManager->getRootSceneNode()->
     createChildSceneNode(Ogre::Vector3(0,0,0));
   ```

2. Create child nodes for the `Sun`, the `Earth`, and the `Moon` entities, so that each new node is a child of the previous node. The `Earth` node will be a child of the `Sun` node, and the `Moon` node will be a child of the `Earth` node.

   ```
   Ogre::SceneNode *SunNode = m_SystemNode->
     createChildSceneNode("Sun", Ogre::Vector3(0,0,0));
   Ogre::SceneNode *EarthNode = m_SystemNode->
     createChildSceneNode("Earth", Ogre::Vector3(50,0,0));
   Ogre::SceneNode *MoonNode = EarthNode->
     createChildSceneNode("Moon", Ogre::Vector3(200,0,0));
   ```

3. Next, create `sphere` entities for the `Sun`, the `Earth`, and the `Moon`, and attach each to its respective scene node:

   ```
   Ogre::Entity *SunEntity = SceneManager->
     createEntity("Sun", "sphere.mesh");
   Ogre::Entity *EarthEntity = SceneManager->
     createEntity("Earth", "sphere.mesh");
   Ogre::Entity *MoonEntity = SceneManager->
     createEntity("Moon", "sphere.mesh");
   ```

```
SunNode->attachObject(SunEntity);
SunEntity->getParentNode()->scale(0.1,0.1,0.1);

EarthNode->attachObject(EarthEntity);
EarthEntity->getParentNode()->scale(0.1,0.1,0.1);

MoonNode->attachObject(MoonEntity);
MoonEntity->getParentNode()->scale(0.5,0.5,0.5);
```

4. Create a member variable named m_RotationAngle of type Ogre::Radian. We will increment this rotation angle, and use it to set the rotation of each of our solar system bodies.

5. Finally, start a timer, and add an event handler named OnTimer. When the timer function is called, update the rotation of scene nodes, so that the Moon orbits the Earth, and both the Moon and the Earth orbit the Sun.

```
Ogre::Quaternion Quaternion;
Quaternion.FromAngleAxis(m_RotationAngle,
  Ogre::Vector3(0.0, 0.0, 1.0));

m_SystemNode->setOrientation(Quaternion);

Ogre::SceneNode *EarthNode =
  (Ogre::SceneNode *)m_SystemNode->getChild("Earth");
EarthNode->setOrientation(Quaternion);

Ogre::SceneNode *MoonNode =
  (Ogre::SceneNode *)EarthNode->getChild("Moon");
MoonNode->setOrientation(Quaternion);

m_RotationAngle += m_AngleIncrement;

Root->renderOneFrame();
```

Ogre 3D uses quaternions to describe the orientation of 3D objects. **Quaternions** are more robust than Euler angles, and have other mathematical properties that make them attractive for use in graphics applications. To create the quaternion that represents the new orientation, we use the Quaternion.FromAngleAxis() method, which takes an angle in radians, and an axis about which to rotate. In our recipe, we are rotating about the z-axis. After creating the quaternion, we apply it to each of the scene nodes, and the result is that each node rotates about its parent node.

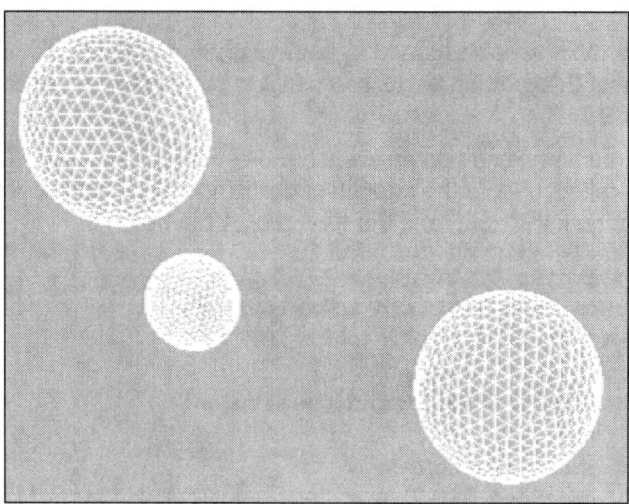

You will see the Sun rotate on its own axis, the rotation of the Earth around the Sun, and rotation of the Moon around the Earth.

How it works...

The scene graph system in Ogre 3D makes it easy to link entities so that they can rotate and move relative to one another. In this recipe, we use quaternions to rotate scene nodes, so that you can easily visualize the effect in a familiar setting – our solar system! Quaternions provide a good mechanism for representing orientations and rotations of objects in three dimensions.

There's more...

You can create scene node hierarchies to simulate the movement and rotation of more complex systems, such as robotic arms or molecular dynamics.

7
Implementing Animations

In this chapter, we will cover the following recipes:

- ▶ Creating skeletal animations
- ▶ Creating morph animations
- ▶ Creating pose animations
- ▶ Creating SceneNode animations
- ▶ Creating numeric value animations
- ▶ Creating linked animations
- ▶ Animation using controllers
- ▶ Creating linked controllers
- ▶ Blending animations
- ▶ Creating animated light

Introduction

In this chapter, we'll explore Ogre 3D's core animation features. Ogre 3D provides many of the most popular animation tools, including skeletal, pose, morph, blending, and linked animations. Using these techniques we will show you how to animate meshes, scene nodes, and lights.

Creating skeletal animations

Skeletal animation is a popular technique for animating a mesh by moving a set of hierarchical bones within the mesh, which in turn moves the vertices of the model according to the bone assignments stored in each vertex. In this recipe, we will use skeletal animation to move the vertices on a simple cube.

Getting ready

To follow this recipe, open the solution located in the `Recipes/Chapter07` folder in the code bundle available on the Packt website.

How to do it...

1. First, create a new Ogre MFC application named `SkeletalAnimation`, by following the *Creating an MFC Ogre application* recipe from *Chapter 1, Delving Deep into Application Design*.

2. In `CSkeletalAnimationView::EngineSetup()`, create `Ogre::ManualObject` with the name `Animation`, for our cube mesh.

```
Ogre::ManualObject* ManualObject = NULL;
ManualObject = SceneManager->createManualObject("Animation");
ManualObject->setDynamic(false);
ManualObject->begin("BaseWhiteNoLighting",
  Ogre::RenderOperation::OT_TRIANGLE_LIST);
```

3. Next, provide the position and triangle information for the first cube face.

```
ManualObject->position(0, 0, 0);
ManualObject->position(1, 0, 0);
ManualObject->position(1, 1, 0);
ManualObject->triangle(0, 1, 2);

ManualObject->position(0, 0, 0);
ManualObject->position(1, 1, 0);
ManualObject->position(0, 1, 0);
ManualObject->triangle(3, 4, 5);
...
...
```

4. Do the same for the remaining cube faces, and then indicate that we are done adding the mesh information, by calling `ManualObject::end()`.

```
ManualObject->end();
```

5. Next, convert the cube `ManualObject`, into a mesh because `ManualObject` doesn't support skeletal animation.

```
Ogre::MeshPtr MeshPtr = ManualObject->convertToMesh("Animation");
Ogre::SubMesh* sub = MeshPtr->getSubMesh(0);
```

6. We also create a local variable named `sub`, which is a pointer to the first and only submesh in our cube mesh. In Ogre 3D, each `Mesh` object is made up of at least one `SubMesh`, which represent the actual vertices of the mesh. The relationship between `Mesh` and `SubMesh` makes sense when you think of it as an entity made up of parts, such as a `car Mesh` would be made up of two `door SubMeshes`, a `frame SubMesh`, four `wheel SubMeshes`, and so on.

7. Create a skeleton object named `Skeleton` by using the aptly named `Ogre::SkeletonManager` singleton instance.

```
Ogre::SkeletonPtr Skeleton =
    Ogre::SkeletonManager::getSingleton().create("Skeleton",
    Ogre::ResourceGroupManager::DEFAULT_RESOURCE_GROUP_NAME);
```

8. Next, create a simple skeleton hierarchy made up of a bone named `Root1` with two child bones, `Child1` and `Child2`.

```
Ogre::Bone *Root1 = NULL;
Ogre::Bone *Child1 = NULL;
Ogre::Bone *Child2 = NULL;

Root1 = Skeleton.getPointer()->createBone("Root");
Root1->setPosition(Ogre::Vector3(0.0, 0.0, 0.0));
Root1->setOrientation(Ogre::Quaternion::IDENTITY);

Child1 = Root1->createChild(1);
Child1->setPosition(Ogre::Vector3(4.0, 0.0, 0.0));
Child1->setOrientation(Ogre::Quaternion::IDENTITY);

Child2 = Root1->createChild(2);
Child2->setPosition(Ogre::Vector3(5.0, 0.0, 0.0));
Child2->setOrientation(Ogre::Quaternion::IDENTITY);
```

9. Assign several vertices from our cube mesh to the bones we just created using the `Ogre::VertexBoneAssignment` class. This structure holds a vertex index, a bone index, and a weight representing the assignment of a vertex to a bone for skeletal animation.

```
Ogre::VertexBoneAssignment Assignment;

Assignment.boneIndex = 0;
Assignment.vertexIndex = 0;
```

The `weight` value indicates how much a vertex should match the movement of the bone it is attached to. The reason for allowing a variable `weight` in the bone assignment is because Ogre 3D supports assigning a vertex to multiple bones, which can improve the distortion characteristics of joints on models. A `weight` value of `0` means that the bone's movement will not affect the vertex at all, while a `weight` value of `1` means the vertex will follow the bone's movement exactly. In this recipe, we will not be using blending, so we'll stick with a `weight` value of `1`.

```
Assignment.weight = 1.0;
```

10. Next, set the default bone position to be the binding pose, that is, the layout in which the vertices were assigned to the bones.

```
Skeleton->setBindingPose();

sub->addBoneAssignment(Assignment);

Assignment.vertexIndex = 1;
sub->addBoneAssignment(Assignment);

Assignment.vertexIndex = 2;
sub->addBoneAssignment(Assignment);
```

11. Create an `Animation` object with the name `HandAnimation`, and add `KeyFrames` to the animation with different positions, for our `Root1` bone.

```
Ogre::Animation *Animation =
  MeshPtr->createAnimation("HandAnimation", 100.0);

Ogre::NodeAnimationTrack *Track = Animation->
  createNodeTrack(0, Root1);

Ogre::TransformKeyFrame *KeyFrame = NULL;

for (float FrameTime = 0.0; FrameTime < 100.0; FrameTime += 0.1)
{
  KeyFrame = Track->createNodeKeyFrame(FrameTime);
  KeyFrame->setTranslate(Ogre::Vector3(10.0, 0.0, 0.0));
}
```

12. Next, indicate that each bone will be manually controlled. This means that we want to alter the bones at runtime, and we don't want the bone positions to be reset by the animation routines.

```
Root1->setManuallyControlled(true);
Child1->setManuallyControlled(true);
Child2->setManuallyControlled(true);
```

13. Normally, when a mesh is loaded from a file, Ogre will pull the skeleton information from the file as well. However, in this recipe, we are creating the skeleton manually for demonstration purposes, so we need to tell the mesh which skeleton to use. Tell the mesh that we want to use our manually created skeleton using the _notifySkeleton method.

```
MeshPtr.getPointer()->_notifySkeleton(Skeleton);
```

14. Next, create an entity using our mesh, and add it to the scene graph.

```
Ogre::Entity *Entity = SceneManager->
   createEntity("Animation", "Animation");

Ogre::SceneNode *SceneNode = SceneManager->
   getRootSceneNode()->createChildSceneNode();


SceneNode->attachObject(Entity);
```

15. Make the skeleton visible using the setDisplaySkeleton method. This is especially useful when attempting to debug animations.

```
Entity->setDisplaySkeleton(true);
```

When the skeleton is set to display, Ogre will render a set of axes at the origin of each bone.

16. Our last step is to enable our custom animation state, set a timer to update the animation time, and render the scene periodically. In CSkeletalAnimationView::EngineSetup() EngineSetup()", enable the HandAnimation state.

```
m_AnimationState = Entity->getAnimationState("HandAnimation");
m_AnimationState->setEnabled(true);
m_AnimationState->setLoop(true);
```

17. In the `CSkeletalAnimationView::OnTimer()` function, modify the time of the animation, and re-render the scene.

```
m_AnimationState->addTime(0.1);
Root->renderOneFrame();
```

How it works...

Skeletal animation refers to the binding of vertices to the bones in a skeleton. Each vertex in an object can have up to four bone influences. Each bone influence is assigned a weight, so that when that bone moves, its influence on the position of the vertex is weighted by that amount. Assigning vertices to multiple bones with varying weights is useful for more realistic deformation, when animating joints.

Ogre 3D uses forward kinematics for animating skeletons similar to how the scene graph is set up. This means that to move a finger downward in a walk cycle, one would calculate the shoulder movement, then the elbow, then the wrist, and finally the finger. The opposite of forward kinematics is inverse kinematics, in which one animates the finger, and the parent bones automatically move to their new position, based on a set of constraints.

OGRE supports the following skeleton animation features:

- Each mesh can be linked to a single skeleton
- Unlimited bones per skeleton
- Hierarchical forward-kinematics on bones
- Multiple named animations per skeleton (for example, `Walk`, `Run`, `Jump`, `Shoot`, and so on)
- Unlimited key frames per animation
- Linear or spline-based interpolation between key frames
- A vertex can be assigned to multiple bones, and assigned weightings for smoother skinning
- Multiple animations can be applied to a mesh at the same time, again with a blend

The most common way of using skeletal animation in Ogre is by creating the model, the skeleton, and the animations in a separate 3D editor, and then exporting the `.mesh` and `.skeleton` files. These files are loaded automatically when you create an entity based on a mesh, which is linked to a skeleton.

Creating morph animations

Sometimes, a mesh cannot be adequately animated using skeletal animation. That's where morph animation comes in. **Morph animation** allows us to store snapshots of vertex positions in each key frame, and then interpolate between them. Because this technique is based on simple key frame snapshots, it is quite fast to use when animating an entire mesh, because it is a simple linear change between key frames. However, this simplistic approach does not support blending between multiple morph animations, so we will not use the `weight` option.

Getting ready

To follow this recipe, open the solution located in the `Recipes/Chapter07` folder in the code bundle available on the Packt website.

How to do it...

1. First, create a new Ogre MFC application named `MorphAnimation`, by following the *Creating an MFC Ogre application* recipe from *Chapter 1*.

2. Create a cube mesh to animate by loading the `cube.mesh` file that comes with the Ogre SDK.

```
Ogre::MeshPtr Mesh =
    Ogre::MeshManager::getSingleton().load("cube.mesh",
    Ogre::ResourceGroupManager::DEFAULT_RESOURCE_GROUP_NAME);

Ogre::SubMesh* SubMesh = Mesh->getSubMesh(0);
```

In the application, the initial cube mesh will look similar to the following screenshot:

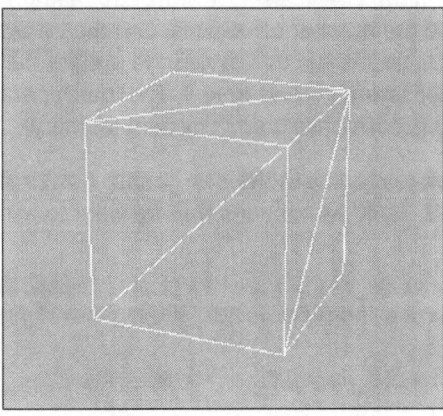

3. Re-organize the cube's geometry, since this mesh has no animations and all vertex elements are packed into one buffer.

```
Ogre::VertexDeclaration* newVertexDeclaration = SubMesh->
  vertexData->vertexDeclaration->
  getAutoOrganisedDeclaration(false, true);
```

4. Create a new vertex declaration for our reorganized buffers.

```
SubMesh->vertexData->reorganiseBuffers(newVertexDeclaration);
```

5. Find the `VES_POSITION` element in the vertex declaration, and then retrieve a pointer to the buffer that holds the position data.

```
const Ogre::VertexElement* PositionElement = SubMesh->
  vertexData->vertexDeclaration->
  findElementBySemantic(Ogre::VES_POSITION);


Ogre::HardwareVertexBufferSharedPtr PositionBuffer =
  SubMesh->vertexData->vertexBufferBinding->
  getBuffer(PositionElement->getSource());
```

6. We will be changing the vertex positions for our morph target. So, create a new position buffer with updated coordinates for each vertex.

```
Ogre::HardwareVertexBufferSharedPtr MorphBuffer =
Ogre::HardwareBufferManager::getSingleton().createVertexBuffer
(
  Ogre::VertexElement::getTypeSize(Ogre::VET_FLOAT3),
  SubMesh->vertexData->vertexCount,
  Ogre::HardwareBuffer::HBU_STATIC, true
);
```

The first parameter in the `createVertexBuffer` method is the vertex size, the second parameter is the number of vertices, and the third parameter is the buffer usage. `HBU_STATIC` means you do not need to update the buffer very often, but you might occasionally want to read from it. The fourth parameter tells the system whether you want this buffer mirrored in system memory.

7. Lock the buffers before reading in the `HBL_READ_ONLY` mode or writing in the `HBL_DISCARD` mode. `HBL_DISCARD` means that we want to write over the existing buffer destructively.

```
float* pSrc = static_cast<float*>(PositionBuffer->
  lock(Ogre::HardwareBuffer::HBL_READ_ONLY));


float* pDst = static_cast<float*>(MorphBuffer->
  lock(Ogre::HardwareBuffer::HBL_DISCARD));
```

8. Next, write the new positions for the new vertex buffer by offsetting x, y, and z values, and then unlock the buffers.

```
for (size_t VertexIndex = 0; VertexIndex < SubMesh->vertexData-
>vertexCount; ++VertexIndex)
{
  *pDst++ = (*pSrc++) + VertexIndex * 10.0f; // x
  *pDst++ = (*pSrc++) + 100.0f; // y
  *pDst++ = (*pSrc++) + VertexIndex * 10.0f; // z
}

PositionBuffer->unlock();
MorphBuffer->unlock();
```

9. Create a morph animation named `testanim`, and indicate that we want the animation length to be `10` seconds.

```
Ogre::Animation* Animation = Mesh->
  createAnimation("testAnim", 10.0f);

Ogre::VertexAnimationTrack* VertexTrack = Animation->
  createVertexTrack(1, SubMesh->vertexData, Ogre::VAT_MORPH);
```

10. Set the first key frame to use the vertex positions in the original position buffer.

```
Ogre::VertexMorphKeyFrame* KeyFrame = VertexTrack-
>createVertexMorphKeyFrame(0);
KeyFrame->setVertexBuffer(PositionBuffer);
```

11. Next, set a key frame at `5` seconds, and set the vertex buffer to our new morphed vertex buffer.

```
KeyFrame = VertexTrack->createVertexMorphKeyFrame(5.0f);
KeyFrame->setVertexBuffer(MorphBuffer);
```

12. Finally, create the final key frame at the end of the animation, using the original position vertex buffer.

```
KeyFrame = VertexTrack->createVertexMorphKeyFrame(10.0f);
KeyFrame->setVertexBuffer(PositionBuffer);
```

13. Export the mesh to a file named `testmorph.mesh`, and create an entity that uses the new mesh file.

```
Ogre::MeshSerializer Serializer;
Serializer.exportMesh(Mesh.get(), "testmorph.mesh");

Ogre::Entity* Entity = SceneManager->
  createEntity("test", "testmorph.mesh");
SceneManager->getRootSceneNode()->
  createChildSceneNode()->attachObject(Entity);
```

14. Activate the `testAnim` animation state that we created.

```
Ogre::AnimationState* animState = Entity->
  getAnimationState("testAnim");
animState->setEnabled(true);
animState->setWeight(1.0f);
m_AnimStateList.push_back(animState);
```

15. Create a timer and an `OnTimer` function to run when the timer message is received. In the `OnTimer` function, increment the animation frame time for each animation state, and then re-render the scene.

```
std::vector<Ogre::AnimationState*>::iterator AnimIterator;

for (AnimIterator = m_AnimStateList.begin(); AnimIterator !=
  m_AnimStateList.end(); ++AnimIterator)
{
  (*AnimIterator)->addTime(0.01);
}

Root->renderOneFrame();
```

How it works...

In Ogre 3D, morph animations work by storing snapshots of the absolute vertex positions in each key frame, and then interpolate between them during the animation. In this recipe, we used the original positions of a cube for the first key frame in our morph animation, and a new set of positions for the second. When we activate our animation state and increment the animation time, Ogre will interpolate the vertex positions for us, so that the vertices morph from one key frame position to the next.

When run, the application will show a normal cube breaking apart into pieces.

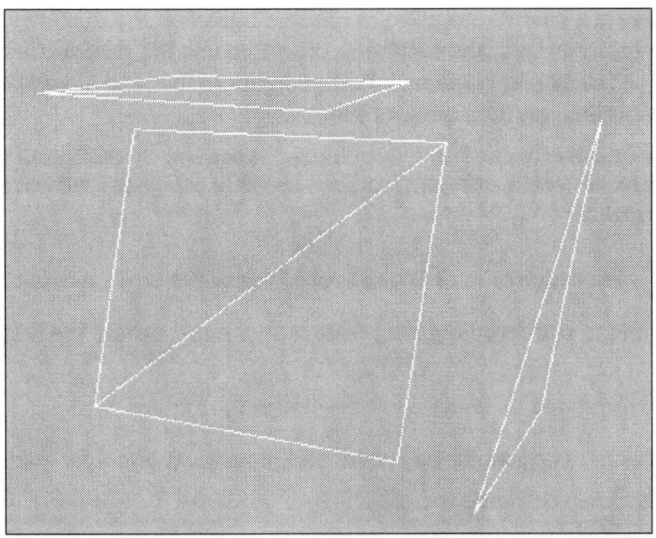

Creating pose animations

Pose animations are very popular for animating faces in various positions to express anger, fear, sorrow, or a mixture of all three. In this recipe, we will show you how to work with pose animations in Ogre 3D. Like morph animation, each animation track uses a single unique set of vertex data, but unlike morph animation, each key frame can reference more than one pose, so they can be blended.

Getting ready

To follow this recipe, open the solution located in the `Recipes/Chapter07` folder in the code bundle available on the Packt website.

How to do it...

1. First, create a new Ogre MFC application named `PoseAnimation`, by following the *Creating an MFC Ogre application* recipe from *Chapter 1*.

2. For this recipe, we will create pose animations using the vertices of a simple cube mesh. So, load the `cube.mesh` file in `CPoseAnimationView::EngineSetup()`, and get a pointer to the first and only `SubMesh` in the file.

```
Ogre::MeshPtr Mesh =
  Ogre::MeshManager::getSingleton().load("cube.mesh",
  Ogre::ResourceGroupManager::DEFAULT_RESOURCE_GROUP_NAME);
Ogre::SubMesh* SubMesh = Mesh->getSubMesh(0);
```

3. Next, generate a new `VertexDeclaration` based on the existing `VertexDeclaration`, and tell the `SubMesh` to use the new declaration. The `VertexDeclaration` contains information about the kind of vertex data stored in the vertex buffers, and the order of the data.

```
Ogre::VertexDeclaration* VertexDeclaration = SubMesh->
  vertexData->vertexDeclaration->getAutoOrganisedDeclaration
(true, true);

SubMesh->vertexData->reorganiseBuffers(VertexDeclaration);
```

4. Now, it's time to start creating the poses for our cube. Create the first pose, and name it `Pose1`.

```
Ogre::Pose* Pose = Mesh->createPose(1, "Pose1");
```

5. Next, add all the vertices for this pose, and provide an offset for each vertex.

```
Ogre::Vector3 offset1(0, 50, 0);

Pose->addVertex(0, offset1);
Pose->addVertex(1, offset1);
Pose->addVertex(2, offset1);
Pose->addVertex(3, offset1);
```

6. Create the second pose named `Pose2`, and add the vertices for this pose with a different offset.

```
Pose = Mesh->createPose(1, "Pose2");
Ogre::Vector3 offset2(100, 0, 0);
Pose->addVertex(3, offset2);
Pose->addVertex(4, offset2);
Pose->addVertex(5, offset2);
```

7. Now that we have a couple of poses to work with, create an animation named `PoseAnimation` with an animation duration of `20` seconds.

```
Ogre::Animation* anim = Mesh->
  createAnimation( "PoseAnimation", 20 );
```

8. Add an animation track to the animation object, and indicate that the track will use pose animation data.

```
Ogre::VertexAnimationTrack* track = anim->
  createVertexTrack( 1, Ogre::VAT_POSE );
```

9. Create all the key frames for the animation, and indicate which pose to use for each key frame.

```
Ogre::VertexPoseKeyFrame *PoseAnimationKeyFrame = track->
  createVertexPoseKeyFrame( 0 );
```

❑ **Frame 1**: Use pose 1 (index 0).

```
PoseAnimationKeyFrame = track->createVertexPoseKeyFrame(3);
PoseAnimationKeyFrame->addPoseReference(0, 1.0f);
```

❑ **Frame 2**: Remove all the poses, and return to default positions.

```
PoseAnimationKeyFrame = track->createVertexPoseKeyFrame(6);
```

❑ **Frame 3**: Bring in pose 2 (index 1).

```
PoseAnimationKeyFrame = track->createVertexPoseKeyFrame(9);
PoseAnimationKeyFrame->addPoseReference(1, 1.0f);
```

❑ **Frame 4**: Remove all poses again.

```
PoseAnimationKeyFrame = track->
    createVertexPoseKeyFrame(12);
```

❑ **Frame 5**: Bring in pose 1 at 50 percent, and pose 2 at 100 percent.

```
PoseAnimationKeyFrame = track->
    createVertexPoseKeyFrame(15);
PoseAnimationKeyFrame->addPoseReference(0, 0.5f);
PoseAnimationKeyFrame->addPoseReference(1, 1.0f);
```

❑ **Frame 6**: Bring in pose 1 at 100 percent and pose 2 at 50 percent.

```
PoseAnimationKeyFrame = track->
    createVertexPoseKeyFrame(18);
PoseAnimationKeyFrame->addPoseReference(0, 1.0f);
PoseAnimationKeyFrame->addPoseReference(1, 0.5f);
```

❑ **Frame 7**: Return to default positions.

```
PoseAnimationKeyFrame = track->
    createVertexPoseKeyFrame(20);
PoseAnimationKeyFrame->addPoseReference(0, 1.0f);
```

10. Export the mesh with the pose animations to a file, and then create an entity using the exported file.

```
Ogre::MeshSerializer Serializer;
Serializer.exportMesh(Mesh.get(), "testpose.mesh");

Ogre::Entity* PoseEntity = SceneManager->
    createEntity("Pose", "testpose.mesh");

Ogre::SceneNode* PoseNode = SceneManager->
    getRootSceneNode()->createChildSceneNode();
PoseNode->attachObject(PoseEntity);
```

In order to update the animation time for the animations associated with our new entity, we will need to get the correct animation state and enable it. Then we can set up a timer, and update the animation.

```
Ogre::AnimationState *PoseAnimationAnimState = PoseEntity->
  getAnimationState("PoseAnimation");

m_AnimStateList.push_back(PoseAnimationAnimState);
PoseAnimationAnimState->setTimePosition(0);

// Sets whether this animation is enabled.
PoseAnimationAnimState->setEnabled( true );
```

11. All that remains to be done is to set up a timer and a timer event handler in which we increment the animation time, and re-render the scene. Create the `CPoseAnimationView::OnTimer()` function with the following code to update the animation time:

```
std::vector<Ogre::AnimationState*>::iterator AnimIterator;

for (AnimIterator = m_AnimStateList.begin(); AnimIterator !=
  m_AnimStateList.end(); ++AnimIterator)
{

  (*AnimIterator)->addTime(0.01);
}

Root->renderOneFrame();
```

When you run the program, the cube will animate between the normal cube shape, which is the default pose, and animate to the deformed cube pose.

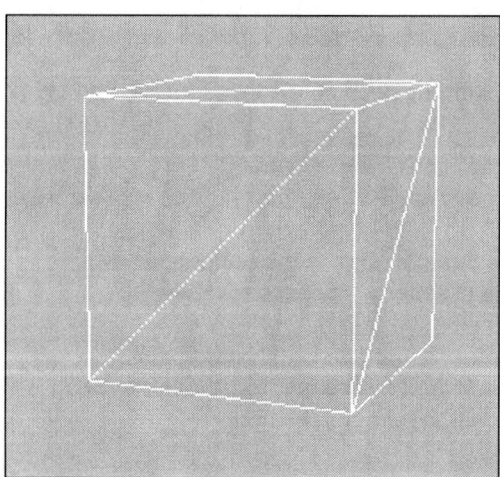

The deformed cube looks somewhat similar to a box with the top open.

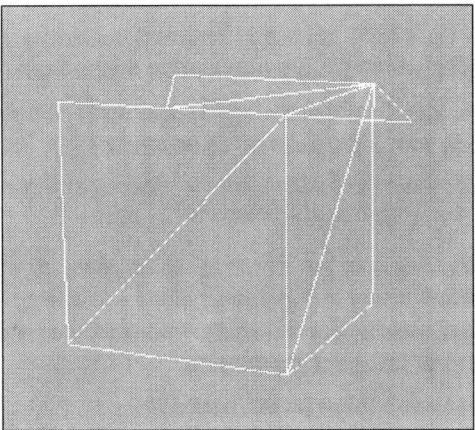

How it works...

In this recipe, we used pose animation to change the shape of a cube mesh using two poses. This technique is very popular when doing facial animation, where the facial expressions are each a separate pose, and then the pose animations are blended together. Poses can be created for a character's mouth, forming every consonant and vowel shape, and then pose animation can blend between each pose to make the mouth sync up with a speech audio file.

There's more...

The Ogre SDK comes with a face mesh named `facial.mesh`, which can be used for experimenting with facial animation.

Creating SceneNode animations

In this recipe, we will show you how to animate a scene node's orientation, scale, and position. Animating scene nodes can be a useful way to move all the entities attached to a scene node on a predetermined path. This type of animation is especially useful for cut-scenes in games, when a number of entities need to be moved around, without being affected by user input.

Getting ready

To follow this recipe, open the solution located in the `Recipes/Chapter07` folder in the code bundle available on the Packt website.

How to do it...

1. First, create a new Ogre MFC application named `SceneNodeAnimation`, by following the *Creating an MFC Ogre application* recipe from *Chapter 1*.

2. In `CSceneNodeAnimationView::EngineSetup()`, create an animation named `SphereAnimation` with a duration of `10` seconds.

```
Ogre::Animation *SphereAnimation = SceneManager->
  createAnimation("SphereAnimation", 10);
```

3. Set the interpolation mode to `IM_SPLINE`, which gives us a smoother-looking animation. The default linear interpolation mode will interpolate values between two adjacent key frames linearly, but the spline interpolation mode will interpolate the data, based on several adjacent key frames.

```
SphereAnimation->setInterpolationMode
  (Ogre::Animation::InterpolationMode::IM_SPLINE);
```

4. Next, create a node animation track for our sphere node, and create the initial key frame.

```
Ogre::NodeAnimationTrack* SphereTrack = SphereAnimation-
>createNodeTrack(1, SphereNode);
Ogre::TransformKeyFrame* SphereKey = SphereTrack-
>createNodeKeyFrame(0);
```

5. Add transform key frames, and change the rotation and position data for the transform key frames at various times in the animation.

```
SphereKey->setRotation(Ogre::Quaternion(1,1.5,0,0));
SphereKey = SphereTrack->createNodeKeyFrame(2.5);
SphereKey->setTranslate(Ogre::Vector3(70,50,-100));
SphereKey = SphereTrack->createNodeKeyFrame(5);
SphereKey->setTranslate(Ogre::Vector3(-1500,1000,-600));
SphereKey = SphereTrack->createNodeKeyFrame(7.5);
SphereKey->setTranslate(Ogre::Vector3(0,-100,0));
SphereKey = SphereTrack->createNodeKeyFrame(10);
SphereKey->setTranslate(Ogre::Vector3(0,0,0));
```

6. Next, create an animation state for our sphere animation, enable it, and set it to loop indefinitely.

```
Ogre::AnimationState *SphereAnimationState = SceneManager->
  createAnimationState("SphereAnimation");
SphereAnimationState->setEnabled(true);
SphereAnimationState->setLoop(true);
```

7. Finally, add a timer and a timer event handler named `OnTimer`. In the `OnTimer` function, advance the sphere animation and re-render the scene.

```
Ogre::AnimationState *AnimationState = SceneManager->
  getAnimationState("SphereAnimation");
AnimationState->addTime(0.01);
Root->renderOneFrame();
```

How it works...

SceneNode animation is very similar to skeleton animation, in which child scene nodes will be affected by their parent node's animation values, just as a child bone in a skeleton is affected by the parent bone. The difference between scene node animation and skeleton animation is that scene nodes have entities attached to them, not vertices, and scene nodes can be scaled, not just moved and rotated. In this recipe, we created an animation track for animating a scene node and added several key frames with various changes in the position. When the application is run, you will see a yellow sphere moving, based on the key frame positions that we set.

Creating numeric value animations

Ogre 3D gives you the ability to animate any value for any class that implements the `AnimableObject` interface. A common use for this is to animate the properties of lights in a scene to change their color or attenuation. In this recipe, we will show you how to use the numeric value animation to change the color of a light, and then access the animated value each frame.

Getting ready

To follow this recipe, open the solution located in the `Recipes/Chapter07` folder in the code bundle available on the Packt website.

How to do it...

1. First, create a new Ogre MFC application named `NumericValueAnimation`, by following the *Creating an MFC Ogre application* recipe from *Chapter 1*.

2. Create a light in `CNumericValueAnimation::EngineSetup` named `AnimatedLight`.

```
Ogre::NumericKeyFrame* kf;
Ogre::Light *Light = SceneManager->createLight("AnimatedLight");
```

3. Next, create an `AnimableValuePtr` for the named value `diffuseColour`, and set the initial value.

```
Ogre::AnimableValuePtr animableValue = Light->
  createAnimableValue("diffuseColour");
animableValue->setValue(lightInitialColor);
animableValue->setCurrentStateAsBaseValue ();
```

4. Next, create an animation named `AnimateValue` with a duration of 5 seconds.

```
Ogre::Animation *Animation = SceneManager->
  createAnimation("AnimateValue", 5);
```

5. Create a `NumericAnimationTrack`, and associate it with `AnimableValue` that we created.

```
Ogre::NumericAnimationTrack *track = Animation->
  createNumericTrack(0, animableValue);
```

6. Next, create key frames for each time index, and set the values for each key frame to a varying color of red.

```
float colourValue = 0.0;

for(int i = 1; i <= 1000; i++)
{
  kf = track->createNumericKeyFrame(i * 0.025);
  colourValue = colourValue + 0.01;
  kf->setValue( Ogre::AnyNumeric(Ogre::ColourValue
    (colourValue, 0.0, 0.0, 1.0)) );
}
```

7. Start a timer, and add a timer event handler named `OnTimer`. In the timer function, get the value from the next `NumericKeyFrame`, and set the background color of the viewport to the same color value as the light.

```
Ogre::Animation *Animation = SceneManager->
  getAnimation("AnimateValue");

Ogre::NumericAnimationTrack *track = Animation->
  getNumericTrack(0);
Ogre::NumericKeyFrame *frame = track->
  getNumericKeyFrame(m_TimeIndex++);
Ogre::AnyNumeric value = frame->getValue();
Ogre::ColourValue color = Ogre::any_cast
  <Ogre::ColourValue>(value);

Viewport->setBackgroundColour(color);

Root->renderOneFrame();
```

How it works...

The attribute we change in this recipe is the light diffuse color. When we create the key frames, we store a new color in each key frame. The key frame `setValue()` function only accepts a value of type `AnyNumeric`, so we must cast our color value to this type first. Then, when the timer function is run, we get the value for the current key frame, and set the background color with that value. The starting background color starts out black and ends bright red.

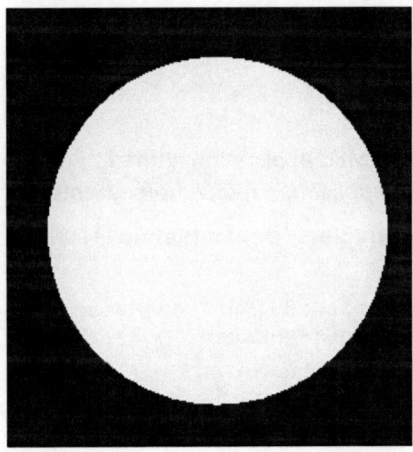

The final frame has a bright red background.

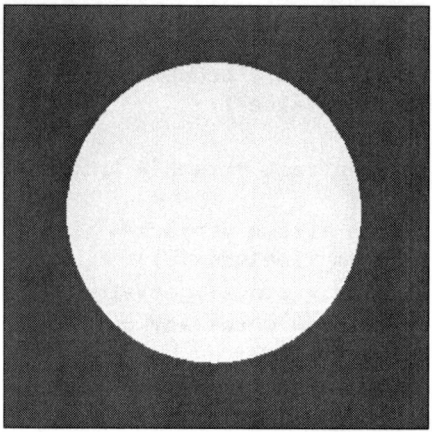

Creating linked animation

Ogre provides a useful method for re-using animations if you have two meshes that have skeletons with identically named bones, and the same bone hierarchy. In this recipe, we'll show you how to link two skeletons, so that we animate the first skeleton using the animations from the second.

Getting ready

To follow this recipe, open the solution located in the `Recipes/Chapter07` folder in the code bundle available on the Packt website.

How to do it...

1. First, create a new Ogre MFC application named `LinkedAnimation` by following the *Creating an MFC Ogre application* recipe from *Chapter 1*.

2. In `CLinkedAnimationView::EngineSetup()`, create two robot entities named `Robot1` and `Robot2`.

   ```
   Ogre::SceneNode *RobotNode1 = SceneManager->getRootSceneNode()->
     createChildSceneNode("Robot1", Ogre::Vector3(-50,0,0));

   Ogre::Entity *RobotEntity1 = SceneManager->
     createEntity("Robot1", "robot.mesh");

   RobotNode1->attachObject(RobotEntity1);
   ```

```
Ogre::SceneNode *RobotNode2 = SceneManager->getRootSceneNode()->
  createChildSceneNode("Robot2", Ogre::Vector3(50,0,0));
Ogre::Entity *RobotEntity2 = SceneManager->
  createEntity("Robot2", "robot.mesh");
RobotNode2->attachObject(RobotEntity2);
```

3. Next, set the skeletons to display their bone positions, so we can better see what is happening in the scene when they animate.

```
Ogre::Skeleton *Skeleton1 = RobotEntity1->getSkeleton();
RobotEntity1->setDisplaySkeleton(true);
Ogre::Skeleton *Skeleton2 = RobotEntity2->getSkeleton();
RobotEntity2->setDisplaySkeleton(true);
```

4. Next, add a linked skeleton animation source to the first skeleton with a scale factor of two. The scale factor is there in case there is a size difference in the two meshes. In this recipe, we are simply scaling the key frames for demonstration purposes. Our linked source is the second skeleton, since we will be using animations from the second skeleton to animate the first.

```
Skeleton1->addLinkedSkeletonAnimationSource(Skeleton2->
  getName(), 2.0);
```

5. Now that the skeletons are linked, we need to rebuild the internal structures for the entity and refresh animation states before we use any of the linked animations. Re-initialize each entity, and refresh the available animation states.

```
RobotEntity1->_initialise(true);
RobotEntity2->_initialise(true);
RobotEntity1->refreshAvailableAnimationState();
```

6. Next, set the animation states for each robot, and enable them. Save the animation states in member variables, so we can update their animation time in a timer function.

```
m_AnimationState1 = RobotEntity1->getAnimationState("Walk");
m_AnimationState1->setEnabled(true);

m_AnimationState2 = RobotEntity2->getAnimationState("Slump");
m_AnimationState2->setEnabled(true);
```

7. Finally, create a timer and a timer event handler named OnTimer. In the timer event handler function, increment the animation time for each animation state, and then re-render the scene.

```
CEngine *Engine = ((CLinkedAnimationApp*)AfxGetApp())->m_Engine;
Ogre::Root *Root = Engine->GetRoot();
m_AnimationState1->addTime(0.01);
m_AnimationState2->addTime(0.01);
Root->renderOneFrame();
```

How it works...

Ogre provides the ability to share animations between meshes, if they have skeletons with identically named bones and the same bone hierarchy. We simply link the two skeletons, refresh the internal structures, and then we can use the linked animations. The usefulness of this is mostly for saving memory and time when animating. For example, let's say your application has 100 cars in it, and they each have the same skeleton. They're all just slightly different sizes. You can use linked animation, so that all your cars share the animations from a single mesh file, instead of including the animation data in every car mesh.

The resulting application shows the two robots, their bone positions, and the linked animation.

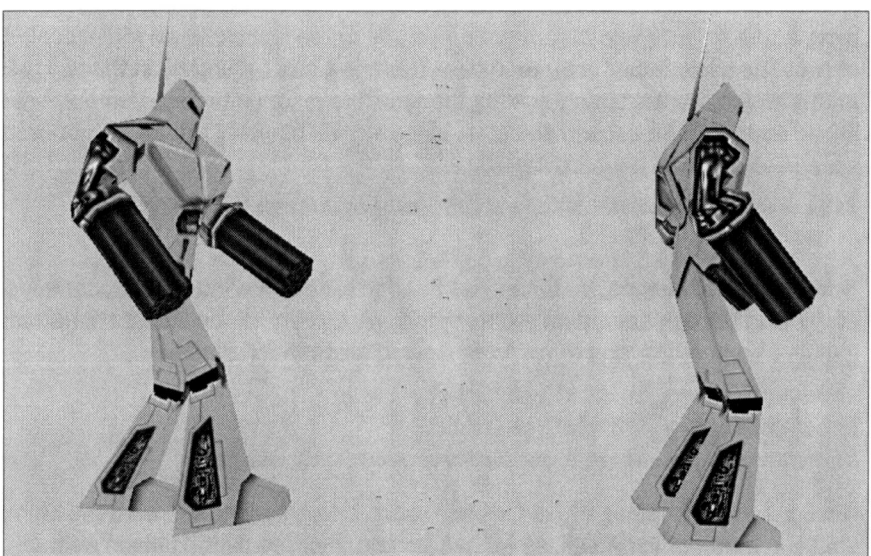

Animation using controllers

You may find in your application that you do not need the key frame animation to achieve a certain effect. One example of this might be to make a light pulse or flicker randomly. You could animate the light with key frames, but that would be time-consuming, and the end result wouldn't be as dynamic. Ogre provides controller functions and values to give us a way to animate object values, based on functions. In this recipe, we'll show you how to use controllers to animate the size of the sphere.

Getting ready

To follow this recipe, open the solution located in the `Recipes/Chapter07` folder in the code bundle available on the Packt website.

How to do it...

1. First, create a new Ogre MFC application named `UsingControllers` by following the *Creating an MFC Ogre application* recipe from *Chapter 1*.

2. Create a class named `SphereScale` with a parent class of `ControllerValue`. Add two member variables: one to store a node pointer, and one to store a scale factor. The constructor will have two parameters for setting the node and the scale, and we'll override the `getValue` and `setValue` functions to manipulate the scale of the node based on the input value.

```cpp
class SphereScale : public ControllerValue<Real>
{
  public:

    SphereScale(Node *Node, Real Scale)
    {
      m_Node = Node;
      m_Scale = Scale;
    }

    Real getValue(void) const
    {
      return m_Scale;
    }

    void setValue(Real value)
    {
      m_Scale = (value / m_Scale) + 0.5;
      m_Node->scale(m_Scale, m_Scale, m_Scale);
    }

    Node *m_Node;
    Real m_Scale;
};
```

When the controller function calls `setValue`, the value is used to calculate the scaling factor for the node.

3. Next, in `CUsingControllersView::EngineSetup()`, create a controller function pointer using the existing `Ogre::WaveformControllerFunction`, and a controller value pointer using our custom `SphereScale` controller value class.

```
Ogre::ControllerFunctionRealPtr func(OGRE_NEW
    Ogre::WaveformControllerFunction(Ogre::WFT_SINE, 0.0, 1.0));

Ogre::ControllerValueRealPtr dest(OGRE_NEW SphereScale(SphereNode,
    1.0));
```

4. Next, create the controller using the controller function and value pointers we just created.

```
Ogre::ControllerManager& ControllerManager =
    Ogre::ControllerManager::getSingleton();

m_SphereController =
    ControllerManager.createController(ControllerManager
    .getFrameTimeSource(), dest, func);
```

The first argument to `createController()` is a call to `getFrameTimeSource()`, which will give us an object that provides the controller with time information.

5. Finally, create a timer and a timer event handler named `OnTimer`. In the timer function, simply re-render the scene. Ogre will use your controller to update the animation every time we render the scene, so we do not need to increment any animation state time or anything like that. Also, add menu items to start and stop the timer, or simply start the timer in the `EngineSetup()` function.

```
CEngine *Engine = ((CUsingControllersApp*)AfxGetApp())->m_Engine;
Ogre::Root *Root = Engine->GetRoot();
Root->renderOneFrame();

CView::OnTimer(nIDEvent);
```

How it works...

Ogre's controller is an abstract concept. You can generate values based on all sorts of standard input such as time, or you can provide your own custom function for input. The values calculated from the input can then be applied to animate any object value. Controllers are extremely flexible, but the way they work can be a bit tough to wrap your head around, so you may want to experiment with other controller functions, and other controller values till you get the hang of it.

Ogre includes several controller functions, such as the `WaveControllerFunction`. So, you don't have to re-invent the wheel when it comes to common types of controllers.

When you run the application, you will see the yellow sphere's scale change based on our controller.

There's more...

The `WaveformControllerFunction` is a predefined controller function, based on a dynamic waveform. When plotted on a graph, the waveform takes the shape of a signal similar to a sine wave.

Waveform function input parameters

There are several factors for the waveform function that affect the output.

- **Wave type**: The shape of the wave
- **Base**: The wave output base value
- **Frequency**: The wave speed in cycles-per-second
- **Phase**: The wave start offset; if you set the phase to `0.5`, then the start position would be half way through the wave
- **Amplitude**: By default, the wave output will be between `0` and `1`, but it is multiplied by the amplitude value, so you can scale the output
- **Duty cycle**: The width of a pulse-width modulation

Waveform types

There are several wave types provided by Ogre.

- `WFT SINE`: Standard sine wave, which smoothly changes from low to high, and back again.
- `WFT_TRIANGLE`: An angular wave with a constant increase/decrease speed with pointed peaks.
- `WFT_SQUARE`: Half of the time is spent at the `min`, and half at the `max` with instant transition between.

- ▶ `WFT_SAWTOOTH`: Gradual steady increase from `min` to `max` over the period, with an instant return to `min` at the end.

- ▶ `WFT_INVERSE_SAWTOOTH`: Gradual steady decrease from `max` to `min` over the period, with an instant return to `max` at the end.

- ▶ `WFT_PWM`: **Pulse Width Modulation** (**PWM**) works similar to `WFT_SQUARE`, except that the high to low transition is controlled by duty cycle. A duty cycle of 50 percent (`0.5`), will give the same output as `WFT_SQUARE`.

See also

In this chapter:

- ▶ *Creating linked controllers*: This recipe shows how to re-use controller values and functions, for use with multiple entities

Creating linked controllers

You will often find that you want to provide a way to animate properties for multiple objects with different animation functions. One common example of this is the animation of the pulsing or the flickering of many lights in a scene, each with a different color. In this recipe, we'll show you how to use a controller to animate the diffuse color property for multiple light entities.

Getting ready

To follow this recipe, open the solution located in the `Recipes/Chapter07` folder in the code bundle available on the Packt website.

How to do it...

1. First, create a new Ogre MFC application named `LinkedControllers`, by following the *Creating an MFC Ogre application* recipe from *Chapter 1*.

2. In `CLinkedControllersView::EngineSetup()`, create a sphere and three billboards, and add them to the scene graph.

```
Ogre::SceneNode *SphereNode = SceneManager->
  getRootSceneNode()->createChildSceneNode("Sphere",
  Ogre::Vector3(0,0,0));

Ogre::Entity *SphereEntity = SceneManager->
  createEntity("Sphere", "sphere.mesh");

SphereEntity->setMaterialName("Wall/White");
SphereNode->attachObject(SphereEntity);
```

```
SphereEntity->getParentNode()->scale(0.5,0.5,0.5);

m_Lights = SceneManager->createBillboardSet("Lights");
m_Lights->setMaterialName("light");
SphereNode->attachObject(m_Lights);

m_RedBillBoard = m_Lights->
  createBillboard(Ogre::Vector3(0, 0, 200));

m_RedBillBoard->setColour(ColourValue::Red);

m_BlueBillBoard = m_Lights->
  createBillboard(Ogre::Vector3(200, 0, 0));

m_BlueBillBoard->setColour(ColourValue::Blue);

m_WhiteBillBoard = m_Lights->
  createBillboard(Ogre::Vector3(-200, 0, 0));


m_WhiteBillBoard->setColour(ColourValue::White);
```

In order to create the billboards, we first had to create a billboard set. Ogre 3D uses billboard sets to manage groups of billboards to speed up rendering, and provides convenience methods for working with multiple billboards.

3. Create three lights for each of the billboards, and place the lights accordingly.

```
m_RedLight = SceneManager->createLight("RedLight");
m_RedLight->setType(Light::LT_POINT);
m_RedLight->setPosition(Ogre::Vector3(0, 0, 200));
m_RedLight->setDiffuseColour(ColourValue::Red);

m_BlueLight = SceneManager->createLight("BlueLight");
m_BlueLight->setType(Light::LT_POINT);
m_BlueLight->setPosition(Ogre::Vector3(200, 0, 0));
m_BlueLight->setDiffuseColour(ColourValue::Blue);

m_WhiteLight = SceneManager->createLight("WhiteLight");
m_WhiteLight->setType(Light::LT_POINT);
m_WhiteLight->setPosition(Ogre::Vector3(-200, 0, 0));
m_WhiteLight->setDiffuseColour(ColourValue::White)
```

4. Next, create a controller class named `LightControl` that derives from `ControllerValue` as shown in the following code snippet:

```
class LightControl : public ControllerValue<Real>
{
  protected:

    Light* m_Light;
    Billboard* m_Billboard;
    ColourValue m_MaxColor;
    Real m_Intensity;

  public:

    LightControl(Light* Light, Billboard* Billboard,
      ColourValue maxColor)
    {
      m_Light = Light;
      m_Billboard = Billboard;
      m_MaxColor = maxColor;
      m_Intensity = 1.0;
    }

    virtual Real  getValue(void) const
    {
      return m_Intensity;
    }

    virtual void  setValue (Real Value)
    {
      m_Intensity = Value;
      ColourValue newColor;

      newColor.r = m_MaxColor.r * m_Intensity;
      newColor.g = m_MaxColor.g * m_Intensity;
      newColor.b = m_MaxColor.b * m_Intensity;

      m_Light->setDiffuseColour(newColor);
      m_Billboard->setColour(newColor);
    }
};
```

Our custom controller takes a light and a billboard pointer as constructor arguments. In the `setValue()` function, we modify the light and billboard color intensity based on the value parameter.

5. Back in `CLinkedControllersView::EngineSetup()`, create three controller function pointers, each with a different waveform type. The waveform for the red light will be a smooth sine wave, the blue light will use a blinking square wave, and the white light will have a punchy triangle waveform.

```
Ogre::ControllerFunctionRealPtr RedFunc(OGRE_NEW
  Ogre::WaveformControllerFunction(Ogre::WFT_SINE));

Ogre::ControllerFunctionRealPtr BlueFunc(OGRE_NEW
  Ogre::WaveformControllerFunction(Ogre::WFT_SQUARE));

Ogre::ControllerFunctionRealPtr WhiteFunc(OGRE_NEW
  Ogre::WaveformControllerFunction(Ogre::WFT_TRIANGLE));
```

6. Next, create three controller values, one for each billboard/light pair.

```
Ogre::ControllerValueRealPtr RedDest(OGRE_NEW
  LightControl(m_RedLight, m_RedBillBoard,
  Ogre::ColourValue::Red));

Ogre::ControllerValueRealPtr BlueDest(OGRE_NEW
  LightControl(m_BlueLight, m_BlueBillBoard,
  Ogre::ColourValue::Blue));

Ogre::ControllerValueRealPtr WhiteDest(OGRE_NEW
  LightControl(m_WhiteLight, m_WhiteBillBoard,
  Ogre::ColourValue::White));
```

7. Create three controllers, one for each light/billboard pair, and specify the frame time source as the input value.

```
Ogre::ControllerManager& ControllerManager =
  Ogre::ControllerManager::getSingleton();

m_RedController =
  ControllerManager.createController(ControllerManager
  .getFrameTimeSource(), RedDest, RedFunc);

m_BlueController =
  ControllerManager.createController(ControllerManager
  .getFrameTimeSource(), BlueDest, BlueFunc);

m_WhiteController =
  ControllerManager.createController(ControllerManager
  .getFrameTimeSource(), WhiteDest, WhiteFunc);
```

8. Finally, create a timer and a timer event handler named `OnTimer`. In the timer function, re-render the scene. Ogre will automatically update the controller values each time the scene is rendered. So, we will see each of the three lights diffuse color, animating according to their waveform.

```
void CLinkedControllersView::OnTimer(UINT_PTR nIDEvent)
{
CEngine *Engine = ((CLinkedControllersApp*)AfxGetApp())->m_Engine;
Ogre::Root *Root = Engine->GetRoot();
Root->renderOneFrame();
CView::OnTimer(nIDEvent);
}
```

How it works...

The Ogre 3D library provides controllers so that we can animate arbitrary properties of objects using our own functions or the built-in ones. In this recipe, we used Ogre's waveform controller functions with our own custom controller class to animate three lights, based on the frame time. One nice side effect of using controllers is that we do not need to manually increment their frame time if we use the `getFrameTimeSource()` function of `ControllerManager`; instead we simply re-render the scene.

The result of our hard work is a scene with three pulsing lights surrounding a sphere. When the animation starts, the lights are dim.

As the animation progresses, the lights change intensity based on their assigned waveform.

Blending animations

In this recipe, we will show you how to blend two animations together. This technique is very useful for making a character transition from a running animation to a standing still animation, or for using one animation to animate a character's upper body, and a different animation to animate the lower body. To show you how the different animation blending modes and weights work, we create a dialog box with controls to modify each of these properties.

Getting ready

To follow this recipe, open the solution located in the `Recipes/Chapter07` folder in the code bundle available on the Packt website.

How to do it...

1. First, create a new Ogre MFC application named `BlendingAnimations`, by following the *Creating an MFC Ogre application* recipe from *Chapter 1*.

2. In `CBlendingAnimationsView::EngineSetup()`, create a robot entity, and add it to the scene.

```
Ogre::SceneNode *RobotNode = SceneManager->
  getRootSceneNode()->createChildSceneNode("Robot",
  Ogre::Vector3(50,0,0));

Ogre::Entity *RobotEntity = SceneManager->
  createEntity("Robot", "robot.mesh");

Ogre::MeshPtr Mesh = RobotEntity->getMesh();
```

```
RobotNode->attachObject(RobotEntity);
RobotEntity->getParentNode()->scale(0.2,0.2,0.2);
```

3. Next, set the robot's skeleton to be visible, and the camera mode to wireframe, so that we can better visualize the blending effect.

```
RobotEntity->setDisplaySkeleton(true);
m_Camera->setPolygonMode(Ogre::PolygonMode::PM_WIREFRAME);
```

When the skeleton is set to display, the bone locations appear as tiny axis arrows in the scene.

4. Create two `Ogre::AnimationState` pointer member variables; one named `m_WalkAnimation` for the `Walk` animation state, and the other named `m_SlumpAnimation` for the `Slump` animation state.

```
m_WalkAnimation = RobotEntity->getAnimationState("Walk");
```

```
m_WalkAnimation->setEnabled(true);

m_SlumpAnimation = RobotEntity->getAnimationState("Slump");
m_SlumpAnimation->setEnabled(true);
```

5. Next, add a menu named **Animation**. Create menu items named **Start walk**, **Start slump**, **Start blend**, **Stop walk**, **Stop slump**, and **Stop blend**. Add event handlers for each of these menu items.

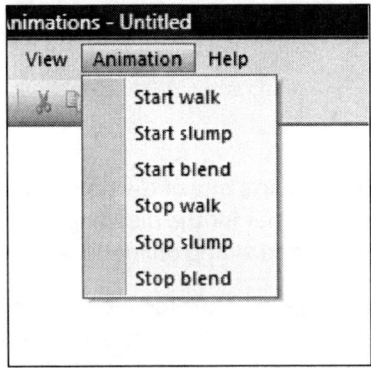

In each event handler add code to start and stop the appropriate timers.

```
void CBlendingAnimationsView::OnAnimationStart()
{
  SetTimer(1, 1, 0);
  KillTimer(2);
  KillTimer(3);
}


void CBlendingAnimationsView::OnAnimationStop()
{
  KillTimer(1);
}


void CBlendingAnimationsView::OnAnimationStartwalk()
{
  SetTimer(2, 1, 0);
  KillTimer(1);
  KillTimer(3);
}


void CBlendingAnimationsView::OnAnimationStartslump()
{
  SetTimer(3, 1, 0);
```

```
     KillTimer(2);
     KillTimer(1);
}

void CBlendingAnimationsView::OnAnimationStopwalk()
{
     KillTimer(2);
}

void CBlendingAnimationsView::OnAnimationStopslump()
{
     KillTimer(3);
}
```

Each event handler stops or starts one of the timers that we will use to update our animations. We use the first timer for the blending animation, and the other two timers are used for the walk and slump animations.

16. Create a dialog box to manage the skeleton blending modes and the weights of each animation. For the bending modes, create radio buttons named **Average** and **Cumulative**. Next, create two sliders with labels **Walk weight** and **Slump weight**.

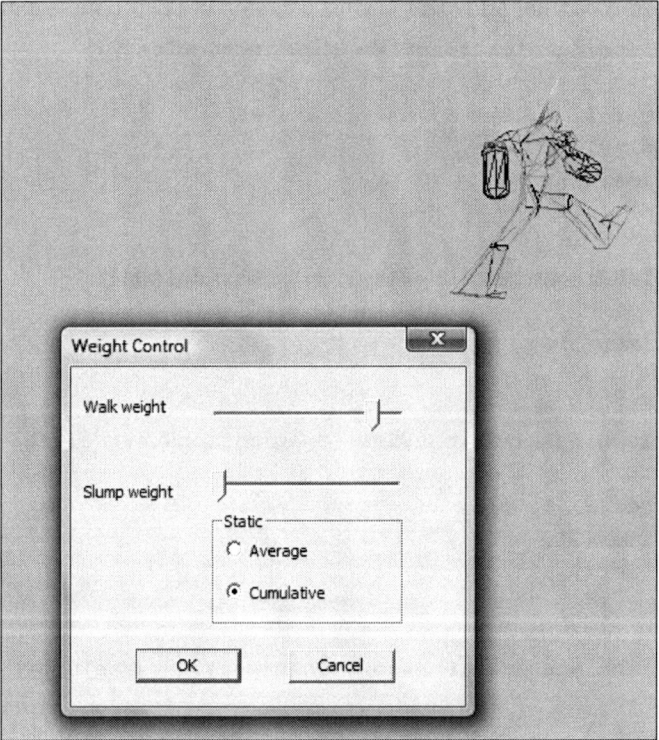

17. Start a timer in `CBlendingAnimationsView::EngineSetup()`, and add a timer
    event handler named `OnTimer`. In the `OnTimer` function, check the state of the
    radio-buttons and the sliders, and update the animation if there are any changes.

```
Ogre::Skeleton *Skeleton = RobotEntity->getSkeleton();

if (m_WeightDlg->m_IsAverage)
{
Skeleton->setBlendMode
    (Ogre::SkeletonAnimationBlendMode::ANIMBLEND_AVERAGE);
}
else
{
Skeleton->setBlendMode
    (Ogre::SkeletonAnimationBlendMode::ANIMBLEND_CUMULATIVE);
}
```

If the **Average** radio button is selected, we set the blending mode to `ANIMBLEND_`
`AVERAGE`, which will result in the final visible animation being a weighted average of
all the animations. If the **Cumulative** radio button is selected, we set the blending
mode to `ANIMBLEND_CUMULATIVE`, which will result in the visible animation being
calculated using the weighted cumulative total of all the animations.

```
double WalkWeight;
double SlumpWeight;

switch(nIDEvent)
{
  case 1:

    WalkWeight = m_WeightDlg->m_WalkWeight.GetPos() / 10.0;
    SlumpWeight = m_WeightDlg->m_SlumpWeight.GetPos() / 10.0;
    m_WalkAnimation->setWeight(WalkWeight);
    m_SlumpAnimation->setWeight(SlumpWeight);

    m_WalkAnimation->addTime(0.01);
    m_SlumpAnimation->addTime(0.01);

  break;

  case 2:

    m_WalkAnimation->addTime(0.01);

  break;
```

```
    case 3:

        m_SlumpAnimation->addTime(0.01);

    break;
}

Root->renderOneFrame();
```

We also check the slider positions, and change the animation weights for the walk and slump animations. The last thing to do is to increment the time for each animation, and re-render the scene.

How it works...

We can use Ogre to blend animations and achieve various effects, by indicating the blend mode and the weights of the animations to be blended. Blended animations are useful for transitioning from one animation to another; for example, a running animation to a standing still one. We can also use blending to use one animation for the top of a character, and one for the bottom. This is commonly used to make the legs run, stand still, or jump, while the top animation does something else, such as a weapon firing animation.

The two animation modes are ANIMBLEND_AVERAGE and ANIMBLEND_CUMULATIVE. For ANIMBLEND_AVERAGE, all the weights must add up to 1.0, and if the sum of all the animation weights is not 1.0, then Ogre normalizes the weights. When using ANIMBLEND_CUMULATIVE, Ogre will use the weight of each animation without any rebalancing. Cumulative blending can be used for skeletal, pose, or morph animations, but only skeletal animations can use the blended average mode.

Creating animated light

In this recipe, we'll show you how to use a node animation track to make a light and a billboard fly around the scene. The method for animating a light is similar to the *Creating SceneNode animations* recipe, except we attach a light to a SceneNode.

Getting ready

To follow this recipe, open the solution located in the Recipes/Chapter07 folder in the code bundle available on the Packt website.

How to do it...

1. First, create a new Ogre MFC application named `AnimatedLight`, by following the *Creating an MFC Ogre application* recipe from *Chapter 1*.

2. In `CAnimatedLightView::EngineSetup()`, create a sphere for the light to fly around, and add it to the scene.

```
Ogre::SceneNode *SphereNode = SceneManager->
  getRootSceneNode()->createChildSceneNode("Sphere",
  Ogre::Vector3(0,0,0));

Ogre::Entity *SphereEntity = SceneManager->
  createEntity("Sphere", "sphere.mesh");

SphereEntity->setMaterialName("Wall/Screen");
SphereNode->attachObject(SphereEntity);

SphereEntity->getParentNode()->scale(0.2,0.2,0.2);
```

3. Next, create a spotlight named `AnimLight`, and add it to the scene.

```
Ogre::Light* AnimatedLight = SceneManager->
  createLight("AnimLight");

AnimatedLight->setType(Ogre::Light::LT_SPOTLIGHT);

AnimatedLight->setDiffuseColour
  (Ogre::ColourValue(0.25f,0.25f,0.0f));

AnimatedLight->setSpecularColour
  (Ogre::ColourValue(0.25f,0.25f,0.0f));

AnimatedLight->setAttenuation(8000,1,0.0005,0);

AnimatedLight->setSpotlightRange(Ogre::Degree(60),
  Ogre::Degree(70));


AnimatedLight->setDirection(Ogre::Vector3::NEGATIVE_UNIT_Y);
```

To make this light a spotlight, we set the type to `LT_SPOTLIGHT`, and provide a direction and spotlight range. The first parameter for `setSpotlightRange()` is the inner cone, and the second parameter is for the outer cone.

4. Next, create a billboard set and add a single billboard to the set to represent the light source. This billboard will automatically face the camera in any position.

```
Ogre::BillboardSet* LightBillboardSet =
  SceneManager->createBillboardSet("LightBillboardSet", 1);

LightBillboardSet->setMaterialName("Examples/Flare");

Ogre::Billboard* LightBillboard = LightBillboardSet->
  createBillboard(0,0,0,Ogre::ColourValue(0.5,0.3,0.0f));
```

5. Next, create a scene node named `AnimLightNode`, and attach the light and the billboard set to it. We will animate this scene node to move the light around the scene.

```
Ogre::SceneNode* AnimLightNode = SceneManager->
  getRootSceneNode()->createChildSceneNode("AnimLightNode");

AnimLightNode->attachObject(AnimatedLight);
AnimLightNode->attachObject(LightBillboardSet);

AnimLightNode->setPosition(20.0, 20.0, 0.0);
AnimLightNode->setScale(0.05f, 0.05f, 0.05f);
```

6. Create an animation instance named `LightAnimation` with a duration of 4 seconds, and use `IM_SPLINE` as the interpolation mode. The spline interpolation will make the changes in direction appear smoother.

```
Ogre::Animation* Animation = SceneManager->
  createAnimation("LightAnimation", 4.0);
Animation->setInterpolationMode(Ogre::Animation::IM_SPLINE);
```

7. Next, create a node animation track, and add five key frames to the animation.

```
Ogre::NodeAnimationTrack* track = Animation->
  createNodeTrack(0, AnimLightNode);

Ogre::TransformKeyFrame* key;

key = track->createNodeKeyFrame(0.0f);
key->setTranslate(Ogre::Vector3(-20.0f, -20.0f, 0.0f));
key->setScale(Ogre::Vector3(0.05f,0.05f,0.05f));
```

```
key = track->createNodeKeyFrame(1);
key->setTranslate(Ogre::Vector3( -20.0f, 20.0f,0.0f));
key->setScale(Ogre::Vector3(0.05f,0.05f,0.05f));

key = track->createNodeKeyFrame(2.0);
key ->setTranslate(Ogre::Vector3( 20.0f, 20.0f, 0.0f));
key->setScale(Ogre::Vector3(0.05f,0.05f,0.05f));

key = track->createNodeKeyFrame(3.0);
key->setTranslate(Ogre::Vector3(20.0f, -20.0f, 0.0f));
key->setScale(Ogre::Vector3(0.05f,0.05f,0.05f));

key = track->createNodeKeyFrame(4.0);
key->setTranslate(Ogre::Vector3(-20.0f, -20.0f,0.0f));
key->setScale(Ogre::Vector3(0.05f,0.05f,0.05f));
```

8. Now create a member variable named `m_LightAnimationState`, and assign it a new animation state named `LightAnimation`. Set the animation state to `loop`, and enable it.

```
m_LightAnimationState = SceneManager->
  createAnimationState("LightAnimation");
m_LightAnimationState->setEnabled(true);
m_LightAnimationState->setLoop(true);
```

9. Finally, create a timer and a timer event handler named `OnTimer`. In `OnTimer`, add code to increment the animation time, and re-render the scene.

```
CEngine *Engine = ((CAnimatedLightApp*)AfxGetApp())->m_Engine;
Ogre::Root *Root = Engine->GetRoot();

m_LightAnimationState->addTime(0.01);

Root->renderOneFrame();
```

How it works...

In this recipe, we used node animation to move a light and a billboard. After creating the light and the billboard, and attaching them to a scene node, we added key frames for an animation, with different positions and scales. When the application runs, the scene node moves according to the positions set in the animation key frames, and we see the light and the billboard flying around.

There's more...

You can use scene node animation to move the light, and a controller to animate the light intensity and color.

See also

In this chapter:

► *Animation using controllers*: This recipe shows how to create an animation controller

8
Flashy Multimedia

In this chapter, we will cover the following recipes:

- ▸ Render to texture
- ▸ Creating a mirror
- ▸ Creating a video
- ▸ Using sounds
- ▸ Using voice
- ▸ Video to texture

Introduction

Have you ever wanted to add video and audio to your 3D application? It may seem a daunting task to get a large video into a 3D application, but we'll show you how. In addition to video, we'll cover the basics of rendering to a texture in Ogre, and show you how to include sound in your application.

Render to texture

In this recipe, we'll introduce Ogre's method of rendering to a texture, by showing you how to render the contents of a camera viewport onto a texture in a 3D scene. This technique is the basis for many useful effects, including shadow maps, GPU-based calculations, deferred rendering, and so on.

Getting ready

To follow this recipe, open the solution located in the `Recipes/Chapter08` folder in the code bundle available on the Packt website.

How to do it...

1. First, create a new Ogre MFC application named `RTT`, by following the *Creating an MFC Ogre application* recipe from *Chapter 1, Delving Deep into Application Design*.

2. In `CMirrorView::EngineSetup()`, add a robot to the scene to give us something to reflect.

```
Ogre::Entity *RobotEntity = m_SceneManager->
  createEntity("Robot", "robot.mesh");

Ogre::SceneNode *RobotNode = m_SceneManager->
  getRootSceneNode()->createChildSceneNode();

RobotNode->attachObject(RobotEntity);
```

3. Next, create a second camera named `RTTCam`. We will use this camera to render the scene for the render texture.

```
m_RTTCamera = m_SceneManager->createCamera("RTTCam");
m_RTTCamera->setNearClipDistance(m_Camera->getNearClipDistance());
m_RTTCamera->setFarClipDistance(m_Camera->getFarClipDistance());

m_RTTCamera->setAspectRatio( (Ogre::Real)
  m_RenderWindow->getViewport(0)->getActualWidth() /(Ogre::Real)
  m_RenderWindow->getViewport(0)->getActualHeight());

m_RTTCamera->setPosition(Ogre::Vector3(200.0, 50.0, 100.0));
m_RTTCamera->lookAt(Center);
```

4. Create a function named `createRTT` in which we will put all the code for displaying a viewport in a texture.

```
void CRTTView::createRTT(Ogre::String planeName,
                         Ogre::String texName,
                         Ogre::Camera* Camera,
                         Ogre::Real sizeX,
                         Ogre::Real sizeY,
                         Ogre::Vector3 position
                         )
{
}
```

5. First, create a plane and add it to the scene. This plane will be our render texture surface, and we will change the texture on it, so that it shows the scene from the view of our RTT camera.

```
m_Plane = new Ogre::MovablePlane(planeName + "_RTTPlane");
m_Plane->d = 0;
m_Plane->normal = Ogre::Vector3::UNIT_Y;

Ogre::MeshManager::getSingleton().createPlane(planeName +
  "_RTTPlane",
  Ogre::ResourceGroupManager::DEFAULT_RESOURCE_GROUP_NAME,
  *m_Plane, sizeX, sizeY,
  1, 1, true, 1, 1, 1, Ogre::Vector3::UNIT_Z);

m_PlaneEntity = m_SceneManager->createEntity(planeName + "_Plane",
  planeName + "_RTTPlane");

Ogre::SceneNode *PlaneNode = m_SceneManager->
  getRootSceneNode()->createChildSceneNode();

PlaneNode->attachObject(m_PlaneEntity);
PlaneNode->attachObject(m_Plane);

PlaneNode->setPosition(position);
```

The createPlane method takes the following parameters: name, group, plane, width, height, number of segments in the x direction, number of segments in the y direction, a flag to create normals, one texture coordinate set, one tile in the u direction, one tile in the v direction, and the up direction of the plane, which is the z-axis.

6. Next, create a TU_RENDERTARGET texture, specify the width and height to be 512 pixels, and the pixel format to be PF_R8G8B8.

```
Ogre::TexturePtr texture =
  Ogre::TextureManager::getSingleton().createManual(texName,
  Ogre::ResourceGroupManager::DEFAULT_RESOURCE_GROUP_NAME,
  Ogre::TEX_TYPE_2D, 512, 512, 0, Ogre::PF_R8G8B8,
  Ogre::TU_RENDERTARGET);
```

The TU_RENDERTARGET texture unit parameter indicates to Ogre that we want this texture to be able to receive the data from a viewport.

7. Now, get the `RenderTarget` for the texture, and add the viewport from our `RTT` camera.

```
Ogre::RenderTarget *RenderTarget = texture->
  getBuffer()->getRenderTarget();


Ogre::Viewport *Viewport = RenderTarget->addViewport(Camera);
```

This instructs Ogre to render the contents of the `RTT` camera viewport into this texture buffer.

8. Next, create a material, and add a texture unit state to the first pass using the same name as we used for the texture that we created. Ogre will use the texture name parameter to link our custom texture to this material.

```
Ogre::MaterialPtr Material = Ogre::MaterialManager::getSinglet
on().create(texName,
  Ogre::ResourceGroupManager::DEFAULT_RESOURCE_GROUP_NAME);


Ogre::TextureUnitState* TextureUnitState =
  Material->getTechnique(0)->
  getPass(0)->createTextureUnitState(texName);
```

9. Set the texture addressing mode to `TAM_CLAMP`, so the texture doesn't repeat at the edges of the plane. Also, set the projective texturing flag to `true`, and indicate the camera to use the perspective. By using the camera perspective to generate projected texture coordinates, we get the impression that our custom texture is projected onto the plane.

```
TextureUnitState->
  setTextureAddressingMode(Ogre::TextureUnitState::TAM_CLAMP);


TextureUnitState->setProjectiveTexturing(true, Camera);
RenderTarget->setAutoUpdated(true);
```

10. Assign the new material to our plane entity.

```
        m_PlaneEntity->setMaterialName(Material.get()->getName());
```

11. If you run the program at this point, the surface will have two problems: it will display itself, and it will display items below the surface. To fix the plane from displaying itself, we need to hide it before the `RTT` camera updates, and reveal it again when the updating is complete.

12. Create a new class named `RTTListener` that derives from `Ogre::RenderTargetListener`, and add the following code to it.

```
class RTTListener : public Ogre::RenderTargetListener
{
  public:
    RTTListener():Ogre::RenderTargetListener()
    {
      m_PlaneEntity = NULL;
    }

    void preRenderTargetUpdate(const Ogre::RenderTargetEvent& evt)
    {
      if (m_PlaneEntity != NULL)
        m_PlaneEntity->setVisible(false);

    }
    void postRenderTargetUpdate(const Ogre::
      RenderTargetEvent& evt)
    {
      if (m_PlaneEntity != NULL)
        m_PlaneEntity->setVisible(true);
    }

  Ogre::Entity *m_PlaneEntity;

};
```

13. Back in `CRTTView::createRTT()`, create an instance of our `RTTListener`. Set the plane entity member variable, and add the listener to our render target.

```
RTTListener *Listener = new RTTListener;
Listener->m_PlaneEntity = m_PlaneEntity;
RenderTarget->addListener(Listener);
```

14. To take care of the surface showing objects below the plane, we set the near clipping plane for the RTT camera to be the plane itself. In this way, everything in front of the near clipping plane will be hidden.

```
Camera->enableCustomNearClipPlane(m_Plane);
```

How it works...

Ogre uses render to texture, to store the contents of camera viewport in a texture. That texture can then be displayed on a mesh in the scene, or used to perform calculations, or for many other useful things. The process requires jumping through the right hoops, to connect a camera with a texture. In this recipe, we created a suitable texture for receiving the contents of a camera viewport, and set up a camera for rendering the scene to that texture. We then created a plane mesh with a material that used this texture, so that we could see the results of our hard work in the application.

There's more...

When the user moves the camera in our application, we should update the position and orientation of the RTT camera to match it. Add the following code to update the RTT camera in all the places where the main camera position or orientation changes.

```
m_RTTCamera->setPosition(m_Camera->getPosition());
m_RTTCamera->setOrientation(m_Camera->getOrientation());
```

Creating a mirror

One common use of render to texture is for creating flat-mirrored surfaces in 3D applications. In this recipe, we'll show you how to create a mirror, by extending on the techniques presented in the *Render to texture* recipe.

Getting ready

To follow this recipe, open the solution located in the `Recipes/Chapter08` folder in the code bundle available on the Packt website.

How to do it...

1. First, create a new Ogre MFC application named `Mirror`, by following the *Creating an MFC Ogre application* recipe from *Chapter 1*.

2. Create a class called `MirrorListener` that derives from `Ogre::RenderTargetListener`. We will use this listener class to hide the mirror entity when the **Render To Texture** (**RTT**) camera renders the scene, and then unhide the mirror when the main camera renders the scene.

```
class MirrorListener : public Ogre::RenderTargetListener
{
  public:

    MirrorListener():Ogre::RenderTargetListener()
    {
      m_PlaneEntity = NULL;
    }

    void preRenderTargetUpdate(const Ogre::RenderTargetEvent& evt)
    {
      if (m_PlaneEntity != NULL)
        m_PlaneEntity->setVisible(false);
    }

    void postRenderTargetUpdate(const Ogre::
RenderTargetEvent& evt)
    {
      if (m_PlaneEntity != NULL)
        m_PlaneEntity->setVisible(true);
    }

    Ogre::Entity *m_PlaneEntity;

};
```

3. Next, in `CMirrorView::EngineSetup()`, create a robot entity, so that we have something to reflect in the scene.

```
Ogre::Entity *RobotEntity = m_SceneManager->createEntity("Robot",
  "robot.mesh");

Ogre::SceneNode *RobotNode = m_SceneManager->
  getRootSceneNode()->createChildSceneNode();

RobotNode->attachObject(RobotEntity);
```

4. Next, create the RTT camera to use for rendering the scene from the mirror perspective.

```
m_MirrorCamera = m_SceneManager->createCamera("MirrorCamera");

m_MirrorCamera->setNearClipDistance(m_Camera
  ->getNearClipDistance());

m_MirrorCamera->setFarClipDistance(m_Camera
  ->getFarClipDistance());

m_MirrorCamera->setAspectRatio( (Ogre::Real)m_RenderWindow
  ->getViewport(0)->getActualWidth() /
  (Ogre::Real)m_RenderWindow->getViewport(0)->getActualHeight());

m_MirrorCamera->setPosition(Ogre::Vector3(200.0, 50.0, 100.0));


m_MirrorCamera->lookAt(Center);
```

5. Now that the mirror camera exists, create a utility function named `createMirror`, and call that function from `EngineSetup`. We'll put all our code for the mirror entity setup in there.

```
createMirror("Mirror","Mirror",m_MirrorCamera, 500, 500,
  Ogre::Vector3(100.0, 0.0, 0.0));
```

6. In `CMirrorView::createMirror()`, create a plane entity for our mirror, and add it to the scene.

```
void CMirrorView::createMirror(Ogre::String planeName,
                               Ogre::String texName,
                               Ogre::Camera* MirrorCamera,
                               Ogre::Real sizeX,
                               Ogre::Real sizeY,
                               Ogre::Vector3 position)
{
  m_MirrorPlane = new Ogre::MovablePlane(planeName +
  "_mirrorplane");
```

```
m_MirrorPlane->d = 0;
m_MirrorPlane->normal = Ogre::Vector3::UNIT_Y;

Ogre::MeshManager::getSingleton().createPlane(planeName +
"_mirrorplane",
  Ogre::ResourceGroupManager::DEFAULT_RESOURCE_GROUP_NAME,
  *m_MirrorPlane, sizeX, sizeY,
  1, 1, true, 1, 1, 1, Ogre::Vector3::UNIT_Z);

m_MirrorEntity = m_SceneManager->createEntity(planeName +
  "_plane", planeName + "_mirrorplane" );

Ogre::SceneNode *mMainNode = m_SceneManager->getRootSceneNode()
  ->createChildSceneNode();

mMainNode->attachObject(m_MirrorEntity);
mMainNode->attachObject(m_MirrorPlane);

mMainNode->setPosition(position);
```

7. Next, create the texture and material to use for the mirror. It is important that we specify the texture type as `TU_RENDERTARGET`, so that Ogre can create a texture that can receive the contents of a camera viewport.

```
Ogre::TexturePtr texture = Ogre::
  TextureManager::getSingleton().createManual(texName + "_rttrex",
  Ogre::ResourceGroupManager::DEFAULT_RESOURCE_GROUP_NAME,
  Ogre::TEX_TYPE_2D,
  512, 512, 0, Ogre::PF_R8G8B8, Ogre::TU_RENDERTARGET );

Ogre::RenderTarget *rttTex = texture->getBuffer()->
  getRenderTarget();

Ogre::Viewport *v = rttTex->addViewport(MirrorCamera);
v->setClearEveryFrame(true);
v->setBackgroundColour(Ogre::ColourValue::White);

Ogre::MaterialPtr mat =
  Ogre::MaterialManager::getSingleton().create(texName + "rttmat",
  Ogre::ResourceGroupManager::DEFAULT_RESOURCE_GROUP_NAME);

Ogre::TextureUnitState* t = mat->getTechnique(0)->getPass(0)->
  createTextureUnitState(texName + "_rttrex");

t->setTextureAddressingMode(Ogre::TextureUnitState::TAM_CLAMP);
t->setProjectiveTexturing(true, MirrorCamera);
rttTex->setAutoUpdated(true);
```

8. Assign the new material to the mirror entity, and add our `MirrorListener`, which will hide and unhide the mirror, depending on which camera is rendering the scene.

```
m_MirrorEntity->setMaterialName(mat.get()->getName());
MirrorListener *Listener = new MirrorListener;
Listener->m_PlaneEntity = m_MirrorEntity;
rttTex->addListener(Listener);
```

9. The last step is to enable reflection for the mirror camera, so that it renders the scene from a reflected perspective, and to enable a custom near plane, so that the mirror camera does not render anything below the mirror surface.

```
MirrorCamera->enableReflection(m_MirrorPlane);
MirrorCamera->enableCustomNearClipPlane(m_MirrorPlane);
}
```

How it works...

In this recipe, we used the same `RTT` technique as the one in the *Render to texture* recipe. The main difference is that for the mirror effect, we enabled the reflection for the mirror camera. So, it always renders the scene from the reflection perspective through the specified plane.

Creating a video

In this recipe, we will show you how to capture the contents of a camera viewport, and use them to create a video file. This technique is especially useful if you want to record a video of your 3D application or game.

Getting ready

To follow this recipe, open the solution located in the `Recipes/Chapter08` folder in the code bundle available on the Packt website.

How to do it...

1. First, create a new Ogre MFC application named `Video`, by following the *Creating an MFC Ogre application* recipe from *Chapter 1*.

2. Add a menu named **Video**, and two sub-items named **Start** and **Stop**.

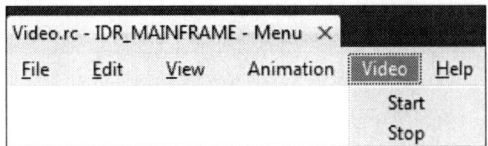

3. Next, create event handlers named `onVideoStart()` and `onVideoStop()` for the two new menu sub-items.

4. In `CVideoView::OnVideoStart`, initialize the AVI library, and create a file stream for writing the AVI file to.

```
void CVideoView::OnVideoStart()
{
  AVIFileInit();

  AVIFileOpen(&aviFile, "output.avi",OF_WRITE | OF_CREATE,NULL);

  int Left;
  int Top;
```

5. Prepare an AVI stream info structure with all the details of the video stream we are about to create.

```
AVISTREAMINFO  psi;
ZeroMemory(&psi,sizeof(psi));

psi.fccType = streamtypeVIDEO;// stream type
```

```
psi.fccHandler = 0;
psi.dwScale = 24;
psi.dwRate = 1000;
psi.dwSuggestedBufferSize = 0;
```

Set the stream type to `streamtypeVIDEO` as we are creating a video stream. The `dwScale` variable is for the time scale for the video. The `dwRate` variable is for setting the rate. The AVI library will obtain the playback rate by dividing `dwRate` by `dwScale`, to get the playback rate in number of samples per second.

6. Next, create the file stream that we will write our render data to, passing in the file handle, the pointer to the new stream interface, and the pointer to the AVI stream info `struct` that we just created.

```
AVIFileCreateStream(aviFile,&aviStream,&psi);

AVIFileRelease(aviFile);

AVIStreamInfo(aviStream,&aviStreamInfo,sizeof(aviStreamInfo));
```

7. Now that the stream has been prepared, start a timer and create a new member function named `OnTimer` to handle the timer event.

```
SetTimer(1, 1, 0);
}
```

8. Create a new member variable named `data` to hold the contents of the viewport in a format that we can write to the video stream.

```
Ogre::uchar *data;
```

9. In `CVideoView::OnTimer()`, copy the contents of the render viewport into our temporary buffer, and write the temporary buffer to the video stream.

```
Ogre::PixelFormat pf = m_RenderWindow->suggestPixelFormat();

m_RenderWindow->getMetrics(mWidth, mHeight, mColorDepth,
  Left, Top);

data = OGRE_ALLOC_T(Ogre::uchar, mWidth * mHeight *
  Ogre::PixelUtil::getNumElemBytes(pf),
  Ogre::MEMCATEGORY_RENDERSYS);

Ogre::PixelBox m_PixelBox(mWidth, mHeight, mColorDepth, pf, data);

switch (nIDEvent)
{
  case 1:
    m_RenderWindow->copyContentsToMemory(m_PixelBox);
```

```
AVIStreamWrite(aviStream, m_FrameNumber++, 1, m_PixelBox.data,
    m_PixelBox.getHeight() * m_PixelBox.getHeight() * 4,
    AVIIF_KEYFRAME, NULL, NULL);
```

In order to get the right size of the data buffer, we get the pixel format for the render window and the window metrics. Next, we create a data buffer using the window metrics to calculate the size. We specify the memory category as `MEMCATEGORY_RENDERSYS` because that category is for render system structures. After creating a data buffer we use Ogre's `PixelBox` utility class to copy the contents of the render window into the data buffer. We then use the `AVIStreamWrite` function to write the data buffer to the video stream. Note that we also increment the frame number member variable here as well. So each time the timer function is run, we are writing the next frame.

10. In `CVideoView::OnVideoStop()`, kill the timer so that we stop writing data to the AVI stream, release the AVI stream, and free the data buffer.

```
void CVideoView::OnVideoStop()
{
    KillTimer(1);

    AVIStreamRelease(aviStream);

    OGRE_FREE(data, Ogre::MEMCATEGORY_RENDERSYS);
}
```

How it works...

In this recipe, we created an AVI video file using the Video for Windows AVI library. The library calls we used were:

- ▶ `AVIFileInit`: It initializes the AVIFile library
- ▶ `AVIFileOpen`: It opens an AVI file, and returns the address of a file interface used to access it
- ▶ `AVIFileCreateStream`: It creates a new stream using an existing file and an `AVISTREAMINFO` structure
- ▶ `AVIStreamInfo`: It obtains the stream header information
- ▶ `AVIStreamWrite`: It writes data to the video stream
- ▶ `AVIStreamRelease`: It releases a stream handle, and closes the stream when all handles are released

In the timer callback function, we allocated space for a data buffer to hold the contents of the render window, and wrote those contents of the buffer to the AVI stream with the correct frame number. When the stop video function is called, we release the AVI stream, and end recording.

You can use this technique to create video demos of your 3D application without any other external screen recording software.

Using sounds

Sounds can be integrated with animations in a variety of ways. In this recipe, we'll show you how to trigger sounds, using controllers. This technique can be useful when you want to play sounds based on the current frame time, or even if you just want to leverage Ogre's existing controller functionality.

Getting ready

To follow this recipe, open the solution located in the `Recipes/Chapter08` folder in the code bundle available on the Packt website.

It may be useful to review the voice and speech recipes from *Chapter 2, Let Us Be Multimodal*, and the controller-based recipes from the *Chapter 7, Implementing Animations*. You'll also need to prepare a set of sound `.wav` files to play.

How to do it...

1. First, create a new Ogre MFC application named `Sounds`, by following the *Creating an MFC Ogre application* recipe from *Chapter 1*.

2. In `CSoundsView::EngineSetup()`, add a robot to the scene, and activate the robot's `Walk` animation state.

```
Ogre::Entity *RobotEntity = m_SceneManager->
    createEntity("Robot", "robot.mesh");

Ogre::SceneNode *RobotNode = m_SceneManager->
    getRootSceneNode()->createChildSceneNode();

RobotNode->attachObject(RobotEntity);

Ogre::AxisAlignedBox Box = RobotEntity->getBoundingBox();
Ogre::Vector3 Center = Box.getCenter();
m_Camera->lookAt(Center);

m_WalkAnimation = RobotEntity->getAnimationState("Walk");
m_WalkAnimation->setEnabled(true);
```

3. In this recipe, we will use the **Microsoft® Speech SDK** to play audio. In `Sounds.h`, include the API header, and create a member variable named `m_cpVoice`.

```
#include <sapi.h>

class CSoundsApp : public CWinAppEx
{
  public:
    //…

    CComPtr<ISpVoice> m_cpVoice;
```

4. In `CSounds::InitInstance()`, prepare the API for use.

```
m_cpVoice.CoCreateInstance(CLSID_SpVoice);
```

5. Back in `CSoundsView::EngineSetup()`, get a pointer to the API interface, so that we can pass it to our controller.

```
CSoundsApp* SoundsApp = (CSoundsApp*)AfxGetApp();
CComPtr<ISpVoice> Voice = SoundsApp->m_cpVoice;
```

6. Next, add a member variable named `m_SoundController` of type `Ogre::Controller<Ogre::Real>*` to `CSoundsView`. Then, in `CSoundsView::EngineSetup()`, create a controller function pointer, a controller value pointer, and a controller using `m_SoundController`.

```
Ogre::ControllerFunctionRealPtr func(OGRE_NEW
  Ogre::WaveformControllerFunction(Ogre::WFT_SAWTOOTH));

Ogre::ControllerValueRealPtr dest(OGRE_NEW
  CSoundController(SoundPath, Voice));

Ogre::ControllerManager& ControllerManager =
  Ogre::ControllerManager::getSingleton();


m_SoundController = ControllerManager
  .createController(ControllerManager.getFrameTimeSource(),
  dest, func);
```

We pass the pointer to the `voice` API to our custom sound controller, so that it can use it to play the audio files based on the controller input values.

7. Next, create a new file named `SoundController.h`, and define a new class named `CSoundController` that derives from `Ogre::ControllerValue` in it. This will be our custom sound controller class that will play sounds based on the value passed in to the `setValue()` function. In this recipe, we use the frame time as the value to select new sounds, so as the application runs and the frame time increments, new sounds will be played.

```cpp
class CSoundController : public ControllerValue<Real>
{
  public:
    CString Sounds[10];

    CString m_SoundPath;
    Real m_SoundIndex;
    CComPtr<ISpVoice> m_Voice;

    CSoundController(CString SoundPath, CComPtr<ISpVoice> Voice)
    {
      m_SoundPath = SoundPath;
      m_Voice = Voice;
      m_SoundIndex = 0;

      Sounds[0] = "boatsteam.wav";
      Sounds[1] = "carcrash.wav";
      Sounds[2] = "earlycarengine.wav";
      Sounds[3] = "ferrari250.wav";
      // …
    }

    Real getValue(void) const
    {
      return m_SoundIndex;
    }
```

You will need to modify the sound filenames in the constructor of `CSoundController` to match the filenames of your sounds.

The `setValue()` function contains the logic for playing a sound based on the input value, which is the frame time. We use an `ISpStream` interface to create an object from a file suitable for SAPI usage, using the `BindToFile` function, which binds the audio stream to the specified file. We then play the file using the `SpeakStream` API function. The sound file to play is chosen using the input `value` parameter.

```cpp
void setValue(Real value)
{
  CComPtr<ISpStream> cpWavStream;
```

```
    int Index = (int)(value * 4);

    if ((int)m_SoundIndex == Index)
    {
      //do nothing
    }
    else
    {
      m_SoundIndex = Index;

      CString SoundPath = m_SoundPath + "\\" + Sounds[Index];

      SPBindToFile(SoundPath, SPFM_OPEN_READONLY, &cpWavStream);

      m_Voice->SpeakStream(cpWavStream, SPF_ASYNC |
        SPF_PURGEBEFORESPEAK, NULL);

      //m_Voice->Resume();
    }
}
```

The SpeakStream function plays the contents of a stream cpWavStream with flags used to control the playback process. The allowed flag values are SPF_ASYNC, which specifies that the call should be asynchronous, and SPF_PURGEBEFORESPEAK, which purges all pending speak requests prior to this call. We use asynchronous playback, because we want the audio to play using a background thread, so that we can continue rendering while the audio is playing.

8. Finally, create a timer and a timer event handler named OnTimer to update the animation time.

```
void CSoundsView::OnTimer(UINT_PTR nIDEvent)
{
  m_WalkAnimation->addTime(0.001);

  CEngine *Engine = ((CSoundsApp*)AfxGetApp())->m_Engine;
  Ogre::Root *Root = Engine->GetRoot();
  Root->renderOneFrame();

  CView::OnTimer(nIDEvent);
}
```

How it works...

The **SAPI** library gives us the functionality to play audio files. In this recipe, we will trigger audio playback by creating a controller with a custom controller value class named CSoundController. Every time the OnTimer function is called, we increment the frame time, and Ogre automatically updates our custom controller and gives it the new frame time. Our custom controller uses that frame time to select a sound file to play.

Using voice

The SAPI can also be used to speak text, which can be useful when you want to make your 3D models talk, or simply to provide a synthesized voice for an AI character in your game. In this recipe, we'll show you how to use the text-to-speech functionality and animation to make two characters speak lines from Shakespeare's Hamlet.

Getting ready

To follow this recipe, open the solution located in the Recipes/Chapter08 folder in the code bundle available on the Packt website.

How to do it...

1. First, create a new Ogre MFC application named Voice, by following the *Creating an MFC Ogre application* recipe from *Chapter 1*.

2. In Voice.h, include the SAPI header, and create a member variable named m_cpVoice for the SAPI interface.

   ```
   #include <sapi.h>

   class CVoiceApp : public CWinAppEx
   {
     public:
       // ...
       CComPtr<ISpVoice> m_cpVoice;
   ```

   The ISpVoice interface enables our application to perform text synthesis operations. With it, our applications can speak text strings and text files, or play audio synchronously or asynchronously.

3. Next, in VoiceView.h, define an ISpObjectToken member variable for each voice. In this recipe, we'll be using two voices.

   ```
   CComPtr<ISpObjectToken> m_cpVoiceToken1;
   CComPtr<ISpObjectToken> m_cpVoiceToken2;
   ```

4. Create an `IEnumSpObjectTokens` member variable for each of the voice object tokens.

   ```
   CComPtr<IEnumSpObjectTokens> m_cpEnum1;
   CComPtr<IEnumSpObjectTokens> m_cpEnum2;
   ```

5. We are going to animate two characters in the scene. So, create two animation state member variables for us to control the animations with. We will also need a member variable named `m_Event` to control the next event in our little play.

   ```
   Ogre::AnimationState *m_WalkAnimation1;
   Ogre::AnimationState *m_WalkAnimation2;
   int m_Event;
   ```

6. In `CVoiceApp::InitInstance()`, prepare the SAPI interface for use.

   ```
   m_cpVoice.CoCreateInstance(CLSID_SpVoice);
   ```

7. In `CVoiceView::EngineSetup()`, create two robot entities, and add them to the scene. Next, get pointers to their `Walk` animation states, and enable each.

   ```
   Ogre::Entity *RobotEntity1 = m_SceneManager->
     createEntity("Robot1", "robot.mesh");

   Ogre::SceneNode *RobotNode = m_SceneManager->getRootSceneNode()->
     createChildSceneNode(Ogre::Vector3(-100, 0, 0));

   RobotNode->attachObject(RobotEntity1);

   Ogre::Entity *RobotEntity2 = m_SceneManager->
     createEntity("Robot2", "robot.mesh");

   RobotNode = m_SceneManager->getRootSceneNode()->
     createChildSceneNode(Ogre::Vector3(0, 0, 0));

   RobotNode->attachObject(RobotEntity2);

   m_WalkAnimation1 = RobotEntity1->getAnimationState("Walk");
   m_WalkAnimation2 = RobotEntity2->getAnimationState("Walk");

   m_WalkAnimation1->setEnabled(true);
   m_WalkAnimation2->setEnabled(true);
   ```

   Now the robots are in the scene, and ready to be animated.

8. The only setup that remains for the SAPI voice tokens is to assign the voice to use. The following code indicates that we want to use the Microsoft® Anna voice, and assign it to our voice token:

```
SpEnumTokens(SPCAT_VOICES, L"Name=Microsoft Anna",
  NULL, &m_cpEnum1);


m_cpEnum1->Next(1, &m_cpVoiceToken1, NULL );


SpEnumTokens(SPCAT_VOICES, L"Name=Microsoft Anna", NULL,
  &m_cpEnum2);


m_cpEnum2->Next(1, &m_cpVoiceToken2, NULL );
```

`SpEnumTokens` enumerates the tokens for the specified category (`voices`). Next retrieves the next object token in the enumeration sequence.

9. Create a menu item named `Animation`, and two sub-items named `Start` and `Stop`, and create event handlers for each. In the event handler for the `Start` sub-item, start a timer, and set our event variable to `0`.

```
void CVoiceView::OnAnimationStart()
{
  m_Event = 0;
  SetTimer(1,1,0);
}
```

10. Next, add a timer event handler function named `OnTimer`, and use the `m_Event` member variable to determine the correct voice to play and use the event ID parameter to set the correct animation.

```
void CVoiceView::OnTimer(UINT_PTR nIDEvent)
{
  switch (nIDEvent)
  {
    case 1: //main loop

    switch(m_Event)
    {
      case 0:

        SetTimer(2,1,0);

        m_Voice->SetVoice(m_cpVoiceToken1);
        m_Voice->Speak(L"Hamlet 0.txt", SPF_ASYNC |
          SPF_IS_FILENAME, NULL);
        m_Event++;
```

```
      break;
    case 1:

      SetTimer(3,1,0);

      m_Voice->SetVoice(m_cpVoiceToken2);
      m_Voice->Speak(L"Hamlet 1.txt", SPF_ASYNC |
        SPF_IS_FILENAME, NULL);
      m_Event++;
    break;
    case 2:

      SetTimer(2,1,0);

      m_Voice->SetVoice(m_cpVoiceToken1);
      m_Voice->Speak(L"Hamlet 2.txt", SPF_ASYNC |
        SPF_IS_FILENAME, NULL);
      m_Event++;
    break;
    case 3:

      SetTimer(3,1,0);

      m_Voice->SetVoice(m_cpVoiceToken2);
      m_Voice->Speak(L"Hamlet 3.txt", SPF_ASYNC |
        SPF_IS_FILENAME, NULL);
      m_Event++;
    break;
    default:
    break;
    }
  break;
  case 2: //first robot speaking

    m_WalkAnimation1->addTime(0.01);
  break;
  case 3: //second robot speaking

    m_WalkAnimation2->addTime(0.01);
  break;
  }
```

We use the SetVoice function to indicate the voice to use for the following call to Speak, which does the actual text-to-speech conversion using the provided text file. We also add time to the animation for the robot that is currently acting. In a real application, it would be more appropriate for the animation to match the dialog, but this gives you the general idea of how to make it work.

How it works...

The SAPI can take a text file or a text string, and speak the text using a voice. The sound playback can be synchronous or asynchronous, but most of the time, you will use asynchronous playback because it plays the audio using a background process, and the `Speak` function returns immediately rather than after the sound playback finishes. If we used the synchronous playback, then rendering would stop while the voice played.

Video to texture

Just as we are able to take the contents of a render window buffer and create a video with it, we can take a frame from a video, and display it in a texture in our 3D application. To play the video in the texture, we simply update the contents of the texture with frames from the video at the correct time. In this recipe, we will show you how to play a movie in a 3D scene using a dynamic texture that we manually update.

Getting ready

To follow this recipe, open the solution located in the `Recipes/Chapter08` folder in the code bundle available on the Packt website.

How to do it...

1. First, create a new Ogre MFC application named `VideoInTexture`, by following the *Creating an MFC Ogre application* recipe from *Chapter 1*.

2. Create a new utility class to manage the video-to-texture functionality, named `CVideoTexture`.

```
class CVideoTexture
{
  public:
    CVideoTexture(void);
    ~CVideoTexture(void);
    CVideoTexture(Ogre::SceneManager *SceneManager, Ogre::Real
      Width, Ogre::Real Height, LPCTSTR szFile);

    Ogre::SceneManager *m_SceneManager;

    int m_FrameNumber;

    PGETFRAME   m_Frame;
    BITMAPFILEHEADER m_BMPFileHeader;
    PAVIFILE    m_aviFile;
```

```
PAVISTREAM   m_aviStream;
AVISTREAMINFO  m_aviStreamInfo;
BITMAPINFOHEADER m_bmpInfo;

Ogre::HardwarePixelBufferSharedPtr m_PixelBuffer;
};
```

3. In the constructor of our new `CVideoTexture` class, create a new texture for us to write the video frame data to.

```
Ogre::TexturePtr VideoTexture =
  Ogre::TextureManager::getSingleton().createManual(
    "Video",
    Ogre::ResourceGroupManager::DEFAULT_RESOURCE_GROUP_NAME,
    Ogre::TEX_TYPE_2D, 640, 480, 0, Ogre::PF_R8G8B8A8,
    Ogre::TU_DYNAMIC_WRITE_ONLY_DISCARDABLE);
```

We set texture type to 2D with a width and height of 640 by 480, a pixel format of PF_R8G8B8A8, and a texture usage mode of TU_DYNAMIC_WRITE_ONLY_ DISCARDABLE. The texture usage mode TU_DYNAMIC_WRITE_ONLY_DISCARDABLE indicates that we intend to update the texture buffer often, and that since we will be updating the entire buffer, there is no need to retain the buffer contents when we are writing to it. We also will not be reading from the texture buffer, which is why we use the write only mode.

4. Store a pointer to the texture pixel buffer in a member variable named `m_PixelBuffer` for easy access.

```
m_PixelBuffer = VideoTexture->getBuffer();
```

5. We need to display the texture on some object in the scene, so create a manual object named `Screen`, and provide the vertex data to create a simple plane out of triangles with the appropriate texture coordinates.

```
Ogre::ManualObject *Screen = SceneManager->
  createManualObject("Screen");

Screen->setDynamic(true);
Screen->begin("Video", Ogre::RenderOperation::OT_TRIANGLE_LIST);

Screen->position(0,0,0);
Screen->textureCoord(0,0);

Screen->position(Width,0,0);
Screen->textureCoord(1,0);

Screen->position(Width,Height,0);
Screen->textureCoord(1,1);
```

```
Screen->triangle(0, 1, 2);

Screen->position(0,0,0);
Screen->textureCoord(0,0);

Screen->position(Width,Height,0);
Screen->textureCoord(1,1);

Screen->position(0,Height,0);
Screen->textureCoord(0,1);

Screen->triangle(3, 4, 5);

Screen->end();
```

6. Next, add the plane to the scene at the origin.

```
Ogre::SceneNode* node = SceneManager->getRootSceneNode()-
    >createChildSceneNode();
node->setPosition(0, 0, 0);
node->attachObject(Screen);
```

7. Before we can use the AVI library, we need to initialize it. After that, open the AVI file, and save a pointer to the AVI stream in a member variable named m_aviStream.

```
AVIFileInit();

AVIFileOpen(&m_aviFile, szFile, OF_READ,NULL);

AVIFileGetStream(m_aviFile, &m_aviStream, streamtypeVIDEO, 0);
AVIFileRelease(m_aviFile);
```

8. Next, use the AVIStreamInfo library function to get the information about the stream that we'll need about the video, and store it in a member variable named m_aviStreamInfo.

```
AVIStreamInfo(m_aviStream, &m_aviStreamInfo,
    sizeof(m_aviStreamInfo));
```

9. After we have the stream info, fill out a BITMAPINFOHEADER struct with the correct height, width, and compression mode, and use AVIStreamGetFrameOpen to indicate to the AVI library the format we want the AVI frame data in.

```
memset(&m_bmpInfo, 0, sizeof(BITMAPINFOHEADER));
m_bmpInfo.biSize = sizeof(BITMAPINFOHEADER) ;
m_bmpInfo.biBitCount = 32;
m_bmpInfo.biCompression = BI_RGB;
m_bmpInfo.biHeight = 480;
m_bmpInfo.biWidth = 640;
```

```
m_bmpInfo.biPlanes = 1;
m_bmpInfo.biSizeImage = 0;

m_FrameNumber = 0;
m_Frame = AVIStreamGetFrameOpen(m_aviStream, &m_bmpInfo);
}
```

10. Now it's time to use our `CVideoTexture` class in our application. In `VideoInTextureView.h`, add a member variable named `m_VideoTexture` that is a pointer to a `CVideoTexture`. Then, in `CVideoTextureView::EngineSetup`, create an instance of the `CVideoTexture`, and pass in the video dimensions and the filename.

```
m_VideoTexture = new CVideoTexture(m_SceneManager, 640.0, 480.0,
  "somename.avi");
```

11. Create a new menu named `Video`, and add two sub-items named `Stop` and `Start`. Add event handlers for `Stop` and Start that activate or de-activate a timer.

```
void CVideoInTextureView::OnVideoStart()
{
  SetTimer(1, 1, 0);
}


void CVideoInTextureView::OnVideoStop()
{
  KillTimer(1);
}
```

12. Create a timer event handler function named `OnTimer`, add the necessary code to retrieve frame data for a specific frame from the AVI stream, write it to the custom texture, and re-render the scene.

```
void CVideoInTextureView::OnTimer(UINT_PTR nIDEvent)
{
  if (m_VideoTexture->m_FrameNumber == m_VideoTexture->
    m_aviStreamInfo.dwLength)
  {
    KillTimer(1);
    return;
  }

  LPBITMAPINFOHEADER lpbi =
    (LPBITMAPINFOHEADER)AVIStreamGetFrame(m_VideoTexture->m_Frame,
    ++m_VideoTexture->m_FrameNumber);

  LPVOID GetFrame = AVIStreamGetFrame(m_VideoTexture->
    m_Frame, ++m_VideoTexture->m_FrameNumber);
```

```
      if (lpbi == NULL)
      {
        KillTimer(1);
        return;
      }

      m_VideoTexture->m_PixelBuffer->
        lock(Ogre::HardwareBuffer::HBL_DISCARD);

      memcpy(m_VideoTexture->m_PixelBuffer->getCurrentLock().data,
        lpbi + lpbi->biSize + 25, lpbi->biSizeImage);

      m_VideoTexture->m_PixelBuffer->unlock();

      Ogre::Root *Root = ((CVideoInTextureApp*)AfxGetApp())->
        m_Engine->GetRoot();

      Root->renderOneFrame();

      CView::OnTimer(nIDEvent);
    }
```

Before we grab the frame data from the AVI stream, we must check if there are no more video frames left. To do that, we check if our current frame number is equal to the `AVIStreamInfo` `dwLength` variable.

If we haven't reached the end of the video, we get the next frame in a decompressed format using `AVIStreamGetFrame`, then write the frame data into the pixel buffer, and re-render the scene.

How it works...

Displaying a video in a 3D scene is a two-step process. First, we must get the frame data from the video file. The second step is to take that frame data, and copy it into a texture. In this recipe, we used the video for Windows AVI library to retrieve the video data from a video file in a format that is decompressed and compatible with Ogre 3D. Then, we copy that raw video frame into the pixel buffer of our texture and re-rendered the scene.

When you run the application, and press the **Video | Start** menu item, you will see the video playing in a texture inside our 3D scene. The applications of this technique are numerous, and honestly, the process is very straightforward. We're simply moving bits around; the difficulty is often in converting from a video file format to one that is supported by Ogre.

9
Queries and Views

In this chapter, we will cover the following recipes:

- ▶ Predefined views
- ▶ Zoom management
- ▶ Zooming to a selected object
- ▶ Orbiting an object
- ▶ Selecting objects
- ▶ Object visibility

Introduction

When creating a 3D application, you inevitably must address the problem of selecting objects in the scene, whether for collision testing, or analyzing. After you have solved the problem of selecting an object, it is often useful to have the ability to rotate around the object to view the object's features, or to zoom in to view features more closely. In this chapter, we will show you how to select objects in a 3D scene, and then manipulate the camera to orbit the object, or zoom in on it.

Predefined views

Modeling and texturing applications, such as many 3D applications, often need to provide a way to view the objects from different perspectives in multiple windows. In this recipe, we will show you how to manipulate a camera to view an object from several perspectives that are commonly used in the 3D utility applications.

Getting ready

To follow this recipe, open the solution located in the `Recipes/Chapter09` folder in the code bundle available on the Packt website.

How to do it...

1. First, create a new Ogre MFC Ribbon application named `ViewManager` by following the *Creating an MFC Ogre application with a Ribbon* recipe from *Chapter 1, Delving Deep into Application Design*.

2. In `CViewManagerView::EngineSetup()`, create a cube entity, and add it to the scene.

   ```
   Ogre::Entity *CubeEntity = m_SceneManager->createEntity("Cube",
     "cube.mesh");

   CubeEntity->setMaterialName("Examples/SceneCubeMap1");

   Ogre::SceneNode *CubeNode = m_SceneManager->
     getRootSceneNode()->createChildSceneNode("Cube");

   CubeNode->attachObject(CubeEntity);
   ```

3. Next, create a toolbar that contains the following bitmap for predefined views:

   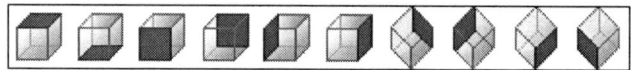

   Each cube represents a predefined view.

4. Next, add a category named `3D View` to the ribbon, and a panel named `3D Views` to the category. Then, add a gallery button to the panel, and apply the toolbar to it.

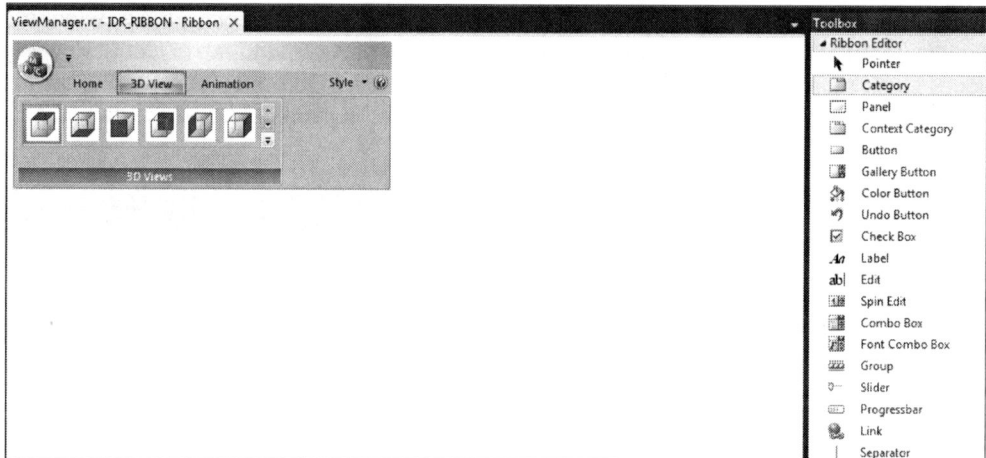

5. Add a second category named `Animation` to the ribbon, and add two buttons named `Start` and `Stop`. Add event handlers for the new buttons that start and stop a timer.

```
void CViewManagerView::OnStartAnimation()
{
  SetTimer(1, 1, 0);
}


void CViewManagerView::OnStopAnimation()
{
  KillTimer(1);
}
```

6. Next, create a timer event handler function named `OnTimer()`, and in it, re-render the scene. If your application has animated objects, this is where you would update the animation frame time.

```
void CViewManagerView::OnTimer(UINT_PTR nIDEvent)
{
  // update any animations here

  CEngine *Engine = ((CViewManagerApp*)AfxGetApp())->m_Engine;
  Ogre::Root *Root = Engine->GetRoot();
  Root->renderOneFrame();

  CView::OnTimer(nIDEvent);
}
```

7. Right-click on the 3D View toolbar, and add an event handler.

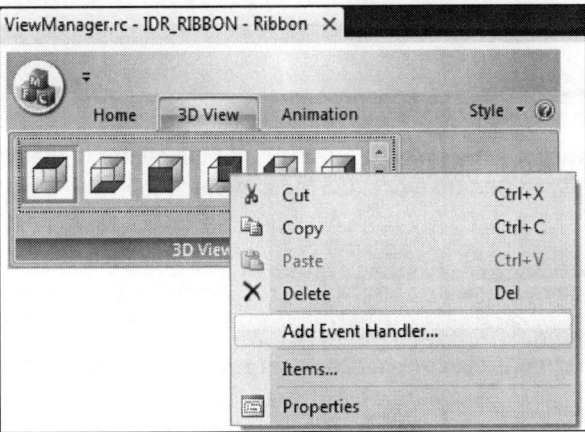

Click on **Add Event Handler...** on the shortcut menu, and the **Event Handler Wizard** will appear.

8. Select the COMMAND message type in the **Message type** box, and CViewManagerView in the **Class list** box. Leave the default name in the **Function handler name** field, then click on **Add and edit** to add the event handler to the project, and open the text editor.

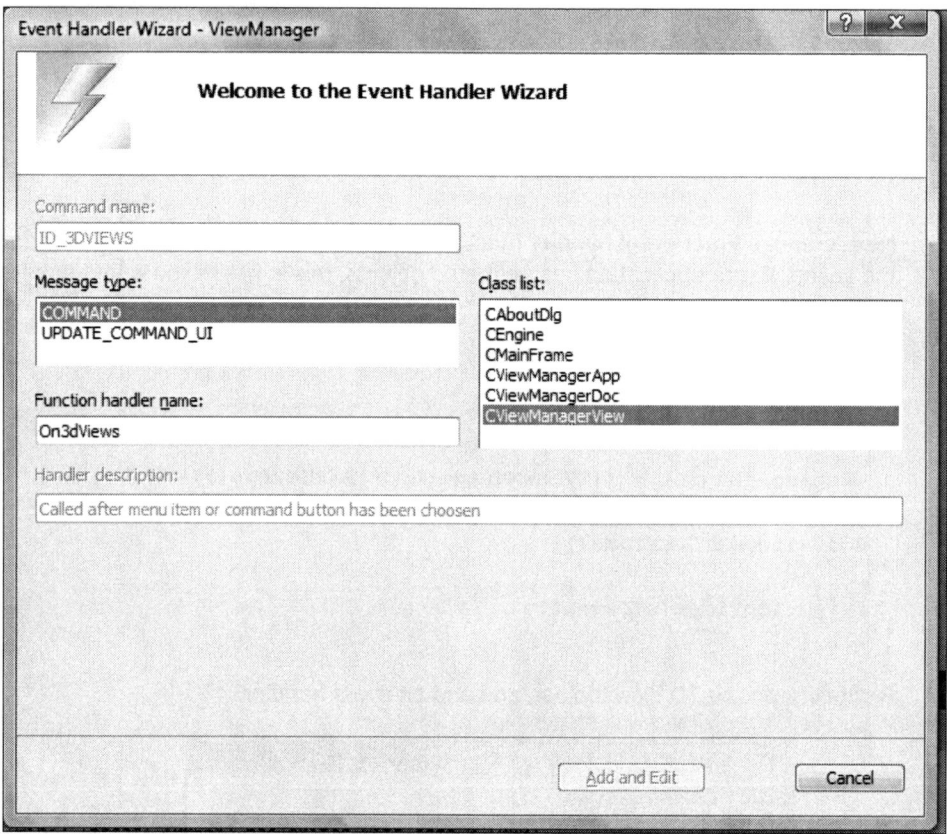

9. In CViewManagerView::On3dViews(), get the center of the cube we want the camera to look at, and then position the camera to look at the cube from the selected perspective.

```cpp
void CViewManagerView::On3dViews()
{
  int ViewIndex =
    CMFCRibbonGallery::GetLastSelectedItem(ID_3DVIEWS);

  CEngine *Engine = ((CViewManagerApp*)AfxGetApp())->m_Engine;
  Ogre::Root *Root = Engine->GetRoot();
```

```cpp
Ogre::SceneNode *CubeNode = m_SceneManager->
  getSceneNode("Cube");

Ogre::AxisAlignedBox Box = m_SceneManager->
  getRootSceneNode()->_getWorldAABB();
Ogre::Vector3 Center = Box.getCenter();
Ogre::Vector3 Position;
Ogre::Vector3 Destination;

switch (ViewIndex)
{
  case 2:

    Position = Center;
    Position.x += 4.0 * Box.getSize().x;
                  Destination = Center;

  break;

  case 3:

    Position = Center;
    Position.x -= 4.0 * Box.getSize().x;
    Destination = Center;

  break;

  // add the other views here...

  case 9:

    CubeNode->roll(Ogre::
      Radian(-atan(sin(Ogre::Math::PI/4.0))));
    CubeNode->yaw(Ogre::Radian(Ogre::Math::PI/4.0));
    Destination = Center;
    Position = m_Camera->getPosition();

  break;
}

m_Camera->setPosition(Position);
m_Camera->lookAt(Destination);
Root->renderOneFrame();
}
```

The position for `top`, `bottom`, `left`, `right`, `front`, and `back` are calculated by adding a predefined amount to x, y or z. To calculate the isometric perspective, we roll the camera, and then yaw to position it over the object looking down at an angle.

How it works...

In this application, you are able to select a predefined view using the buttons in the ribbon. When a button is pressed, we move the camera to the appropriate location, and re-render the scene. All of the predefined views are standard in most 3D utility applications, including the isometric view.

 An isometric view is one in which the coordinate axes appear equally foreshortened, and the angles between the projection of the x, y, and z axes are all 120 degrees.

When the application runs the initial view will be slightly off-center.

When a 3D View button is pressed, the camera view will update to show the new perspective. In the following image, the front perspective is shown:

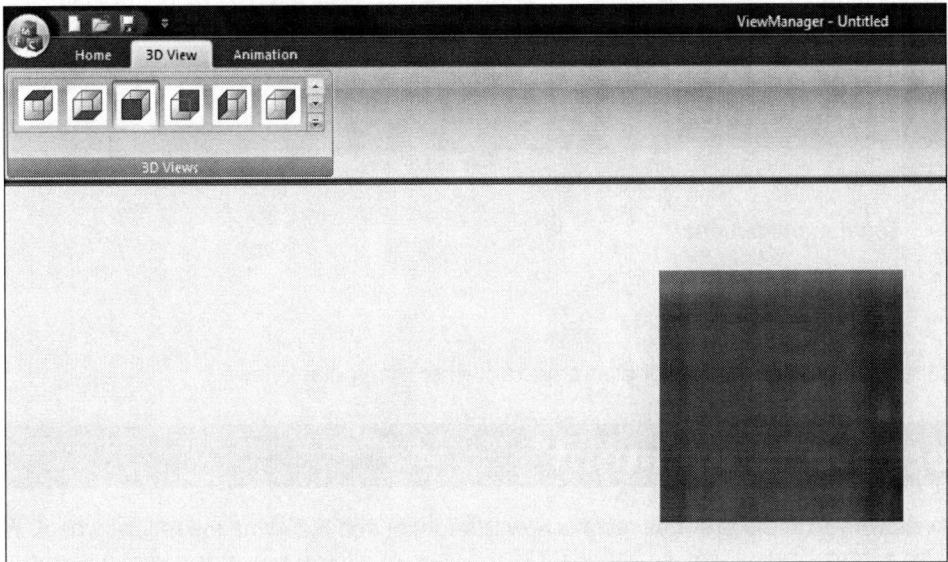

By pressing the last button in the 3D View panel, you will see an isometric view of the cube.

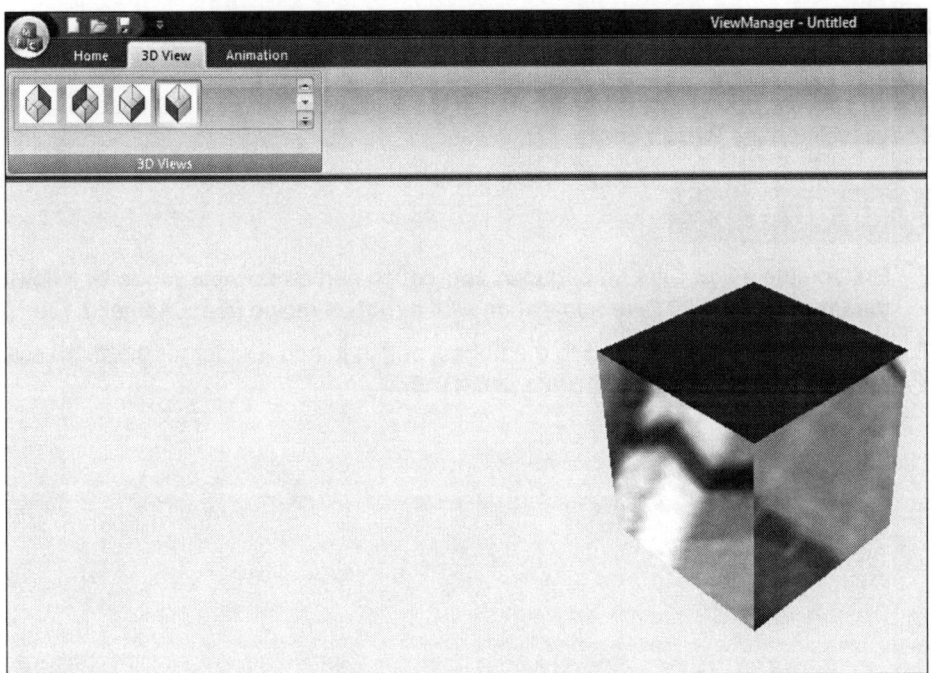

There's more...

In addition to these predefined views, it is often useful to allow the user to create their own saved perspectives, so that they can return to a view quickly.

See also

In this chapter:

- ▸ *Zoom management*
- ▸ *Zooming to a selected object*
- ▸ *Orbiting an object recipes*

These recipes provide instructions on ways to further manipulate views.

Zoom management

We've shown you in the previous recipes how to zoom in and out using the mouse wheel. We can also automatically zoom, so a model fills the view, or allow the user to select a rectangular region of the view to zoom in on. In this recipe, we'll show you how to manipulate the 3D camera to implement these useful zoom tools.

Getting ready

To follow this recipe, open the solution located in the `Recipes/Chapter09` folder in the code bundle available on the Packt website.

How to do it...

1. First, create a new Ogre MFC Ribbon application named `ZoomManager` by following the *Creating an MFC Ogre application with a Ribbon* recipe from *Chapter 1*.

2. Add a category named `Zoom` to the ribbon, and in it, add a slider for the zoom scale and two buttons named `Extents` and `Window`.

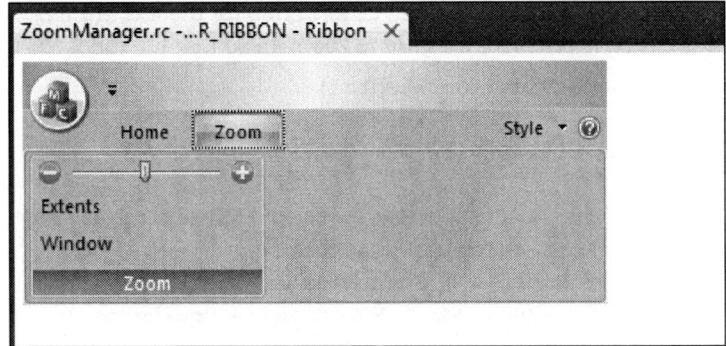

3. Next, add an event handler for the slider named OnZoom. In the OnZoom method, adjust the camera's proximity to the object based on the slider position.

```cpp
void CZoomManagerView::OnZoom()
{
  CMainFrame *MainFrame = (CMainFrame *)(
    (CZoomManagerApp*)AfxGetApp())->GetMainWnd();

  CMFCRibbonBar* RibbonBar = MainFrame->GetRibbonBar();
  CMFCRibbonSlider* ZoomSlider = DYNAMIC_DOWNCAST(
    CMFCRibbonSlider, RibbonBar->FindByID(ID_ZOOM));

  CEngine *Engine = ((CZoomManagerApp*)AfxGetApp())->m_Engine;
  Ogre::Root *Root = Engine->GetRoot();

  int Pos = ZoomSlider->GetPos();
  int Min = ZoomSlider->GetRangeMin();
  int Max = ZoomSlider->GetRangeMax();

  int Middle = (Max + Min) / 2;
  ZoomSlider->SetPos(Middle);
  Ogre::Vector3 CameraMove(0.0, 0.0, 0.0);

  Pos = Pos - Middle;
  CameraMove[2] = 0.1 * Pos;
  m_Camera->moveRelative(CameraMove);

  if (Root != NULL)
  {
    Root->renderOneFrame();
  }
}
```

4. Next, create an event handler named `OnExtents` for the `Extents` ribbon button. When this button is pressed, we want to zoom in, so that the robot fills the screen.

```
void CZoomManagerView::OnExtents()
{
    Ogre::Radian fieldOfView = m_Camera->getFOVy();

    CEngine *Engine = ((CZoomManagerApp*)AfxGetApp())->m_Engine;
    Ogre::Root *Root = Engine->GetRoot();
    Ogre::Entity* Robot = m_SceneManager->getEntity("Robot");
    Ogre::AxisAlignedBox Box = Robot->getBoundingBox();

    Ogre::Vector3 Center = Box.getCenter();
    Ogre::Vector3 Size = Box.getSize();
    float Width = Size[0];
    float Length = Size[1];

    float Height = 0.5 * std::max(Width, Length) /
      Ogre::Math::Sin(fieldOfView / 2.0);

    m_Camera->setPosition(Center[0], Center[1], Height);
    m_Camera->lookAt(Center);
    Root->renderOneFrame();
}
```

Here, we get the coordinates for the center of the robot entity, and then position the camera so that the robot fills the screen. The technique used here is to position the camera at the center of the robot, and then move the camera away along one axis until the robot fills the screen. When calculating the correct amount to move the camera away from the center using the robot's bounding box width, height and the camera's field of view, we must take into account the camera's field of view, because a larger field of view will show much more of the scene than a small field of view.

5. Next, add an event handler named `OnWindow` for the **Window** button. When the user presses this button, we want to turn on the selection mode. In selection mode, the user can click-and-drag to select an area of the screen to zoom in on.

```
void CZoomManagerView::OnWindow()
{
    m_SelectMode = true;
}
```

6. Add an event handler named `OnLButtonDown` for the "left mouse button down" event. If selection mode is active, start recording the selection bounds using a `CRect` member variable, and draw the bounds on the screen.

```
void CZoomManagerView::OnLButtonDown(UINT nFlags, CPoint point)
{
```

```
    if (m_SelectMode)
    {
      m_Start = point;
      m_rubberBand.SetRect(m_Start, m_Start);

      CClientDC dc(this);
      dc.DrawFocusRect(m_rubberBand);
    }

    CView::OnLButtonDown(nFlags, point);
  }
```

7. Next, add another event handler named OnMouseMove for the "mouse move" event. When the selection mode is active, update the selection CRect, and re-draw it on the screen.

```
void CZoomManagerView::OnMouseMove(UINT nFlags, CPoint point)
{
  if (m_SelectMode)
  {
    m_rubberBand.SetRect(m_Start, point);
    CClientDC dc(this);

    dc.DrawFocusRect(m_rubberBand);
    Invalidate(FALSE);
  }

  CView::OnMouseMove(nFlags, point);
}
```

8. Create an event handler named OnLButtonUp for the "left mouse button up" event. If the selection mode is active, and the user releases the left mouse button, use the selected region to reposition the camera, so that the region fills the screen.

```
void CZoomManagerView::OnLButtonUp(UINT nFlags, CPoint point)
{

  if (m_SelectMode)
  {
    m_SelectMode = false;
    Invalidate(FALSE);

    CRect rect;
    GetClientRect(&rect);
    Ogre::Vector3 Position = m_Camera->getPosition();
```

```
        float ratio = std::min(m_rubberBand.Width()/
          rect.Width(), m_rubberBand.Height()/rect.Height());
        Position[2] *= ratio;
        m_Camera->setPosition(Position);
        CEngine * Engine = ((CZoomManagerApp*)AfxGetApp())->m_Engine;
        Ogre::Root *Root = Engine->GetRoot();
        Root->renderOneFrame();
    }
    CView::OnLButtonUp(nFlags, point);
}
```

To calculate the new camera position, multiply the camera's z position by the ratio of the selected width divided by the screen width, or the selected height divided by the screen height – whichever is smaller.

How it works...

When you start the application, you will see the slider and two buttons in the ribbon. You will also see the robot entity from far away.

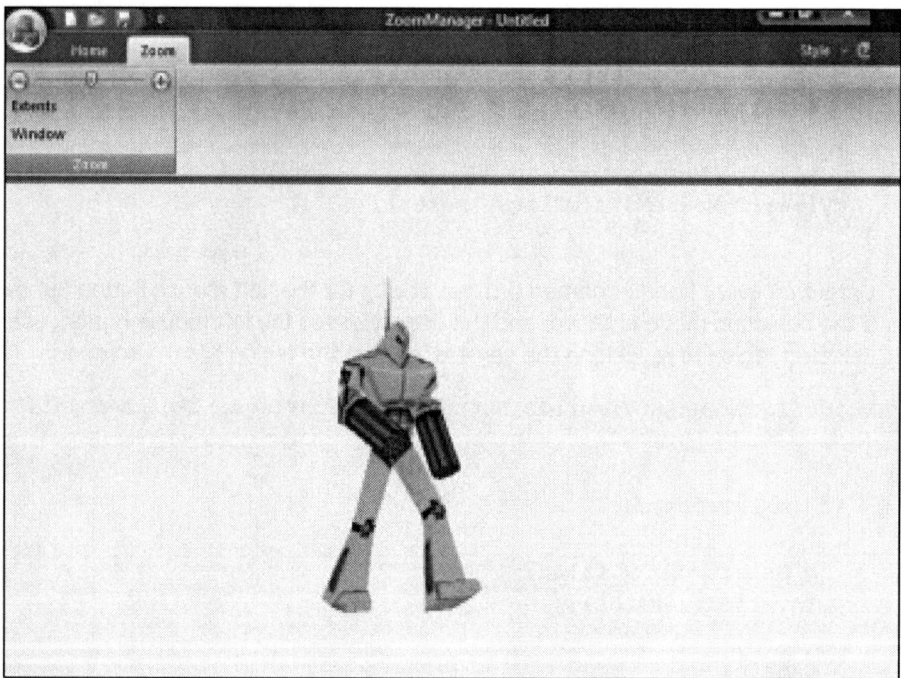

When the user increases the value of the zoom slider, the camera is repositioned closer to the robot.

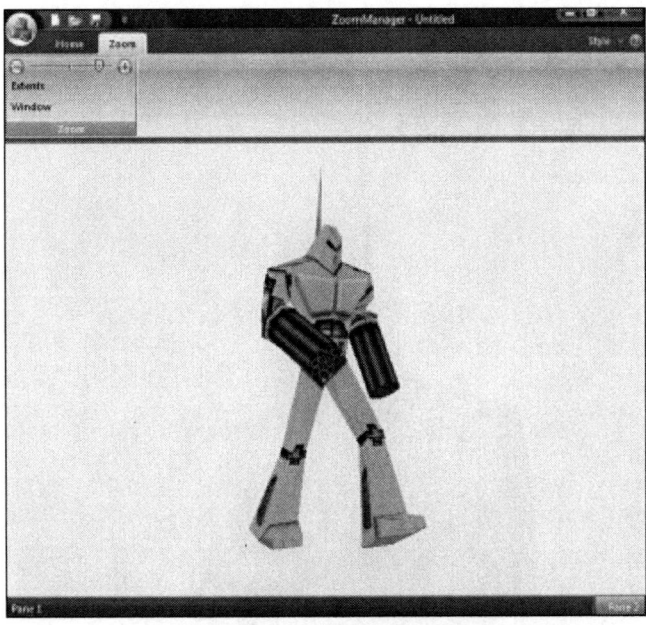

When the user presses the **Extents** button, the camera is positioned so that the robot entity fills the screen.

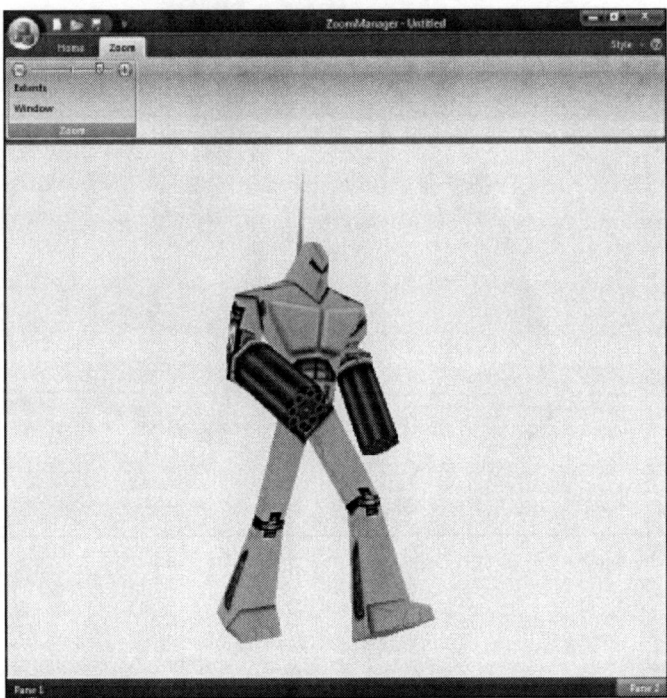

The **Window** button enables zooming to a selectable area. Before zooming, the scene looks similar to the following image:

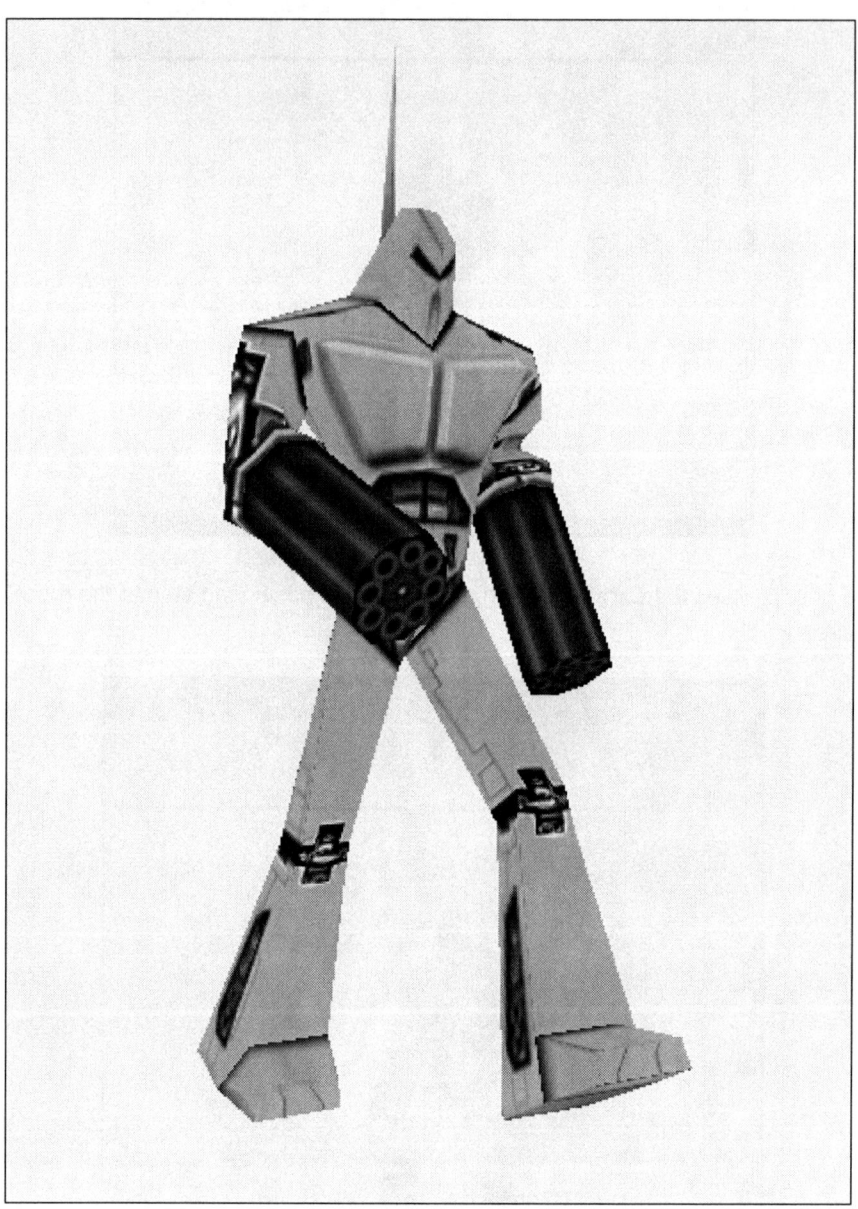

The robot entity is fully visible and the selection mode is active. When the user clicks-and-drags to select a zoom region, a rectangle is drawn on the screen to highlight that region.

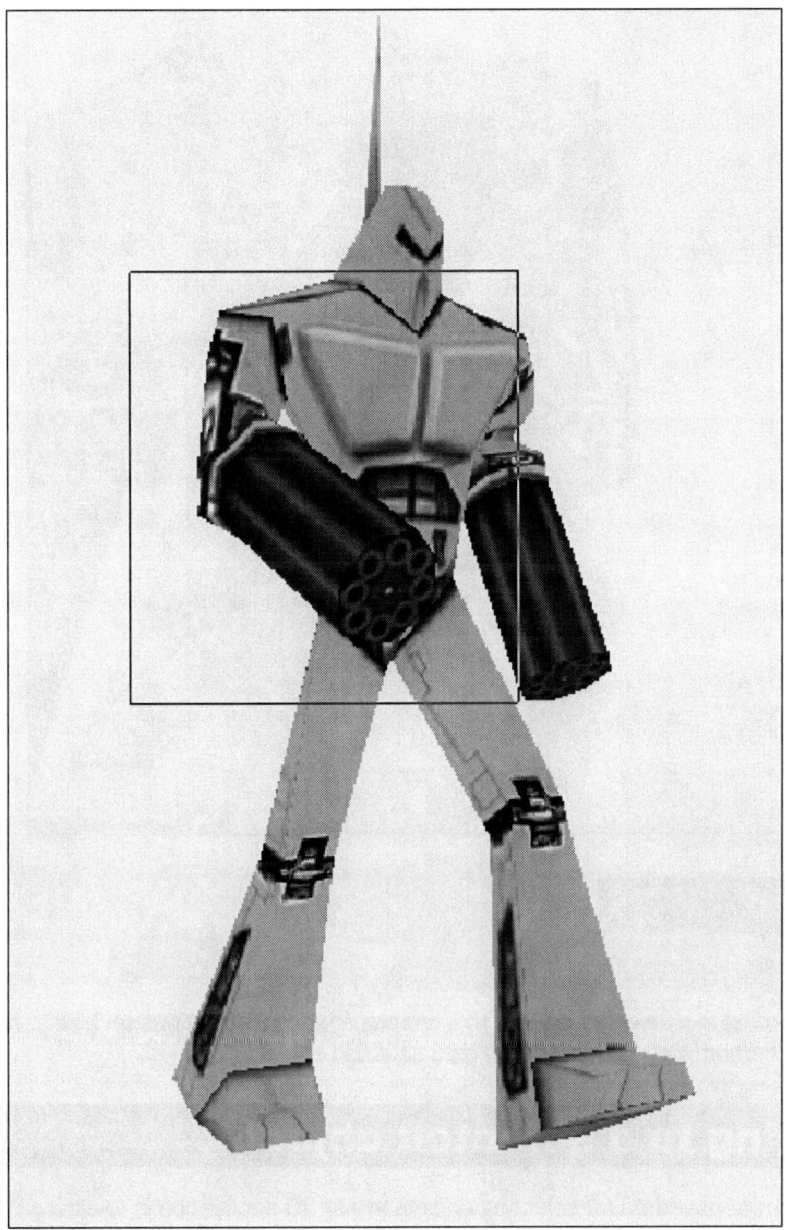

After the region is selected, and the user releases the left mouse button, the camera is repositioned so that the selected region fills the screen.

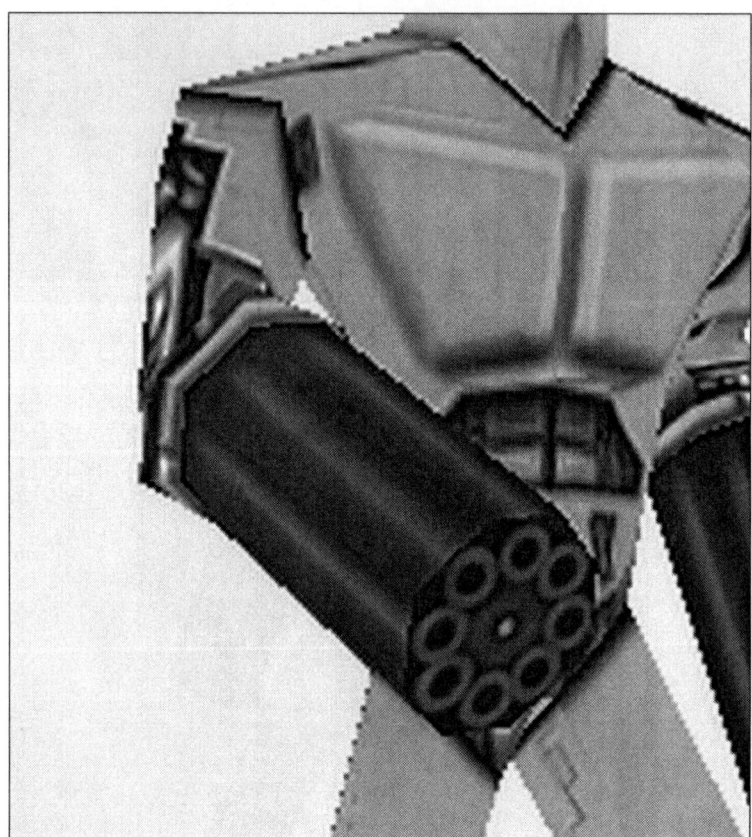

See also

In this chapter:

> ▸ *Zooming to a selected object*: This recipe provides instructions on how to manipulate the camera view so it zooms in on a selected object

Zooming to a selected object

The most common method for selecting objects in any 3D application is to click on it with the mouse, or highlight it with a selection region. In this recipe, we will show you how to determine which object the user clicked on, and how to adjust the camera so that the selected object fills the screen.

Getting ready

To follow this recipe, open the solution located in the `Recipes/Chapter09` folder in the code bundle available on the Packt website.

It may help to also review the *Collision detection* recipe from *Chapter 6, Learning to Move*, as we will be using a similar ray casting function.

How to do it...

1. First, create a new Ogre MFC Ribbon application named `ViewForObject` by following the *Creating an MFC Ogre application with a Ribbon* recipe from *Chapter 1*.

2. In `CViewForObjectView::EngineSetup()`, create four robots for the user to click on.

```
gre::Entity *RobotEntity;
Ogre::SceneNode *RobotNode;

for (int RobotIndex = 0; RobotIndex < 4; RobotIndex++)
{
  char Number[20];
  itoa(RobotIndex, Number, 10);
  Ogre::String RobotName = "Robot";
  RobotName += Ogre::String(Number);
  RobotEntity = m_SceneManager->
    createEntity(RobotName, "robot.mesh");

  RobotNode = m_SceneManager->getRootSceneNode()->
    createChildSceneNode(Ogre::Vector3(RobotIndex * 100,
    RobotIndex * 100, 0));


  RobotNode->attachObject(RobotEntity);
```

3. Add a boolean member variable to the `CViewForObjectView` class named `m_SelectionMode` to keep a track of the selection state. Then, create a ribbon category named `View`, and add a panel named `Select` to it. Add a button named `Select` to the `Select` panel, and create an event handler named `OnSelect` for it. When the `select` button is pressed, turn on the selection mode.

```
void CViewForObjectView::OnSelect()
{
  m_SelectionMode = true;
}
```

4. Next, add an event handler named `OnLButtonDown` for the "left mouse button down" event. When selection mode is active, we'll get the mouse position when the user clicks and searches for an entity at that point. If we find an entity, then we'll zoom in on it.

```
void CViewForObjectView::OnLButtonDown(UINT nFlags, CPoint point)
{
  if (m_SelectionMode)
  {

    Ogre::Entity *SelectedEntity = GetEntity(point);

    if (SelectedEntity != NULL)
    {
      Ogre::Vector3 Center = SelectedEntity->
        getParentNode()->getPosition();

      Ogre::Real Radius = SelectedEntity->getBoundingRadius();

      m_Camera->setPosition(Ogre::Vector3(Center.x,
        Center.y + 0.5 * Radius, Center.z + Radius));

      m_Camera->lookAt(Ogre::Vector3(Center.x,
        Center.y + 0.5 * Radius, Center.z));

      CEngine * Engine = ((CViewForObjectApp*)AfxGetApp())
        ->m_Engine;

      Ogre::Root *Root = Engine->GetRoot();
      Root->renderOneFrame();
    }
  }
}
```

The `GetEntity` function returns a 3D vector that is the center of the entity mesh under the cursor. Using the center position, we move the camera, so it looks at that entity and is close enough to it that the entity fills the screen.

5. Next, create a utility function named `GetEntity` in which we will use ray casting to find any entities under the mouse cursor.

```
Ogre::Entity* CViewForObjectView::GetEntity(CPoint point)
{
  Ogre::Camera *Camera = m_SceneManager->getCamera("Camera");
  Ogre::Entity *Entity = NULL;
  Ogre::RaySceneQueryResult Result;
  CRect    rect;
```

```
this->GetClientRect(&rect);

Ogre::Ray SearchRay = Camera->
  getCameraToViewportRay(((float)point.x)/((float)rect.Width()),
  ((float)point.y)/((float)rect.Height()));

Ogre::RaySceneQuery *ObjectRaySceneQuery = m_SceneManager->
  createRayQuery(SearchRay);

ObjectRaySceneQuery->setSortByDistance(true);

Result = ObjectRaySceneQuery->execute();

Ogre::RaySceneQueryResult::iterator Iterator;
Iterator = Result.begin();

Ogre::String ObjectName = Iterator->movable->getName();
Ogre::MovableObject *MovableObject = Iterator->movable;

Entity = static_cast<Ogre::Entity*>(MovableObject);
return Entity;
}
```

To define the ray, we scale the mouse cursor coordinates by the screen size, so that they are between 0 and 1. The `getCameraToViewportRay()` function returns a ray based on these normalized screen coordinates. Next, we create a ray query with our ray, and execute it. We return the first entity in the query results, or NULL if there are no results.

How it works...

When you run the application, you will see four robots in various positions on the screen, and the new ribbon panel and button. Pressing the **Select** button activates selection mode. In selection mode, we run a ray scene query every time the user clicks on the screen based on the mouse cursor position. If an entity is hit by the ray scene query, we zoom in on that entity.

The following screenshots shows what the application looks when you first run it, and when the selection mode is not active:

After the **Select** button is pressed, and the user clicks on a robot, the camera gets repositioned, so that robot fills the screen. The next screenshot is from the application after the user has clicked on a robot while in the selection mode:

Orbiting an object

Being able to constrain the camera so that it rotates about an object is very useful and saves time when you wish to view or manipulate the object from various perspectives. **Orbiting** is a technique in which the user drags the mouse to move the camera at a fixed distance about a point, while keeping the camera focused on the point. In this recipe, we'll show you how to implement tools for orbiting and for constraining the orbit to a single axis.

Getting ready

To follow this recipe, open the solution located in the `Recipes/Chapter09` folder in the code bundle available on the Packt website.

How to do it...

1. First, create a new Ogre MFC Ribbon application named `OrbitView` by following the *Creating an MFC Ogre application with a Ribbon* recipe from *Chapter 1*.

2. In `COrbitViewView::EngineSetup()`, create a robot entity, add it to the scene, and make the camera look at the center of the robot.

```
Ogre::Entity *RobotEntity = m_SceneManager->
  createEntity("Robot", "robot.mesh");

Ogre::SceneNode *RobotNode = m_SceneManager->
  getRootSceneNode()->createChildSceneNode("Robot");

RobotNode->attachObject(RobotEntity);

Ogre::AxisAlignedBox Box = RobotEntity->getBoundingBox();
Ogre::Vector3 Center = Box.getCenter();

m_Camera->setPosition(Ogre::Vector3(Center[0], Center[1],
  Center[2] + 500.0));

m_Camera->lookAt(Center);
```

3. Next, create a toolbar with three buttons to control the mouse navigation.

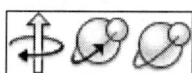

4. Next, add a category named `View` to the ribbon with a panel named `Orbit`. Then, add a button named `gallery` to the Orbit panel.

5. Add an event handler named `OnOrbit()` for the gallery button. Also, create a Boolean member variable named `m_Orbit`. When the user presses the `gallery` button, set `m_Orbit` to `true`, indicating that we are in the orbit mode.

```
void COrbitViewView::OnOrbit()
{
  int ViewIndex =
    CMFCRibbonGallery::GetLastSelectedItem(ID_ORBIT);
```

```
    switch (ViewIndex)
    {
      case 0:

        m_Orbit = true;

      break;
    }
  }
```

6. In `COrbitViewView::EngineSetup()`, create a scene node named `CameraNode`, and attach the camera to it. We will use this node to rotate the camera around the target.

```
CameraNode = m_SceneManager->getRootSceneNode()->
  createChildSceneNode("CameraNode", Ogre::Vector3::ZERO);


CameraNode->attachObject(m_Camera);
```

7. Add an event handler named `OnLButtonDown` for the "left mouse button down" event. In this new method, store the mouse cursor coordinates in a member variable named `m_MousePosition`, and set the `m_MouseNavigation` variable to `true`.

```
void COrbitViewView::OnLButtonDown(UINT nFlags, CPoint point)
{
  m_MousePosition = point;
  m_MouseNavigation = true;

  CView::OnLButtonDown(nFlags, point);
}
```

8. Next, create an event handler named `OnMouseMove` for the "mouse move" event. Inside `OnMouseMove`, add code to move the camera based on the active mode.

```
void COrbitViewView::OnMouseMove(UINT nFlags, CPoint point)
{
  Ogre::Vector3 CameraMove(0.0, 0.0, 0.0);

  CEngine * Engine = ((COrbitViewApp*)AfxGetApp())->m_Engine;
  if (Engine == NULL)
  return;
  Ogre::Root *Root = Engine->GetRoot();
  if (m_Camera == NULL)
  return;

  if (m_MouseNavigation)
  {
```

```
      if (m_Orbit)
      {
        Ogre::SceneNode* CameraNode = m_SceneManager->
          getSceneNode("CameraNode");

        CameraMove[1] = m_MousePosition.y - point.y;
        m_Camera->moveRelative(CameraMove);

        CameraNode->
          yaw(Ogre::Radian(0.001 * (m_MousePosition.x - point.x)));
      }

      else
      {
        CameraMove[0] = -(m_MousePosition.x - point.x);
        CameraMove[1] = m_MousePosition.y - point.y;
        m_Camera->moveRelative(CameraMove);
      }

      m_MousePosition = point;
      Root->renderOneFrame();
    }

    CView::OnMouseMove(nFlags, point);
  }
```

If the orbit mode is active, then rotate the camera about the camera scene node using yaw only. If it is not in the orbit mode, simply move the camera on the x and y axes.

How it works...

In this recipe, we pan the camera in the x and y axes when the user clicks on the screen, and drags the mouse in the viewport. We also added an orbit button, which activates the orbit mode when clicked. In the orbit mode, the camera will rotate about the object when the user clicks-and-drags the mouse cursor on the robot. In both the modes, we simply move the camera using the moveRelative() function, and in the orbit mode, we also use the yaw() function to rotate the camera.

When you run the application, you will see our familiar robot on a green background. Click-and-drag the mouse on the robot to move the camera.

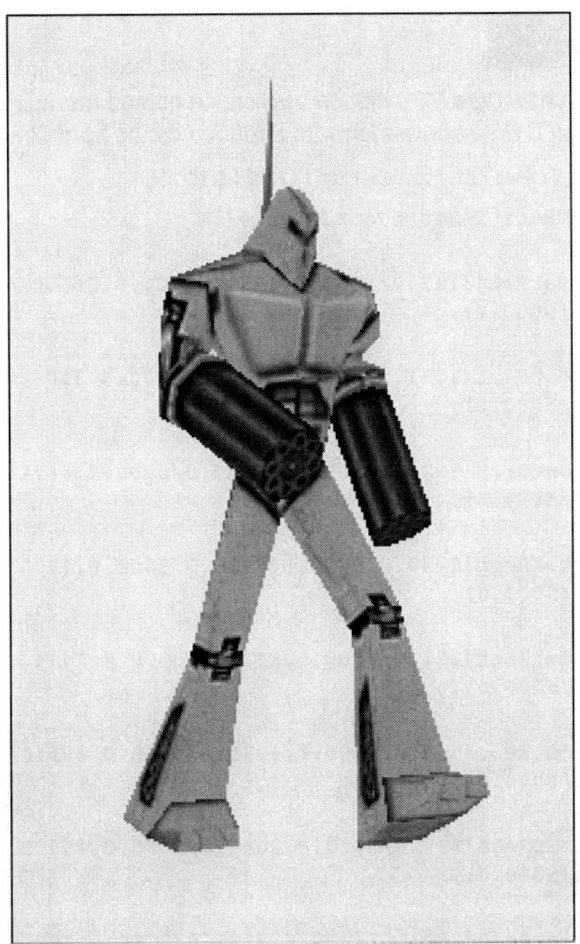

Selecting objects

In addition to the ray casting collision detection method, Ogre 3D also provides a way to find all the entities that are inside or touching a bounding box. In this recipe, we'll show you how to use the bounding box scene query to select entities in a scene. We'll also show you how to use the query mask parameter to filter the results by entity type.

Getting ready

To follow this recipe, open the solution located in the `Recipes/Chapter09` folder in the code bundle available on the Packt website.

How to do it...

1. First, create a new Ogre MFC Ribbon application named `Nearest` by following the *Creating an MFC Ogre application with a Ribbon* recipe from *Chapter 1*.

2. In `CNearestView::EngineSetup()`, add a robot.

```
Ogre::FloatRect TextureCoordinates[]=
{
  Ogre::FloatRect(113.0/5000.0,121.0/5000.0,851.0/5000.0,
    1073.0/5000.0),

  Ogre::FloatRect(1021.0/5000.0,114.0/5000.0,3386.0/5000.0,
    1984.0/5000.0),

  Ogre::FloatRect(3825.0/5000.0,1049.0/5000.0,4871.0/5000.0,
    3588.0/5000.0),

  Ogre::FloatRect(1739.0/5000.0,2418.0/5000.0,2796.0/5000.0,
    4774.0/5000.0),

  Ogre::FloatRect(221.0/5000.0,2723.0/5000.0,1464.0/5000.0,
    3795.0/5000.0),

  Ogre::FloatRect(505.0/5000.0,4391.0/5000.0,805.0/5000.0,
    4662.0/5000.0),

  Ogre::FloatRect(339.0/5000.0,2085.0/5000.0,482.0/5000.0,
    2216.0/5000.0),

  Ogre::FloatRect(2803.0/5000.0,3355.0/5000.0,3891.0/5000.0,
    4912.0/5000.0)
};

Ogre::Entity *RobotEntity = m_SceneManager->
  createEntity("Robot", "robot.mesh");

Ogre::SceneNode *RobotNode = m_SceneManager->
  getRootSceneNode()->createChildSceneNode();

RobotNode->attachObject(RobotEntity);
Ogre::AxisAlignedBox Box = RobotEntity->getBoundingBox();
Ogre::Vector3 Center = Box.getCenter();
m_Camera->lookAt(Center);
```

3. Next, add a billboard set named `Tree`, and add a single billboard to the sets.

```
Ogre::BillboardSet *Trees = m_SceneManager->
  createBillboardSet("Trees");

Trees->setTextureCoords(TextureCoordinates, 8);
Trees->setMaterialName("Trees");
Trees->setCastShadows(true);
Trees->setSortingEnabled(true);
Trees->setBillboardType(Ogre::BBT_ORIENTED_COMMON);

Ogre::Vector3 TreePosition(0.0, 0.0, 0.0);
Ogre::Billboard* Tree = Trees->createBillboard(TreePosition);
Tree->setDimensions(20.0, 100.0);
Tree->setTexcoordIndex(0);

Ogre::SceneNode *TreeNode = m_SceneManager->getRootSceneNode()->
  createChildSceneNode();

TreeNode->setPosition(0.0, 0.0, -100.0);
TreeNode->setDirection(Ogre::Vector3::NEGATIVE_UNIT_Y);
TreeNode->attachObject(Trees);
```

4. Next, add a manual object entity named `Screen`.

```
Ogre::ManualObject *Screen = m_SceneManager->
  createManualObject("Screen");

Screen->setDynamic(true);

Screen->begin("BaseWhiteNoLighting",
  Ogre::RenderOperation::OT_TRIANGLE_LIST);

Screen->position(0,0,0);
Screen->textureCoord(0,0);

Screen->position(100.0,0,0);
Screen->textureCoord(1,0);

Screen->position(100.0, 100.0 ,0);
Screen->textureCoord(1,1);

Screen->triangle(0, 1, 2);

Screen->position(0,0,0);
Screen->textureCoord(0,0);
```

```
Screen->position(100.0, 100.0, 0);
Screen->textureCoord(1,1);

Screen->position(0, 100.0,0);
Screen->textureCoord(0,1);

Screen->triangle(3, 4, 5);

Screen->end();

Ogre::SceneNode* node = m_SceneManager->getRootSceneNode()->
  createChildSceneNode();

node->setPosition(-50.0, 0, -20.0);
node->attachObject(Screen);
```

5. Add a category named `Select` to the ribbon, with a set of checkboxes and a button also named `Select` as shown in the following screenshot:

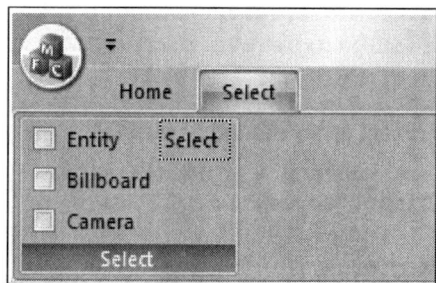

6. Add event handlers for each checkbox. In each event handler, activate the appropriate query mask.

```
void CNearestView::OnEntity()
{
   m_QueryMask |= Ogre::SceneManager::ENTITY_TYPE_MASK;
}

void CNearestView::OnBillboard()
{
   m_QueryMask |= Ogre::SceneManager::FX_TYPE_MASK;
}

void CNearestView::OnCamera()
{
   m_QueryMask |= Ogre::SceneManager::FRUSTUM_TYPE_MASK;
}
```

7. Add an event handler named `OnSelect` for the `Select` button.

```
void CNearestView::OnSelect()
{
// ...
}
```

8. In `CNearestView::OnSelect()`, update the scene graph, and then get the axis aligned, bounding the box for all the entities in the world.

```
m_SceneManager->_updateSceneGraph(m_Camera);


Ogre::AxisAlignedBox Box = m_SceneManager->getRootSceneNode()->
   _getWorldAABB();
```

9. Next, create an axis aligned box scene query using the bounding box from the root scene node, and use the query mask to filter the results, so that we only get the entities selected by the active checkboxes.

```
Ogre::AxisAlignedBoxSceneQuery* Query = m_SceneManager->
   createAABBQuery(Box, m_QueryMask);
Ogre::SceneQueryResult &Result = Query->execute();
```

10. Iterate over the results, and hide all the entities.

```
Ogre::SceneQueryResultMovableList::iterator Iterator;

for (Iterator = Result.movables.begin(); Iterator !=
   Result.movables.end(); Iterator++)
{
   Ogre::String ObjectName = (*Iterator)->getName();
   Ogre::MovableObject *Object = (*Iterator);

   Object->setVisible(false);
}
Ogre::Root *Root = ((CNearestApp*)AfxGetApp())->m_Engine->
   GetRoot();

Root->renderOneFrame();
}
```

How it works...

In this recipe, we created controls that allow the user to filter the types of entities that are affected by the `select` button. To filter out certain types of entities we use a query mask, which is a bit mask, when running the axis aligned bounding box query. When certain bits are set in the mask, those entities are filtered in the results.

Ogre 3D provides the following query masks:

- ▶ `WORLD_GEOMETRY_TYPE_MASK`: This mask is for world geometry
- ▶ `ENTITY_TYPE_MASK`: This mask filters entities
- ▶ `FX_TYPE_MASK`: This mask filters effects, such as billboards and particle systems
- ▶ `STATICGEOMETRY_TYPE_MASK`: This mask filters static geometry
- ▶ `LIGHT_TYPE_MASK`: This mask filters lights
- ▶ `FRUSTUM_TYPE_MASK`: This mask filters frustum-based classes, such as cameras

If you like, you can define your own masks, and then set the query flags for your entities using the `setQueryFlags()` method.

To indicate which entities are selected, we hide them from view, and then re-render the scene.

When you run the application, you will see a robot entity, a billboard, and a manual object on the screen. Select one or more of the checkboxes, and press the `select` button to see the results.

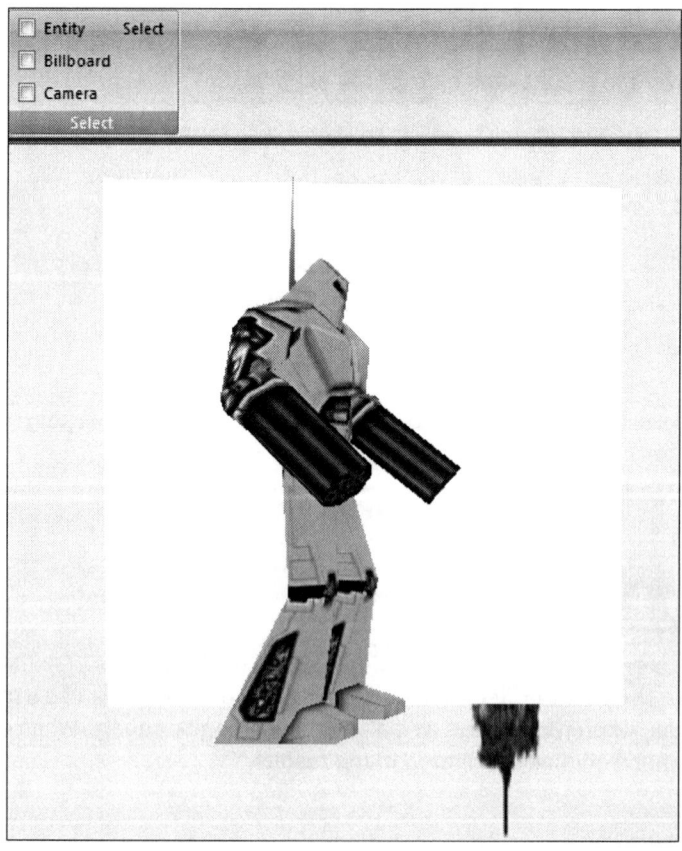

Object visibility

In addition to determining objects that a user clicks on, collision detection can also tell us if there is an obstacle between two objects, or if one object is "looking" at another object. This can be useful in a game for checking if a non-player character can see the player's character, or as a rudimentary check to see if two objects are separated by a wall. In this recipe, we'll use **collision detection** to show when a robot is looking at another robot, and if its view is obstructed.

Getting ready

To follow this recipe, open the solution located in the `Recipes/Chapter09` folder in the code bundle available on the Packt website.

How to do it...

1. First, create a new Ogre MFC Ribbon application named `Visibility` by following the *Creating an MFC Ogre application with a Ribbon* recipe from *Chapter 1*.

2. In `CVisibilityView::EngineSetup()`, create two robots, and add them to the scene.

```
Ogre::Entity *RobotEntity1;
Ogre::Entity *RobotEntity2;

Ogre::SceneNode *RobotNode1;
Ogre::SceneNode *RobotNode2;
Ogre::Quaternion Quaternion(Ogre::Quaternion::IDENTITY);

RobotEntity1 = m_SceneManager->createEntity("Robot1",
  "robot.mesh");

RobotNode1 = m_SceneManager->getRootSceneNode()->
  createChildSceneNode("Robot1",Ogre::Vector3::ZERO,
  Ogre::Quaternion::IDENTITY);

RobotNode1->attachObject(RobotEntity1);

RobotEntity2 = m_SceneManager->createEntity("Robot2",
  "robot.mesh");

Quaternion.FromAngleAxis(Ogre::Radian(Ogre::Math::PI),
  Ogre::Vector3::NEGATIVE_UNIT_Y);
```

```
RobotNode2 = m_SceneManager->getRootSceneNode()->
  createChildSceneNode("Robot2", Ogre::Vector3(200.0, 0.0, 0.0),
  Quaternion);

RobotNode2->attachObject(RobotEntity2);
```

We rotate the second robot to face the first one, by creating a **Quaternion** that represents a `180` degree rotation about the y-axis.

3. Next, create an object between the two robots to represent the obstructing object.

```
Ogre::Entity *WallEntity;
Ogre::SceneNode *WallNode;

Ogre::Real Height = 0.75 * RobotEntity1->getBoundingRadius();
Ogre::Vector3 Center1 = RobotNode1->getPosition();
Ogre::Vector3 Center2 = RobotNode2->getPosition();

Center1[1] += Height;
Center2[1] += Height;

WallEntity = m_SceneManager->createEntity("Wall",
  Ogre::SceneManager::PrefabType::PT_SPHERE);

WallNode = m_SceneManager->getRootSceneNode()->
  createChildSceneNode("Wall", 0.5 * (Center1 + Center2),
  Quaternion);

WallNode->attachObject(WallEntity);
WallEntity->setVisible(false);
```

4. Create a line between the two robots that we will reveal to indicate that the second robot can see the first one.

```
Ogre::ManualObject *Ray = m_SceneManager->
  createManualObject("Ray");

Ray->begin("BumpyMetal", Ogre::RenderOperation::OT_LINE_LIST);
Ray->position(Center1);
Ray->position(Center2);
Ray->end();
Ray->setVisible(false);

RobotNode2->attachObject(Ray);
```

5. Define a query mask named `COLLIDABLE`, and set the query masks of our objects, so that only the wall and the first robot have the `COLLIDABLE` mask.

```
#define COLLIDABLE 1
RobotEntity1->setQueryFlags(COLLIDABLE);
WallEntity->setQueryFlags(COLLIDABLE);
RobotEntity2->setQueryFlags(0);
Ray->setQueryFlags(0);
```

6. Create a toolbar with the following graphic. Next, add a category named `Visibility` to the ribbon with a `panel` and a `gallery` button.

7. Add an event handler named `OnCheckVisibility()` for the toolbar button.

```
void CVisibilityView::OnCheckVisibility()
{
//…
}
```

8. First, get the index of the button that was pressed in the toolbar.

```
int ViewIndex = CMFCRibbonGallery::GetLastSelectedItem(ID_CHECK);
```

9. Prepare some temporary variables that we will be using for collision detection.

```
Ogre::Quaternion Quaternion;
CEngine *Engine = ((CVisibilityApp*)AfxGetApp())->m_Engine;
Ogre::Root *Root = Engine->GetRoot();
Ogre::Entity * WallEntity;
Ogre::Entity * RobotEntity1 = m_SceneManager->getEntity("Robot1");
Ogre::Entity * RobotEntity2 = m_SceneManager->getEntity("Robot2");

Ogre::SceneNode *RobotNode2 = (Ogre::SceneNode *)m_SceneManager->
  getRootSceneNode()->getChild("Robot2");


Ogre::ManualObject *Ray = (Ogre::ManualObject*)RobotNode2->
  getAttachedObject("Ray");
```

10. Hide the visibility ray by default.

```
Ray->setVisible(false);
```

If the first button was pressed, check if robot 2 is looking at robot 1.

```
switch (ViewIndex)
{
```

```
case 0:
{
  //check visibility
  Ogre::Entity *Entity = NULL;
  Ogre::RaySceneQueryResult Result;

  Ogre::SceneNode *RobotNode1 = (Ogre::SceneNode
    *)m_SceneManager->getRootSceneNode()->getChild("Robot1");

  Ogre::Real Height = 0.75 * RobotEntity1->getBoundingRadius();
  Ogre::Vector3 Center1 = RobotNode1->getPosition();
  Ogre::Vector3 Center2 = RobotNode2->getPosition();

  Center1[1] += Height;
  Center2[1] += Height;

  Ogre::Ray SearchRay;
  SearchRay.setOrigin(Center2);

  SearchRay.setDirection(RobotNode2->
    _getDerivedOrientation().xAxis());

  Ogre::RaySceneQuery *ObjectRaySceneQuery = m_SceneManager->
    createRayQuery(SearchRay,COLLIDABLE);

  ObjectRaySceneQuery->setSortByDistance(true);
  Result = ObjectRaySceneQuery->execute();

  if(!Result.empty()) {
    Ogre::RaySceneQueryResult::iterator Iterator;
    Iterator = Result.begin();

    Ogre::String ObjectName = Iterator->movable->getName();

    if(ObjectName.compare("Robot1") == 0) {
      Ray->setVisible(true);
    }
  }
}
break;
```

To check if the robots are looking at each other, we create a ray scene query with our custom query mask. When the query is executed, we will only get objects in the results that match our query mask. If the first object we get back is the robot, then the robots are looking at each other, and we reveal the visibility ray.

If the second button is pressed, toggle the sphere's visibility.

```
case 1:
  WallEntity = m_SceneManager->getEntity("Wall");
  m_IsWallExists = !m_IsWallExists;
  WallEntity->setVisible(m_IsWallExists);
  //wall is visible
break;
```

If the third button is pressed, rotate robot 2.

```
case 2:
  // rotate robot
  RobotEntity = m_SceneManager->getEntity("Robot2");

  if (m_IsRotated)
  {
    Quaternion.FromAngleAxis(Ogre::Radian(0.0),
      Ogre::Vector3::NEGATIVE_UNIT_Y);
}

  else
  {
    Quaternion.FromAngleAxis(Ogre::Radian(Ogre::Math::PI),
      Ogre::Vector3::NEGATIVE_UNIT_Y);
  }

  RobotEntity->getParentNode()->setOrientation(Quaternion);

  m_IsRotated = !m_IsRotated;
break;
}
```

11. Finally, re-render the scene to show the results.

```
Root->renderOneFrame();
```

How it works...

In this recipe, we used ray casting to detect when the two robots are looking at each other. We used a custom query mask, so that our ray casting results only return the entities that we are interested in. If the first ray casting result is the other robot, then we know that the robots are looking at each other, otherwise the robots are not facing each other, or there is an object blocking their view.

When you first run the program and press the visibility button, you will see the two robots and the line between them, which indicates that they can see each other.

When the `wall` button is pressed, a large sphere appears between the two robots. If you press the `visibility` button, the line between the robots will not appear, meaning that the robots cannot see each other.

When the `rotate` button is pressed, the second robot is rotated to face away from the first robot.

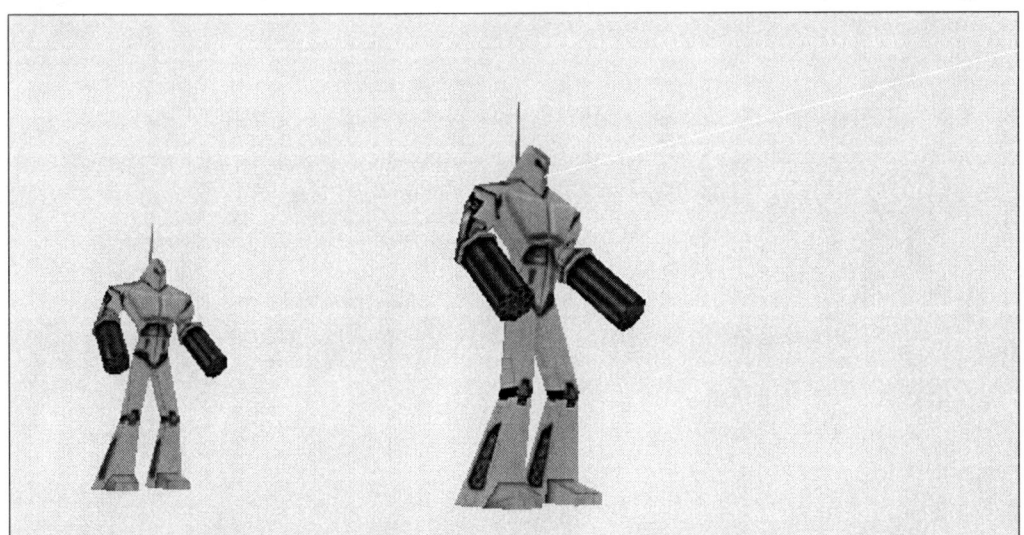

There's more...

We only use a single ray in this recipe to detect if one object can "see" another object. However, it would be more accurate if we used a cone or a frustum to detect visibility. Ogre has a `Frustum` class that contains the functionality to do this kind of visibility testing, and the `Camera` class derives from it.

Index

Y

Z

Thank you for buying
OGRE 3D 1.7 Application Development Cookbook

About Packt Publishing

Packt, pronounced 'packed', published its first book "*Mastering phpMyAdmin for Effective MySQL Management*" in April 2004 and subsequently continued to specialize in publishing highly focused books on specific technologies and solutions.

Our books and publications share the experiences of your fellow IT professionals in adapting and customizing today's systems, applications, and frameworks. Our solution based books give you the knowledge and power to customize the software and technologies you're using to get the job done. Packt books are more specific and less general than the IT books you have seen in the past. Our unique business model allows us to bring you more focused information, giving you more of what you need to know, and less of what you don't.

Packt is a modern, yet unique publishing company, which focuses on producing quality, cutting-edge books for communities of developers, administrators, and newbies alike. For more information, please visit our website: www.packtpub.com.

About Packt Open Source

In 2010, Packt launched two new brands, Packt Open Source and Packt Enterprise, in order to continue its focus on specialization. This book is part of the Packt Open Source brand, home to books published on software built around Open Source licences, and offering information to anybody from advanced developers to budding web designers. The Open Source brand also runs Packt's Open Source Royalty Scheme, by which Packt gives a royalty to each Open Source project about whose software a book is sold.

Writing for Packt

We welcome all inquiries from people who are interested in authoring. Book proposals should be sent to author@packtpub.com. If your book idea is still at an early stage and you would like to discuss it first before writing a formal book proposal, contact us; one of our commissioning editors will get in touch with you.

We're not just looking for published authors; if you have strong technical skills but no writing experience, our experienced editors can help you develop a writing career, or simply get some additional reward for your expertise.

Ogre 3D 1.7 Beginner's Guide

ISBN: 978-1-84951-248-0　　　　Paperback: 300 pages

Create real-time 3D applications using Ogre 3D from scratch

1. Easy-to-follow introduction to OGRE 3D

2. Create exciting 3D applications using OGRE 3D

3. Create your own scenes and monsters, play with the lights and shadows, and learn to use plugins

4. Get challenged to be creative and make fun and addictive games on your own

Blender 2.5 Materials and Textures Cookbook

ISBN: 978-1-84951-288-6　　　　Paperback: 312 pages

Over 80 great recipes to create life-like Blender objects

1. Master techniques to create believable natural surface materials

2. Take your models to the next level of realism or artistic development by using the material and texture settings within Blender 2.5

3. Take the hassle out of material simulation by applying faster and more efficient material and texture strategies

Please check **www.PacktPub.com** for information on our titles

Lightning Source UK Ltd.
Milton Keynes UK
UKOW021501080512

192172UK00003B/184/P